...D ON THE
...ORK TIMES
...SELLING
*THE UNTOLD HISTORY
OF THE UNITED STATES*

THE CONCISE UNTOLD HISTORY OF THE UNITED STATES

THE COMPANION TO ...
DOCUMENTAR...

D0049889

OLIVER STONE & PETER KUZNICK

Praise for Oliver Stone and Peter Kuznick's
New York Times **bestseller**
THE UNTOLD HISTORY OF THE UNITED STATES

"There is much here to reflect upon. Such a perspective is indispensable.
. . . At stake is whether the United States will choose to be the policeman
of a 'Pax Americana,' which is a recipe for disaster, or partner with other
nations on the way to a safer, more just and sustainable future."

—Douglas Brinkley, *New York Times*
bestselling author of *The Great Deluge*

"Howard [Zinn] would have loved this. . . . It's compulsive reading:
brilliant, a masterpiece!"

—Daniel Ellsberg, national bestselling author of
Secrets: A Memoir of Vietnam and the Pentagon Papers

"As riveting, eye-opening, and thought-provoking as any history book
you will ever read. . . . Can't recommend it highly enough."

—Glenn Greenwald, *The Guardian*

"Richly provocative . . . invigorating."

—*Kirkus Reviews*

"Stone and Kuznick have taken almost everything compelling about the last ninety years of American foreign policy and put it all in one place."

—**Jon Schwarz, MichaelMoore.com**

"A phenomenally great book. . . . Honest history that tears through myths and presents a reality not expected by most Americans—and backs it up with well-documented facts."

—**David Swanson, author of** *War Is a Lie*

"This is a must read! This book shakes so many of the assumptions that have anchored U.S. foreign policy."

—**Bill Fletcher, BlackCommentator.com**

"Oliver Stone and Peter Kuznick have done what many would consider impossible. They have written a political history of the United States in the 20th Century that tells us exactly how the United States became an empire through conscious decisions, and how the struggle to maintain that empire will go on despite which political party holds office. It is a brilliant survey."

—**Lloyd C. Gardner, author of** *The Road to Tahrir Square*

"A thought-provoking rebuttal to the nationalist myths that are far too often served up as history. Stone and Kuznick remind us that, until Americans have the courage to confront reality, they will remain trapped by their illusions."

—**Lawrence S. Wittner, author of** *One World or None: A History of the World Nuclear Disarmament Movement Through 1953*

"Stone and Kuznick provide a boldly critical view of the most painful aspects of American history. Their perspective on nuclear danger is especially illuminating."

—**Robert Jay Lifton, author of** *Thought Reform and the Psychology of Totalism*

"Stone and Kuznick peel away layers of misleading myth. . . . Some will be surprised, others angry. Most will understand their nation much better."

—Jeff Madrick, author of *Taking America*

"It's time for serious people to confront rather than avoid or attempt to denigrate the profound challenges raised by Stone and Kuznick. They are asking (and answering!) all the right questions."

—Gar Alperovitz, author of *The Decision to Use the Atomic Bomb*

"The immense contribution of *The Untold History of the United States* is to shatter the conventional wisdom, challenging readers to re-conceptualize the American role in the world. . . . For students of US history, this is an invaluable work."

—Carolyn Eisenberg, author of *Drawing the Line: The American Decision to Divide Germany, 1944–1949*

"A fascinating and provocative work. This courageous and clear-minded account . . . is a milestone in a surprisingly small genre of books, namely, critical history written of and for the people. It should have the widest possible reading."

—Bruce Cumings, author of *The Korean War*

"Beautifully illustrated, well-argued, and compellingly written."

—Marilyn Young, author of *The Vietnam Wars*

"One of the most important books of our time. Oliver Stone and Peter Kuznick disabuse us of the popular notion that this country has always been a force for good in the world."

—Marjorie Cohn, author of *Cowboy Republic: Six Ways the Bush Gang Has Defied the Law*

"The most comprehensive and incisive critique yet written of American foreign policy since World War II."

—Allan Lichtman, author of *White Protestant Nation*

THE CONCISE UNTOLD HISTORY

of the

UNITED STATES

OLIVER STONE

and

PETER KUZNICK

GALLERY BOOKS

New York   London   Toronto   Sydney   New Delhi

G

Gallery Books
A Division of Simon & Schuster, Inc.
1230 Avenue of the Americas
New York, NY 10020

First Gallery Books trade paperback edition October 2014

GALLERY BOOKS and colophon are registered trademarks of Simon & Schuster, Inc.

For information about special discounts for bulk purchases, please contact Simon &
Schuster Special Sales at 1-866-506-1949 or business@simonandschuster.com.

The Simon & Schuster Speakers Bureau can bring authors to your live event. For
more information or to book an event, contact the Simon & Schuster Speakers
Bureau at 1-866-248-3049 or visit our website at www.simonspeakers.com.

Interior design by Jason Snyder
Cover design by Jason Gabbert
I Want You for the U.S. Army Recruitment Poster by James Montgomery Flagg © Corbis

Manufactured in the United States of America

1   3   5   7   9   10   8   6   4   2

Library of Congress Cataloging-in-Publication Data

Stone, Oliver.
The untold history of the United States / Oliver Stone and Peter Kuznick.
—1st Gallery Books hardcover ed.
p. cm.
Companion to the documentary series of the same name.
1. United States—History—20th century. 2. United States—History—21st century.
3. United States—Politics and government—20th century. 4. United States—Politics
and government—2001-2009. I. Kuznick, Peter J. II. Title.
E741.S76 2011
973.91—dc23
2011051642

ISBN 978-1-4767-9166-1
ISBN 978-1-4767-9167-8 (ebook)

To our children—Tara, Michael, Sean, Lexie, Sara, and Asmara—
and the better world that they and all children deserve.

ACKNOWLEDGMENTS

A project of this scope required the support, assistance, and forbearance of a large number of people. On the film side, we'd like to thank the following: Fernando Sulichin for finding the financing and maintaining his composure through difficult times; Rob Wilson and Tara Tremaine were anchors from the beginning, culling archives around the world; Alex Marquez edited on and off through four years and many late nights, aided at various intervals by Elliot Eisman, Alexis Chavez, and Sean Stone; on the aural side, Craig Armstrong, Adam Peters, and Budd Carr—and Wylie Stateman; in the administrative grapple, Evan Bates and Suzie Gilbert; and Steven Pines for managing the money out of thin air. Many thanks to Showtime, through two different administrations—David Nevins for his insights; and the help of Bryan Lourd, Jeff Jacobs, Simon Green, and Kevin Cooper.

On the book side, we are indebted to Peter's colleagues and graduate students in American University's History Department. Max Paul Friedman lent his expertise on the history of U.S. foreign policy, reading the entire manuscript with painstaking care, challenging some of our interpretations and saving us from errors both large and small. Because U.S.-Soviet and U.S.-Russian relations figure so prominently in our story, we drew heavily on the expertise of Russian historian Anton Fedyashin, who was always ready to answer questions and check Russian language sources to make sure we got things right. Among Peter's other colleagues who responded with generosity to questions regarding their own fields of historical scholarship were professors Mustafa Aksakal, Richard Breitman, Phil Brenner, Ira Klein, Allan Lichtman, Eric Lohr, and Anna Nelson.

Among the graduate students, Eric Singer and Ben Bennett were indispensable. They took vast amounts of time out of their own research and writing to help with a variety of research tasks. Eric was a master at tracking down obscure information that no one else could find. Ben, among his many contributions, took charge of finding the visuals that add such an important dimension to this book. Other current and former Ph.D. students who worked extensively on this project include Rebecca DeWolf, Cindy Gueli, Vincent Intondi, Matt Pembleton, Terumi Rafferty-Osaki, and Jay Weixelbaum. Additional research assistance and fertile leads were provided by Daniel Cipriani, Nguyet Nguyen, David Onkst, Allen Pietrobon, Arie Serota, and Keith Skillin.

Numerous friends and colleagues also provided invaluable assistance along the way. Daniel Ellsberg was extremely generous with his insights, suggestions, critical readings, and enthusiastic support. His knowledge of much of this history remains unsurpassed. Among the other scholars who gave generously of their time and expertise, answered questions, and suggested documents are Gar Alperovitz, Robert Berkowitz, Bill Burr, Bob Dreyfuss, Carolyn Eisenberg, Ham Fish, Michael Flynn, Irena Grudzinska Gross, Hugh Gusterson, Anita Kondoyanidi, Bill Lanouette, Milton Leitenberg, Robert Jay Lifton, Arjun Makhijani, Ray McGovern, Roger Morris, Satoko Oka Norimatsu, Robert Norris, Robert Parry, Leo Ribuffo, Jonathan Schell, Peter Dale Scott, Mark Selden, Marty Sherwin, Chuck Strozier, Janine Wedel, and Larry Wittner.

Because the project has taken as long as it has, we were sad to lose four of our biggest supporters along the way—Howard Zinn, Bob Griffith, Charlie Wiener, and Uday Mohan.

Barbara Koeppel provided additional assistance with the visuals and captions. Erin Hamilton offered valuable insights on Chile. Matt Smith and Clement Ho of the American University library were extremely helpful with finding sources and providing other assistance.

The team at Gallery Books did everything they could to meet our often unwieldy requests as we rushed to complete the two projects on schedule. We are especially indebted to our editor, Jeremie Ruby-Strauss, and his assistant, Heather Hunt. We would also like to thank Louise Burke, Jen Bergstrom, Jessica Chin, Emily Drum, Elisa Rivlin, Emilia Pisani, Tricia Boczkowski, Sally Franklin, Jen Robinson, Larry Pekarek, and Davina Mock.

Peter's daughter Lexie and his wife, Simki Kuznick, helped with research and footnoting and Simki pored patiently over numerous drafts of this manuscript with the skill of an editor and the eye of a poet.

CHAPTER ONE

*T*he 2000 presidential election between George Bush and Al Gore confronted the American people with a stark choice between two different visions of the future. Few remember that exactly one hundred years before, the American people had been asked to make a similar choice. They were asked to decide whether the United States should be a republic or an empire.

Incumbent Republican president William McKinley's vision of the American future lay in "Free Trade" and overseas empire. By contrast, Democrat William Jennings Bryan was an outspoken anti-imperialist.

Few noticed a third choice—Socialist presidential candidate Eugene V. Debs. The socialist movement represented the new working class. To socialists, empire meant one thing and one thing only—exploitation.

McKinley ran touting a soaring economy and a victory over Spain in the war of 1898. McKinley believed that America must expand to survive.

Bryan, a Nebraska populist known as "the Great Commoner," was an enemy of industrial tycoons and bankers. He was convinced that McKinley's vision would bring disaster. He quoted Thomas Jefferson's comment that "If there be one principle more deeply rooted than any other in the mind of every American, it is that we should have nothing to do with conquest."

Having now annexed several foreign colonies—the Philippines, Guam, Pago Pago, Wake and Midway islands, Hawaii, and Puerto

The presidential election of 1900 pitted Republican William McKinley (left), a proponent of American empire and a staunch defender of the eastern establishment, against Democrat William Jennings Bryan (right), a midwestern populist and outspoken anti-imperialist. With McKinley's victory, Bryan's warnings against American empire would, tragically, be ignored.

Rico—and asserted practical control over Cuba, the United States was about to betray its most precious gift to mankind.

While most Americans thought the United States had fulfilled its "manifest destiny" by spreading across North America, it was William Henry Seward, secretary of state to both Abraham Lincoln and Andrew Johnson, who articulated a far more grandiose vision of American empire. He set his sights on acquiring Hawaii, Canada, Alaska, the Virgin Islands, Midway Island, and parts of Santo Domingo, Haiti, and Colombia. A lot of this dream would actually come true.

But while Seward dreamed, the European empires acted. Britain led the way in the last thirty years of the nineteenth century, gobbling up 4.75 million square miles of territory, an area significantly larger than the United States. Britain, like the Romans of yore, believed her mission was to bring civilization to mankind. France added 3.5 million square miles. Germany, off to a late start, added one million. Only Spain's empire was in decline.

By 1878, European empires and their former colonies controlled 67 percent of the earth's land surface. And by 1914, they controlled an astounding 84 percent. By the 1890s, Europeans had carved up 90 percent of Africa, the lion's share claimed by Belgium, Britain, France, and Germany.

The United States was anxious to make up for lost time, and, although empire was a hostile concept to Americans, most of whom had come from immigrant stock, it was now an era dominated by the robber barons—in particular, an aristocracy known as the "400," with their huge estates, private armies, and legions of employees. Men like J. P. Morgan, John D. Rockefeller, and William Randolph Hearst held enormous power.

The capitalist class, haunted by visions of the revolutionary workers who formed the Paris Commune of 1871, conjured up similar nightmarish visions of radicals upsetting the system in the United States. These radicals or communards were also called communists more than fifty years before the Russian Revolution of 1917.

Jay Gould's fifteen-thousand-mile railroad network epitomized the worst of the robber barons. Gould was perhaps the most hated man in America, having once boasted that he could "hire one half of the working class to kill the other half."

When the financial panic of "Black Friday" 1893 hit Wall Street, it triggered the nation's worst depression to date. Mills, factories, furnaces, and mines shut down everywhere in large numbers. Four million workers lost their jobs. Unemployment reached 20 percent.

The American Railway Union headed by Eugene Debs responded to layoffs and pay cuts by George Pullman's Palace Car Company and shut down the nation's railroads. Federal troops were sent in on the side of the railroad magnates. Dozens of workers were killed and Debs spent six months in jail.

The socialists, trade unionists, and reformers at home protested that capitalism's cyclical depressions resulted from the underconsumption of the working class. In his pioneering photography, Jacob Riis shocked the nation by documenting the misery of New York City's poor. Working-class leaders were arguing for redistributing wealth at home so that working people could afford to buy the goods they produced in America's farms and factories.

But the 400—the oligarchs—responded that this was a form of socialism. They said there could be a bigger pie for all and argued that the U.S. had to compete with foreign empires and dominate the trade of the world so that foreigners would absorb America's growing surplus. The profit was clearly abroad—in trade, cheap labor, and cheap resources.

The chief prize was China. To tap this vast market, the U.S. would need a modern, steam-powered navy and bases around the world to compete with the British Empire, with its major concession at the port of Hong Kong. Russia, Japan, France, and Germany were all clawing to get in.

Businessmen began pressing for a canal across Central America, which would help open the door to Asia.

In 1898, in this climate of global competition, the United States annexed Hawaii. Almost one hundred years later, a U.S. congressional resolution apologized "to Native Hawaiians" for the deprivation of their right "to self-determination."

Cuba, less than one hundred miles from the shores of Florida, had revolted against the corrupt Spanish rule, and the Spanish reacted by incarcerating much of the population in concentration camps where ninety-five thousand died of disease. As the fighting increased, powerful bankers and businessmen, like Morgan and the Rockefellers, who had millions invested on the island, demanded action from the president—to safeguard their interests.

President McKinley sent the USS *Maine* to Havana harbor as a signal to the Spanish that the U.S. was keeping an eye on American interests.

On a night in February 1898, with the tropical heat more than one hundred degrees, the *Maine* suddenly exploded, killing 254 seamen, allegedly sabotaged by the Spanish. The U.S. "Yellow Press," led by William Randolph Hearst's *New York Journal* and Joseph Pulitzer's *New York World*, led a crazed tabloid reaction and created a vigilante climate for war.

The *Journal* cried: "Remember the Maine, To Hell With Spain!"

Millions read it, convinced that Spain, this decaying Catholic power, was capable of any evil deed to preserve her empire. When McKinley declared war, Hearst took credit: "How do you like the *Journal*'s war?" he asked.

Often remembered by Teddy Roosevelt's symbolically colorful charge up San Juan Hill, the Spanish-American War was over in three months. Secretary of State John Hay called it a "splendid little war." Out of almost fifty-five hundred U.S. dead, fewer than four hundred died in battle, the rest succumbing to disease.

Sixteen-year-old Smedley Darlington Butler lied about his age and signed up with the marines. He would become one of America's most famous military heroes, winning two medals of honor in a career that would span America's early descent into global empire.

With victory, American businessmen swept in, grabbing assets where they could, essentially making Cuba into a protectorate. United Fruit Company locked up two million acres of land for sugar production. By 1901, Bethlehem Steel and other U.S. businesses owned over 80 percent of Cuban minerals.

More than seventy years later, in 1976, an under-reported official investigation by the navy found that the most probable cause of the sinking of the *Maine* was a boiler that exploded in the tropical heat, causing the ship's ammunition store to explode. As with Vietnam and the two Iraq wars, the U.S., basing its reaction on false intelligence, went to war because it wanted to.

In the glow of victory, however, the U.S. found itself with a much bigger problem. It had acquired from the Spanish a gigantic but ramshackle land mass in the Far East—the Philippine Islands—which were viewed as an ideal refueling stop for China-bound ships. As in the invasion of Baghdad in 2003, the fighting there began successfully. Commodore George Dewey had destroyed the Spanish fleet in Manila Bay in May 1898. One anti-imperialist noted, "Dewey took Manila with the loss of one man, and all our institutions."

The Anti-Imperialist League, founded in Boston in 1898, sought to block U.S. annexation of the Philippines and Puerto Rico. Its ranks included Mark Twain, who famously asked, "Shall we go on conferring our

Civilization upon the peoples that sit in darkness, or shall we give those poor things a rest?"

President McKinley chose the former, opting finally for annexation. "There was nothing left for us to do," he declared, "but to take them all, and to educate the Filipinos, and uplift and civilize and Christianize them and by God's grace do the very best we could by them, as our fellow-men for whom Christ also died."

McKinley ran into one major problem—the Filipinos themselves. Under the fiery leadership of Emilio Aguinaldo, the Filipinos had established their own republic in 1899, after being freed from Spain, and, like the Cuban rebels, expected the United States to recognize it. They had overestimated their ally. And now they fought back. After one protest, Americans lay dead on the streets of Manila. America's Yellow Press cried out for vengeance against the barbarians. Torture, including waterboarding, became routine. The insurgents, or "our little brown brothers" as William Howard Taft, the governor-general of the Philippines, called them, were pumped full of salt water until they swelled up like toads to "make them talk." One soldier wrote home, "We all wanted to kill 'niggers.' . . . This shooting human beings beats rabbit hunting all to pieces."

It was a war of atrocities. When rebels ambushed American troops on the island of Samar, Colonel Jacob Smith ordered his men to kill everyone over the age of ten and turn the island into "a howling wilderness."

More than four thousand U.S. troops would not return from this guerilla war, which lasted three and a half years. Twenty thousand Filipino guerillas were killed, and as many as two hundred thousand civilians died—many from cholera. But because of distorted press reports, mainland Americans comforted themselves with the thought that they had spread civilization to a backward people.

American society grew more callous from this war. The doctrine of Anglo-Saxon superiority that justified a nascent empire was also poisoning social relations at home as southern racists, resorting to similar arguments, intensified their campaign to reverse the outcome of the American Civil War and passed new Jim Crow laws enforcing white supremacy and segregation.

ABOVE: *Plowing on a Cuban sugar plantation.*

RIGHT: *The United Fruit Company office building in New Orleans. The Spanish-American War proved quite profitable for American businessmen. Once the war in Cuba ended, United Fruit took 1.9 million acres of Cuban land at 20 cents an acre.*

In China, a similar yearning for independence led to the homegrown Boxer Rebellion of 1898 to 1901. Nationalist-minded Chinese rose up with fury to murder missionaries and throw out all foreign invaders. McKinley sent five thousand American troops to help the Europeans and the Japanese defeat the rebels.

Lieutenant Smedley Butler was in the invading force leading his

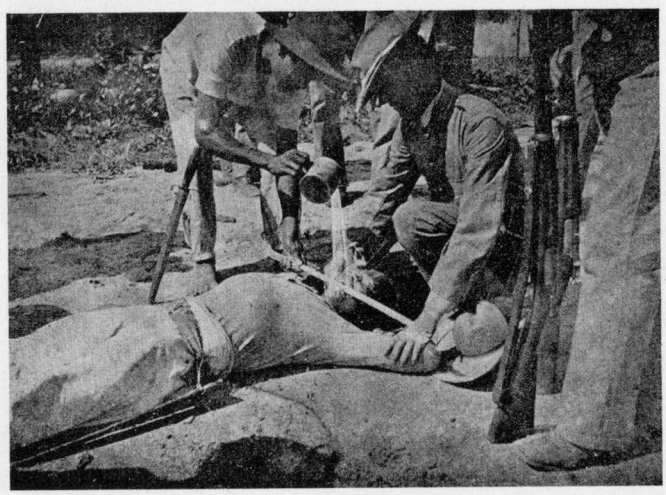

During the Spanish-American War in the Philippines, atrocities were common. U.S. troops employed the torture we now called waterboarding. One reporter wrote "our soldiers pumped salt water into men to 'make them talk.'"

Marines into Beijing where he saw firsthand the way the victorious Europeans treated the Chinese. He was disgusted.

Thus, as in 2008, the 1900 American election took place with U.S. troops tied down in numerous countries—in this case, China, Cuba, and the Philippines. And yet, McKinley, basking in the glow of victory over Spain, beat Bryan by a wider margin than he had in 1896. Socialist Eugene Debs barely registered with under one percent. Americans had clearly endorsed McKinley's vision of trade and empire.

At the height of his popularity, in 1901, McKinley was assassinated by an anarchist. The assassin had complained about American atrocities in the Philippines. The new president, Theodore Roosevelt, an even more unabashed imperialist, continued McKinley's expansionist policies. And Roosevelt, orchestrating a revolution in Panama, a province of Colombia, signed a treaty with the newly created Panamanian government to lease the Canal Zone, receiving the same rights of intervention the U.S. had forced upon Cuba. The canal was built with great difficulty and finally opened in 1914.

The bodies of dead Filipinos. A Philadelphia reporter wrote that soldiers stood Filipinos on a bridge, shot them, and floated the corpses down the river for all to see.

In the years to follow, U.S. Marines were repeatedly sent in to protect U.S. business interests in what were now called "Banana Republics," considered backward and in need of strong rule by sometimes brutal dictators able to force U.S. business interests down the throats of resistant workers and peasants.

Cuba. Honduras. Nicaragua. The Dominican Republic. Haiti. Panama. Guatemala. Mexico. U.S. occupations often lasted for years, sometimes for decades.

No one had more firsthand experience intervening in other countries than Smedley Butler, now a major general in the Marine Corps. He was adored by his men, who called him "Old Gimlet Eye" after a wound sustained in Honduras. And at the end of his long and highly decorated service, he reflected upon his years in uniform. In his book, *War Is a Racket*, he wrote, "I spent thirty-three years and four months in active military service as a member of this country's most agile military force, the Marine Corps. I served in all commissioned ranks from Second Lieutenant to Major-General. And during that period, I spent most of my

General Smedley Butler fought in the Philippines, China, and Central America. He wrote that he was "a high class muscle-man for Big Business, for Wall Street and for the Bankers . . . a gangster for capitalism."

time being a high class muscle-man for Big Business, for Wall Street and for the Bankers. In short, I was a racketeer, a gangster for capitalism. I suspected I was just part of a racket at the time. Now I am sure of it. Like all the members of the military profession, I never had a thought of my own until I left the service. . . . I helped make Mexico, especially Tampico, safe for American oil interests in 1914. I helped make Haiti and Cuba a decent place for the National City Bank boys to collect revenues in. I helped in the raping of half a dozen Central American republics for the benefits of Wall Street. The record of racketeering is long. I helped purify Nicaragua for the international banking house of Brown Brothers in 1909–1912. I brought light to the Dominican Republic for American sugar interests in 1916. In China I helped to see to it that Standard Oil went its way unmolested. During those years, I had, as the boys in the back room would say, a swell racket. Looking back on it, I feel that I could have given Al Capone a few hints. The best he could do was to operate his racket in three districts. I operated on three continents."

His outspokenness over the years would cost Butler dearly when he was passed over as commandant of the Marine Corps, which he left in 1931 under a cloud of contention.

If "war [was] a racket" as Butler said, World War I was among the most dismal episodes of racketeering in human history. One of the lesser-known facts of this story is that on the eve of World War I, the banks of the British Empire were in crisis. Britain's economic model of cannibalizing the economies of increasing parts of the globe in order to survive and not investing in its own homegrown manufacturing was failing. Cycles of depression came and went.

In contrast, the newly unified German Empire was leading the nations of continental Europe in a move away from free trade to protectionist measures that encouraged the growth of a domestic industrial base not as dependent on colonization.

Germany was competing in the production of steel, electrical power, chemical energy, agriculture, iron, coal, and textiles. Its banks and railroads were growing, and in the battle for oil, the newest strategic fuel that was necessary to power modern navies, Germany's merchant fleet was rapidly gaining on Britain's. England, now heavily dependent on oil imports from the U.S. and Russia, was desperate to find potential new reserves in the Middle East, which was part of the tottering Ottoman Empire.

And when the Germans began building a railroad to import this oil from Baghdad to Berlin through their alliances with this Ottoman Empire, Britain was deeply opposed. The interests of their nearby Egyptian and Indian empires were threatened. Enormous unrest in the Balkans, particularly in Serbia, helped block the Berlin-Baghdad railroad from completion.

In fact, it was a minor affair in Serbia that finally set off the chain of events of World War I, when Archduke Franz Ferdinand, heir to the Austro-Hungarian Empire, and his wife were assassinated on the streets of Sarajevo in the baking summer of 1914. The situation deteriorated quickly and a series of complex alliances between competing economic empires led to the greatest war yet in human history.

The war was a slaughter from beginning to end on a level

incomprehensible to the public. In the first battle of the Marne, in 1915, the British, the French, and the Germans suffered five hundred thousand casualties each. The war lasted beyond all expectations. In one brutal single day at the Somme, Britain lost sixty thousand. France and Germany suffered almost a million casualties during the Battle of Verdun in 1916.

Repeatedly ordering its soldiers to charge into the teeth of German machine guns and artillery, France ultimately lost half of its young men between the ages of fifteen and thirty. Germany first used poison gas at the second Battle of Ypres in April 1915, following an abortive attempt at Bolimów on the eastern front, blanketing French troops along four miles of trenches. The *Washington Post* reported that French soldiers were driven insane or died from agonizing suffocation, their bodies turned black, green, or yellow.

The British retaliated with gas at Loos in September, only to see the winds shift and the gas blown back into the British trenches, resulting in more British casualties than German. In 1917, Germany unleashed even more potent mustard gas weapons against the British, again at Ypres.

Novelist Henry James wrote: "The plunge of civilization into this abyss of blood and darkness is a thing that so gives away this whole long age during which we have supposed the world to be gradually bettering."

Woodrow Wilson was the embodiment of Henry James's prewar ideal of hope and civilization. First elected president in 1912, he echoed most Americans' sympathy for the Allies (Britain, France, Italy, Japan, and Russia) against the Central Powers (Germany, Austria, Hungary, and Turkey) but he didn't join the war, explaining, "We have to be neutral. Since otherwise, our mixed populations would wage war on each other."

He won re-election in 1916 with the slogan "He kept us out of war," but he would soon reverse course.

Wilson was an interesting man. He had been president of Princeton University and governor of New Jersey. Descended from Presbyterian ministers on both sides of his family, he exhibited a strong moralistic streak and sometimes a self-righteous inflexibility.

He shared a missionary's sense of America's global role and believed in the export of democracy—even to countries unwilling to receive it. He

U.S. soldiers undergoing anti-gas training at Camp Dix, New Jersey. Despite being proscribed by civilizations for centuries, chemical warfare became widespread during World War I. Thousands died from poisonous gas attacks.

shared as well his southern forebears' sense of white racial superiority, taking steps to resegregate the federal government. When a delegation of African Americans petitioned him, he replied: "Segregation is not a humiliation, but a benefit."

The old anti-imperialist William Jennings Bryan, now serving as Wilson's secretary of state, tried to maintain America's sense of neutrality in the war, but Wilson rejected his efforts to bar U.S. citizens from traveling on ships of belligerent nations.

Britain, which for nearly a century had controlled the Atlantic with its superior naval power, had launched a blockade of Northern Europe. Germany retaliated with a highly effective U-boat campaign that seemed to tilt the balance of power on the high seas. In May 1915, a German

U-boat sank the British liner *Lusitania*, leaving 1,200 dead including 128 Americans. It was a shock. Some called for America to go to war. But, despite initial disclaimers, it was found that the ship was indeed in violation of neutrality laws and carrying a large cargo of arms to Britain.

Bryan demanded that Wilson condemn the British blockade of Germany as well as the German attack, seeing both as infringements of neutral rights. When Wilson refused, Bryan resigned in protest, fearing that Wilson was inching toward war. He was right. Wilson was increasingly coming to believe that if the U.S. did not join the war, it would be denied a role in shaping the postwar world.

And in January 1917, he dramatically delivered the first formal presidential address to the Senate since the days of George Washington. He called for "peace without victory" based on core American principles of self-determination, freedom of the seas, and an open world with no entangling alliances. The centerpiece of such a world would be a league of nations to enforce the peace. Wilson's idealism has always been suspect because it seemed to be consistently undermined by his politics. American neutrality in this war was in effect more a principle than a practice.

J. P. Morgan and Rockefeller of Standard Oil had been the two titans of American finance since the Civil War. Morgan died in 1913, but his son, J. P. Morgan, Jr., effectively served as America's banker to the British Empire between 1915 and 1917, when the U.S. entered the war.

Initially, the United States would not allow American bankers to float loans to the belligerents, knowing that this would undermine America's stated neutrality, but, in September 1915, in his first term, Wilson, ignoring Bryan's advice, reversed himself. And in that month, Morgan floated a $500 million loan to Britain and France. By 1917, the British War Office had borrowed close to $2.5 billion from the House of Morgan and other Wall Street banks. Only $27 million had been loaned to Germany.

By 1919, after the war, Britain found itself owing the United States a staggering sum of $4.7 billion—$61 billion in today's dollars. Morgan also became the sole purchasing agent for the British Empire in the U.S., placing some $20 billion in purchase orders and taking a 2 percent commission on the price of all goods, favoring friends like the owners of Du Pont Chemical and Remington and Winchester Arms.

Socialist Eugene Debs had consistently urged workers to oppose the war, observing: "Let the capitalists do their own fighting and furnish their own corpses and there will never be another war on the face of the earth."

Whether for financial or idealistic reasons, in April 1917, Woodrow Wilson asked Congress for a declaration of war, saying, "The world must be made safe for democracy." Six senators voted against it, including Robert La Follette of Wisconsin, as did fifty representatives in the House, including Jeannette Rankin of Montana, the first woman ever elected to Congress.

Opponents attacked Wilson as a tool of Wall Street. "We are putting a dollar sign on the American flag," charged Senator George Norris of Nebraska. Opposition ran deep, but Wilson got his wish.

Yet, despite government appeals for a million volunteers, reports of the horrors of trench warfare dampened enthusiasm and only seventy-three thousand men signed up in the first six weeks, forcing Congress to institute a draft.

As 1918 dawned, it looked as if the Central Powers might indeed win the war and defeat the Allies, which threatened to leave U.S. bankers in a huge financial hole. America rallied with patriotic Liberty Bond drives. And many of the nation's leading progressives—including John Dewey and Walter Lippmann—took Wilson's side. But it was the midwestern Republicans like La Follette and Norris who understood that the war was a death knell for meaningful reform at home.

And Congress confirmed this in passing some of the most repressive legislation in the country's history—the Espionage Act of 1917 and the Sedition Act of 1918—which curbed speech and created a climate of intolerance toward dissent.

University professors who opposed the war were either fired or cowed into silence. Hundreds were jailed for speaking out, including Industrial Workers of the World (IWW) leader "Big Bill" Haywood. Eugene Debs protested repeatedly and was finally arrested in June 1918, saying, "Wars throughout history have been waged for conquest and plunder, and that is war in a nutshell. . . . The master class has always declared the wars; the subject class has always fought the battles."

Before being sentenced, Debs eloquently addressed the courtroom, "Your honor, years ago I recognized my kinship within all living beings,

Wisconsin's Robert "Fighting Bob" La Follette was one of six senators who voted against U.S. entry into World War I.

and I made up my mind that I was not one bit better than the meanest on earth. I said then, and I say now, that while there is a lower class, I am in it; while there is a criminal element, I am of it; while there is a soul in prison, I am not free."

The judge sentenced Debs to ten years in prison. He served three, from 1919 to 1921.

With Wilson's permission, the Department of Justice destroyed the IWW—the Wobblies. While some Americans marched off to war to the strains of the hit song "Over There," the Wobblies responded with a parody of "Onward Christian Soldiers" titled "Christians at War," which ended with "History will say of you: 'That pack of God damned fools.'"

One hundred sixty-five of their leaders were charged with conspiring to hinder the draft and encourage desertion. Big Bill Haywood fled to revolutionary Russia; others followed.

German-Americans were singled out with particular animosity. Schools, many of which now demanded loyalty oaths from teachers, banned German from their curricula and orchestras dropped German

Under the 1917 Espionage Act, the U.S. imprisoned hundreds of draft protesters, including IWW leader "Big Bill" Haywood and Socialist Eugene Debs. Debs (pictured here addressing a crowd in Chicago in 1912) had urged workers to oppose the war, proclaiming, "Let the capitalists do their own fighting and furnish their own corpses and there will never be another war on the face of the earth."

composers from their repertoires. Just as French fries would later be renamed freedom fries by congressional xenophobes furious at French opposition to the invasion of Iraq in 2003, during World War I, hamburgers were renamed "liberty sandwiches" and sauerkraut was called "liberty cabbage." German measles became "liberty measles" and German shepherds became "police dogs."

The war years were to bring unprecedented collusion between large corporations and the government in an attempt to stabilize the economy, control unfettered competition, and guarantee profits to munition makers, who were sometimes characterized as "merchants of death."

It was more than a year after declaring war that U.S. troops finally arrived in Europe in May 1918, six months before the war's end, when they helped beleaguered French forces turn the tide along the Marne River. With its manpower and its industrial might, the U.S. presence had an enormous psychological effect on the war and demoralized the Germans, who finally surrendered.

The long, dreary war ended on November 11, 1918. The losses were staggering. Of the 2 million American soldiers who reached France, over 116,000 died and 204,000 were wounded. European losses were truly beyond reason, up to an estimated 8 million soldiers and 6 to 10 million civilians dead—the latter often due to disease and starvation. But, as happened in World War II, no people suffered more in this war than the Russians, with 1.7 million dead and almost 5 million wounded.

Those who survived were living in a new world order. Britain and France had been badly weakened. The German Empire had collapsed. The Austro-Hungarian Empire, more than fifty years old, was over, resulting in the chaotic restructuring of Eastern Europe. And the great polyglot Ottoman Empire of Arabs, Turks, Kurds, Armenians, Muslims, Christians, and Jews, which had lasted for six hundred years, now crumbled.

In Russia, a mysterious group of revolutionaries known as the Bolsheviks, promising bread, land, and peace, took power in October 1917 in the ruined realm of Tsar Nicholas II, who had lost the army in the slaughterhouse of World War I and with it the trust of both soldiers and workers who were fed up by the brutality of this war.

The Bolsheviks were deeply inspired by a German-Jewish intellectual, Karl Marx, calling for the social and economic equality of man. And they immediately set out to reorganize Russian society at its roots—nationalizing banks, distributing land and estates to the peasants, putting workers in control of factories, and confiscating church property.

And in March 1918, eight months before the end of World War I and almost two months before U.S. troops saw action in France, Bolshevik leader Vladimir Lenin signed a peace treaty with Germany, pulling Russian troops from the war. Woodrow Wilson and the Allies were furious.

The Bolsheviks were vowing to destroy the old secretive ways of capitalism and empire building, throwing them into the dustbin of history. They were promising, incredibly, world revolution, and uprisings ensued in Budapest, Munich, and Berlin. The remaining European empires, Belgium, Britain, and France, trembled.

Not since the French Revolution, some 125 years before, had Europe been so profoundly shaken and changed. Inspired by the Russian Revolution, a wave of hope gripped colonized and oppressed peoples on six continents.

Vladimir Lenin and the Bolsheviks seized control of Russia on November 7, 1917, dramatically altering the course of world history. Lenin's vision of worldwide communist revolution would capture the imagination of workers and peasants around the globe, posing a direct challenge to Woodrow Wilson's vision of liberal capitalist democracy.

In one brazen act, Lenin's Red Guard ransacked the old foreign office and published what was found—a web of secret agreements between the European Allies, dividing the postwar map into exclusive zones of influence. Much as the United States would react to the Wikileaks publications of its diplomatic cables in 2010, the Allies were outraged by this violation of the old diplomatic protocol, which now exposed the hollowness of Woodrow Wilson's call for "self-determination" after the war.

Wilson, appalled as he was by Lenin's actions, was already aware of and disgusted by what the French and British had secretly agreed to. But, nonetheless, he sent American troops into battle on behalf of the French and British empires.

The conservative counter-revolution against the Bolsheviks was ferocious. Separate armies were attacking the new Russia from all directions—Native Russians and Cossacks, the Czech legion, Serbs, Greeks, Poles in the West, the French in Ukraine, and some seventy thousand

Japanese in the Far East. In reaction, Lenin's revolutionary coleader Leon Trotsky ruthlessly put together a Red Army of approximately 5 million men. The outspoken and influential ex–lord of the Admiralty Winston Churchill said, "Bolshevism ought to be strangled in its cradle."

An estimated forty thousand British troops arrived in Russia, some deployed to the Caucasus to protect the oil reserves at Baku. Though most of the fighting would be over by 1920, pockets of resistance persisted until 1923. In a foreshadowing of what was to come some sixty years later, Muslim resistance in Central Asia lasted into the 1930s.

Wilson initially hesitated to join the invading forces, rejecting the notion of overthrowing the new regime, but ended up sending more than thirteen thousand American troops and helping arm and finance the anti-Bolshevik forces. Senator Robert La Follette deplored this action as a mockery of Wilson's idealism.

To deny the counter-revolutionaries their major rallying point, in July 1918, in a devastating shock to the ways of prewar Europe, Lenin ordered the execution of the tsar and his family. Exiled into the interior, they were all summarily shot and brutally finished off with bayonets in the cellar.

Lenin's secret police, the Cheka, was successful in mopping up many of the Bolsheviks' remaining enemies. Tales of the "Red Terror," often exaggerated, were carried west. And when Wilson allowed U.S. troops to remain in Russia until 1920, it deeply poisoned the beginnings of any U.S.-Soviet relationship. The U.S. would not recognize Soviet Russia until Franklin Roosevelt's presidency in 1933.

When he arrived in Europe in December 1918 for the Paris Peace Conference, Wilson was mobbed by adoring crowds. Two million cheered him in Paris. When he entered Rome, the streets were sprinkled with golden sand, as per ancient tradition. The Italians proclaimed him "The God of Peace."

Twenty-seven nations met in Paris on January 12, 1919. Wilson was the star. The world was going to be remade. Wilson considered himself the "personal instrument of God" and the Peace Conference was the crowning moment of his divine mission. It was indeed his most glorious moment, but, as with Alexander in Babylon, Caesar in Rome, and Napoleon on the frontiers of Europe, a zenith of success had been reached.

President Woodrow Wilson speaking at the Greek Theatre in Berkeley, California, September 1919. Reelected president in 1916 on the slogan "He kept us out of war," Wilson entered World War I in 1917, hoping to give the United States a hand in shaping the postwar world. Through this and other actions, Wilson put his personal stamp on the office and the country to a much greater extent than his immediate predecessor or his successors.

In reinterpreting World War I ideologically, along the lines of the wars of the French Revolution a century earlier, Wilson was claiming that this was a war to change humanity, a war to end all wars. In an address to the United States Senate that year, he was to say that America's road on the world stage "has come about by no plan of our conceiving, but by the hand of God. . . . It was of this that we dreamed in our birth. America shall in truth show the way." In Wilson's view, America's manifest destiny was no longer a case of continental expansion. It was now a divinely ordained mission to humanity. This idea of saving humanity became essential to the American national myth in all subsequent wars.

In an attempt to counter Lenin's revolutionary appeal, Wilson had, one year earlier, while the war was still raging, announced a set of

From left to right: British Prime Minister David Lloyd George, Italian Premier Vittorio Orlando, French Premier Georges Clemenceau, and Wilson at the Paris Peace Conference. At the conference, most of the lofty rhetoric of Wilson's 14 Points was rejected by the other Allies, who were out for revenge, new colonies, and naval dominance in the postwar world.

international democratic principles, including free trade, open seas, and open agreements between nations that would become the basis of a new international peace. He called this the 14 Points.

The Germans surrendered on the basis of Wilson's 14 Points, believing he would guard them from dismemberment by the Allies. They even changed their form of government, adopting a republic, and opposed the kaiser, who soon disappeared into exile. The United States was the new dominant force in the world. Although it had been a debtor nation in 1914, owing $3.7 billion, by 1918, it had become a creditor nation and was owed $3.8 billion by its allies.

Nonetheless, the old, multinational empires that had stood since the Middle Ages had no interest in Wilson's idealism—they wanted revenge and money and colonies. British prime minister Lloyd George noted that in the United States "not a shack" had been destroyed. French prime minister Georges Clemenceau, whose country had lost over one million soldiers, commented: "Mr. Wilson bores me with his 14 Points; why, God Almighty has only ten!" As a result of this attitude, several of Wilson's ill-defined 14 Points would be removed from the Treaty of Versailles.

Britain, France, and Japan divided the former German colonies in Asia and Africa, and, paying lip service to the promised self-determination of the Arabs who had revolted against the Ottoman Empire, Winston Churchill and the Foreign Office divided that empire, creating new client-states such as Mesopotamia, which was arbitrarily renamed Iraq.

The prospect of a future Jewish homeland in Palestine was also established in a letter from British foreign secretary Arthur Balfour to the Jewish banker Lord Rothschild. A protectorate was established by the League of Nations over Palestine. Approximately 85 percent of the native population was Palestinian Arab and fewer than 8 percent Jewish,

The old empires sanitized their actions by calling these new colonies "mandates," and Wilson went along with it by arguing that the Germans had ruthlessly exploited their colonies, whereas the Allies had treated their colonies humanely—an assessment that was greeted with incredulity by the inhabitants of French Indochina.

Ho Chi Minh as a young man rented a tuxedo and bowler hat and visited Wilson carrying a petition for Vietnamese independence. Like other Third World leaders in attendance, Ho would learn that liberation would only come through armed struggle—not Woodrow Wilson's largesse.

Although Lenin was not invited to Paris, Russia's presence cast a pall over the meetings. Lenin called Wilson a "smoother over." He said, "only genuine revolutionaries may be trusted!" And as the delegates sat, communists took over Bavaria and Hungary and threatened Berlin and Italy.

Lenin's call for worldwide revolution was heard in the Third World, in lands as far away as China and Latin America.

Focused intently on his League of Nations, which he considered essential to preventing future war, Wilson failed to secure the kind of nonpunitive treaty he publicly advocated.

Britain and France perversely applied Wilson's concept of self-determination against Germany—leaving millions of citizens stranded

French Indochina's Ho Chi Minh rented a tuxedo and bowler hat and visited Wilson and the U.S. delegation to the Paris Peace Conference, carrying a petition demanding Vietnamese independence. Like most of the other non-Western world leaders in attendance, Ho would learn that liberation would come through armed struggle, not the colonizers' largesse.

outside their new, shrunken border. In its famous war-guilt clause, the Treaty of Versailles placed the entire blame for starting the war on Germany, and not the other colonial empires, and required it to pay almost $33 billion to the Allies in war reparations—more than double what Germany expected.

Prominent in Wilson's delegation was Thomas Lamont, the House of Morgan's leading partner, upon whom Wilson relied. Lamont made sure that Germany's payments to Britain and France would, in turn, allow them to repay the fortune they had borrowed on Wall Street to survive the war. In reality, then, the entire new structure of international finance was built on the shaky foundation of German war reparations, which would shortly contribute to a German economic collapse out of which Adolf Hitler would emerge.

In years to come, the U.S. Congress would investigate the machinations of the so-called merchants of death. These were the industrialists

THE GAP IN THE BRIDGE.

As this December 1919 Punch *cartoon shows, Congress's rejection of U.S. participation in the League of Nations rendered the League largely ineffectual. Wilson had helped guarantee the League's defeat by silencing potential anti-imperialist allies during the war.*

and bankers who had made obscene profits from the war. No one was convicted, nothing proven. But there remained a lingering populist feeling of distrust for World War I. Many, including congressional leaders, felt that millions had been sacrificed in a financial boondoggle for bankers and other war profiteers. The bitterness of this feeling was intense.

Wilson came home to a country where American labor was rife with discontent and desperate for reform. In the year 1914, by example, as many as 35,000 workers were killed in industrial accidents. Over 4 million workers went on strike in 1919 alone: 365,000 steel workers, 450,000 miners, 120,000 textile workers. In Seattle, a general strike shut down the entire city. In Boston, even the police force walked out, leading the *Wall Street Journal* to warn: "Lenin and Trotsky are on the way."

President Wilson, in response, wanted to discredit Lenin's message. Communism was a European madness, he insisted, not an American one. In the so-called Red Summer of 1919, race riots exploded out of

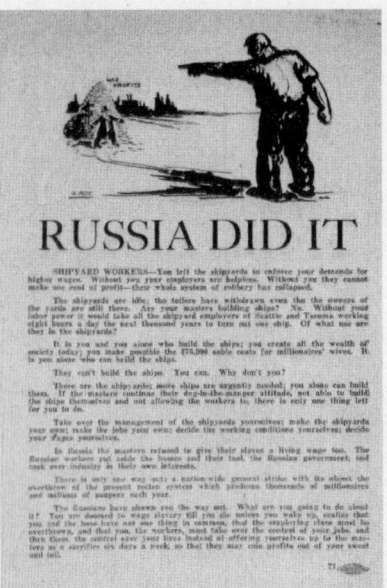

RUSSIA DID IT

In 1919, more than 4 million U.S. workers struck for higher wages, better conditions, and organizing rights. As illustrated by this leaflet from the Seattle General Strike, the Russian Revolution helped inspire this intensified labor militancy.

control in Chicago and several other cities, including Washington, D.C. Federal troops arrived to restore order.

President Wilson continued to travel the land, arguing that the U.S. needed to ratify the Versailles Treaty and establish the League of Nations to ensure his vision of world peace. Progressive Republicans denounced Wilson's League of Nations as a League of Imperialists, bent upon defeating revolutions and defending their own imperial desires. Critics demanded changes, but no modifications were acceptable to Wilson.

His health began to suffer and, at a final speech in Pueblo, Colorado, in September 1919, he collapsed. He suffered a severe stroke and was incapacitated for the rest of his life.

In November 1919, Attorney General A. Mitchell Palmer unleashed federal agents in the first of a series of raids on radical and labor organizations across the country. The operation was run by the twenty-four-year-old director of the Justice Department's Radical Division—J. Edgar Hoover. Somewhere between three and ten thousand dissidents were arrested, many incarcerated without charges for months. Hundreds of foreign-born radicals, including Russian-born Emma Goldman, were deported as civil liberties were increasingly abused and dissent was identified with un-Americanism.

The Senate rejected the Versailles Treaty by seven votes. The League of Nations was born but was crippled without the participation of the United States. Wilson died in 1924, a broken man.

By the early 1920s, the America of Jefferson, Lincoln, and William Jennings Bryan had ceased to exist. It had been replaced by the world of Morgan, Wall Street bankers, and huge corporations. Wilson had hoped to transform the world, but his record is much less positive. While supporting self-determination and opposing formal empire, he intervened repeatedly in other nations' internal affairs, including those of Russia, Mexico, and throughout Latin America. While encouraging reform, he maintained a deep mistrust of the kind of fundamental, and at times revolutionary, change that would actually improve people's lives. While endorsing human brotherhood, he believed nonwhites were inferior and resegregated the federal government. While extolling democracy and the rule of law, he oversaw egregious abuses of civil liberties.

Wilson's failures capped a period in which America's unique mixture of idealism, militarism, avarice, and diplomacy propelled the country toward becoming a new empire. The public in 1900 had rejected William Jennings Bryan and embraced William McKinley's vision of trade and prosperity and, in so doing, legitimized the U.S.'s imperial conquests. The 1900 election had indeed started the United States on a trajectory from which there was no turning back.

CHAPTER TWO

As the troops returned from overseas following the war, Republican presidential candidate Warren G. Harding was promising a "return to normalcy," ushering in one of the most conservative eras in American history. But the Teapot Dome scandal engulfed his administration and revealed the interior secretary to be in the pay of Big Oil, which had been plundering public lands. And the 1920s would turn out to be a decade of bold cultural experimentation mixed with political conservatism—an old culture of scarcity versus a new culture of abundance. This would be baptized "the Roaring Twenties."

Moral reformers feared that the Doughboys, having discovered what some called the "French Way," would foist their new appetite for oral sex as well as their diseases on innocent American girls. The licentious French had, after all, offered to set up brothels for American soldiers, like the ones that serviced their own fighting men, with the idea that it would maintain health standards and morale. But U.S. officials adamantly refused. And back home, moral crusaders had exploited wartime anxieties to shut down red light districts around the country, driving prostitutes underground and forcing them to seek protection from gangsters and pimps.

In 1919, the Eighteenth Amendment was ratified, banning the manufacture and sale of alcohol in the United States—a reform backed by women's temperance groups, certain Protestant denominations, the reborn Ku Klux Klan, and some progressives. But, as with the War on

Drugs later in the century, alcohol remained readily available for all who wanted it, and the War on Alcohol ended up producing fantastic profits for a new stratum of criminals dominated by Italian, Irish, and Jewish immigrant gangs.

Smedley Butler had seen some of the worst of the violence of World War I and the corruption that ensued. But now on sabbatical from the military, he was assigned to the streets of Philadelphia. Butler closed six hundred speakeasies—including two patronized by the city's elite—who had him fired. "Cleaning up Philadelphia," he noted, "was harder than any battle I was ever in."

Other repressive aspects of the new American life included immigration reform laws that imposed strict quotas on Southern and Eastern Europeans and entirely banned immigration from Japan, China, and East Asia.

Anti-Semitism infested postwar America. Some associated Jews with communism and radicalism. Others thought Jews exerted too much influence in Hollywood, business, and academia. Harvard slashed admission of Jewish freshmen from 28 percent in 1925 to 12 percent in 1933. Other top universities followed suit.

Other measures were taken to eliminate "undesirables." In 1911, as governor of New Jersey, eugenics enthusiast Woodrow Wilson had signed a law authorizing sterilization of convicts, epileptics, and the feebleminded. Over the following decades, some sixty thousand Americans would be sterilized, more than a third of them in California. Sexually active women were particularly targeted. Future German leader Adolf Hitler followed U.S. developments closely and claimed to model some of his own "master race" strategies on U.S. programs that he lauded but criticized for only going halfway. He would go further. Much further.

Between 1920 and 1925, 3 to 6 million Americans joined the racist, anti-Semitic, anti-Catholic Ku Klux Klan, which dominated politics in Indiana, Colorado, Oregon, Oklahoma, and Alabama, and sent hundreds of delegates to the 1924 Democratic convention. It is astonishing to think that in 1925 a quarter-million people watched thirty-five thousand Klansmen march and rally through Washington, D.C.

Hatred stalked the heartland. Fourteen-year-old Henry Fonda, the future movie star, recalled watching a lynching in Omaha, Nebraska, from his father's printing plant: "It was the most horrendous sight I'd ever seen. We locked the plant, went downstairs, and drove home in silence. My hands were wet and there were tears in my eyes. All I could think of was that young black man dangling at the end of a rope."

Hundreds more African Americans would suffer a similar fate. Often advertised widely in advance and memorialized on postcards and in sound recordings, lynchings became perverse rituals of desecration replete with dismemberment and castration and preserving body parts as souvenirs.

Backwoods Bible colleges proliferated. Anti-intellectualism abounded. In 1925, a Tennessee schoolteacher named John Thomas Scopes was prosecuted, convicted, and fined for teaching Darwin's evolution theories in school.

World War I marked the ascendancy of the U.S. and Japan, the war's two real victors. It had brought America an unprecedented collusion of bankers, businessmen, and government officials, in an attempt to fix the economy and guarantee profits. By 1925, the U.S. was producing over 70 percent of the world's oil, which had powered the allied wartime navies, airplanes, tanks, and other motorized vehicles. New York had replaced London as the center of the world economy. The size of the U.S. economy dwarfed that of its closest rivals.

Cynical and disillusioned from a brutal war, people were hungry to experience life in a way they had never done before.

A new materialism reigned based on credit, radios, movie palaces, and a golden age of advertising that perfected the capitalist art form of manipulating not only consumer hopes and fantasies but also fears and insecurities. Henry Ford sold 15 million Model-Ts before switching in 1927 to the more fashionable Model-A.

Jazz, with its roots in the African-American South, became wildly popular. Flappers, petting, speakeasies, the Harlem Renaissance, sports, and wild new movies with and without sound flourished.

Rebellious younger writers came on the scene. New expressionism emerged in the works of e. e. cummings, John Dos Passos, T. S. Eliot, Ernest Hemingway, Ezra Pound, William Faulkner, Lawrence Stallings,

Sinclair Lewis, Eugene O'Neill, Willa Cather, Langston Hughes, and Dalton Trumbo. Many of them, despairing of the shallowness of American culture, relocated to Europe.

F. Scott Fitzgerald wrote in 1920, "Here was a new generation . . . grown up to find all gods dead, all wars fought, all faiths in man shaken." Gertrude Stein, a lesbian writer living in Paris, told Hemingway and his drunken friends, "All of you young people who served in the war. You are a lost generation."

As the 1920s progressed, prosperity came to rest increasingly on the shakiest of foundations—unprecedented borrowing, massive speculation, and German war reparations. Agriculture was depressed throughout the decade. Auto manufacturing and road building slowed. Housing investment declined and the gap between rich and poor grew sharply. Capital scrambled for profitable speculative outlets.

To help pay Germany's war reparations, German foreign minister Walther Rathenau, a prominent Jewish industrialist, expanded economic, diplomatic, and even military ties with communist Russia—forging a bridge between the two nations that had been left out of Versailles—in order to rebuild their war-ravaged societies. This infuriated not only England and France but members of Germany's thuggish right-wing Freikorps, who were already up in arms about Germany paying its reparations. They assassinated Rathenau in 1922.

Germany's economy suffered an inflation unlike any ever experienced in history. Wheelbarrows full of worthless German marks were burned for firewood.

By 1923, a bankrupt Germany could no longer pay reparations to France and Britain, which, in turn, asked for relief on the billions in war debts they owed the U.S. government. "Absolutely not," replied the spartan new Republican president Calvin Coolidge.

By 1924, Europe's economies teetered on the edge of collapse. Then, and again four years later, commissions of bankers and businessmen, led by Morgan and his allies, drew up plans for German economic recovery that would guarantee continued, though more manageable, reparations payments. In essence, the U.S. was loaning money to Germany so that it could pay reparations to France and Britain, which then used the money to service their war debts to the U.S. The bankers got rich; people stayed poor. By 1933, Germany, though paying enormous reparations, owed even more money to the Allies than it had in 1924. It was in this climate of economic crisis in the West and communist revolution in the East that a new monster was born—it was called Nazism.

Separate and apart from Germany, in Italy in 1922, Benito Mussolini and his Fascisti took power and decimated the communists in bloody street battles.

And as 1925 came to an end, it was the Morgan bank that loaned Mussolini's government $100 million to repay its war debts to Britain. Morgan was very pleased with Mussolini's repressive labor policies.

"Nazis" stormed the city of Munich in 1923—led by World War I corporal Adolf Hitler. His followers included war veterans unable to adjust to civilian life who clamored for the chance to put down communist uprisings and later formed the backbone of his storm troopers. For his part in the failed coup, Hitler spent nine months in jail, refining his views. His shrill assertion that the German military had won the war only to be stabbed in the back by politicians at home was gaining more and more adherents. Hitler's cause would be greatly advanced when in 1929 the central bankers walked head-on into an unforeseen disaster—the Great Depression.

Montagu Norman, who ruled the private Bank of England from 1920 to 1944, was a paranoid anticommunist/anti-Semite who traveled incognito to avoid assassination. He asked the governor of the New York Federal Reserve bank to raise interest rates to slow Wall Street's soaring stock speculation. Ironically, Norman had been instrumental in convincing the previous governor to lower the rates two years earlier, which fueled the orgy of speculation that now rattled the system. Morgan's senior partner Thomas Lamont considered Norman "the wisest man he had ever met."

But the U.S. stock market, as it would in 2008, had diverted its money and credit away from production into speculation, borrowing to the hilt, in order to loot the economy for huge profit.

When the English and American banks raised their rates, the credit of the world tightened quickly and "too big to fail" American banks went into a panic. Huge banks in Austria and Germany followed.

The crash ended American loans to Germany. And Germany's industry collapsed entirely in the winter of 1931–32. Unemployment soared to over 30 percent, putting millions of angry young men in the streets. Capitalists and conservative politicians feared an imminent communist coup, and Hitler, Germany's most virulent anticommunist, was invited by the ruling classes into the government. Although still representing a radical minority party, in January 1933, Hitler became chancellor of Germany.

In his riveting speeches, Hitler touched a deep chord with many Germans, promising them something they could barely remember—pride.

But disorder followed Hitler's rise to power when the Reichstag, the National Parliament, mysteriously burned down. Hitler readily blamed the communists and many were thrown in concentration camps.

He quickly began a massive program of rearmament, which he made public in 1935. And once Hjalmar Schacht became his minister of economics, he received vital bank credits from Montagu Norman, who in 1934 told a Morgan partner, "Hitler and Schacht are the bulwarks of civilization in Germany. . . . They are fighting the war of our system of society against communism."

Many American bankers agreed, trusting their friend Schacht and hoping that Hitler would repay at least some of the reparations and also crush the German communists.

America was in deep crisis as well. Republican Herbert Hoover struggled ineffectively to quell the Great Depression.

More than twenty thousand, possibly as many as forty thousand, angry American veterans known as the "Bonus Army" descended on Washington, demanding war service bonuses not due to be paid until the year 1945. They set up a tent city on the Anacostia Flats in Washington. They brought their wives and children. They lived by military discipline—with daily parade and a strict "no drinking" rule.

General Smedley Butler arrived to lend moral support. "I know who's made this country worth livin' in!" he told them. "It's just you fellas. Look, it makes me so damn mad a whole lot of people speak of you as 'tramps.' By God, they didn't speak of you as tramps in 1917 and '18. Take it from me, this is the greatest demonstration of Americanism we have ever had—pure Americanism." He was mobbed by veterans wanting to speak to him. Until late that morning, he sat with them in their tents, listening to their tales of lost jobs, distressed families, and old battle wounds.

After demonstrators clashed with District police, President Hoover ordered General Douglas MacArthur to restore order. Convinced that the Bonus Army was the vanguard of a communist coup, MacArthur, not for the only time in his storied career, disobeyed presidential orders and rousted the veterans with tanks, bayonets, and tear gas.

MacArthur, whose aides included future generals Dwight Eisenhower and George Patton, pursued the fleeing veterans across the river and set their makeshift city aflame. It was the first time since the Civil War that American soldiers had knowingly attacked and wounded other American soldiers.

But when the Bonus Army marched again the next year into Washington, there was a new president in the White House, who sent First Lady Eleanor Roosevelt to help serve the veterans three hot meals a day with coffee. One veteran remarked, "Hoover sent the army, Roosevelt sent his wife." Several days later, the Bonus Army voted to disband. The new president put many of the veterans to work in the Civilian Conservation Corps.

It was in his famous inaugural address in March 1933 that Franklin Delano Roosevelt rallied the nation with his declaration "that the only thing we have to fear is fear itself." It was the signature line of his extraordinary life. In truth, he was facing a disaster. Unemployment stood at 25 percent. The gross national product had fallen 50 percent. Farmers lost 60 percent of their income. Industrial production dropped over 50 percent. Between 1930 and 1932, 20 percent of U.S. banks had failed. Breadlines formed in every town to feed the starving. Homeless walked the streets and slept in vast shanty-towns known as "Hoovervilles." There was no safety net to assist the desperate. Misery was everywhere.

Roosevelt united Americans around a message of inclusion—the opposite of Hitler's. "The measure of the restoration," he said, "lies in the extent to which we apply social values more noble than mere monetary profit."

In this vein, he called for "strict supervision of all banking and credits and investments" and "an end to speculation with other people's money." He proclaimed a New Deal. And although he could have nationalized the

Franklin Delano Roosevelt and Herbert Hoover en route to the U.S. Capitol for Roosevelt's inauguration, March 4, 1933. The inauguration sparked great optimism. Will Rogers commented on Roosevelt's early days, "If he burned down the capitol, we would cheer and say, 'Well, we at least got a fire started anyhow.'"

banks with hardly a word of protest, he chose a much more conservative course of action. He declared a four-day national bank holiday, conferred with the nation's top bankers on his first full day in office, and signed the emergency Banking Act, which was written largely by the bankers themselves. The banking system was essentially restored without radical change. And despite being accused of betraying his class, Roosevelt would, ironically, save capitalism from the capitalists themselves.

Recognizing the failures of unfettered capitalism, Roosevelt unleashed the powers of the federal government. In his first hundred days in office, he passed legislation that established the Agricultural Adjustment Administration to save farming, the Civilian Conservation Corps to put young men to work in the forests and parks, the Federal Emergency Relief Administration to provide federal assistance to the states, the Public Works Administration to coordinate large-scale public works projects,

A run on a bank, February 1933. Between 1930 and 1932, one-fifth of U.S. banks failed. By the time Roosevelt was inaugurated, banking had been halted completely or sharply limited everywhere.

and the National Recovery Administration (NRA) to promote economic recovery, and he passed the Glass-Steagall Banking Act, which separated investment and commercial banking and instituted federal insurance of bank deposits.

He also repealed Prohibition and stated "now would be a good time to have a beer."

Roosevelt assembled a team of visionaries. Among them were Harry Hopkins, Roosevelt's chief aide, National Youth Administrator Aubrey Williams, Rexford Tugwell, Adolf Berle, and Secretary of the Interior Harold Ickes. There was also the formidable Frances Perkins, the U.S. secretary of labor and the first woman ever appointed to the cabinet. They became known as the New Dealers.

Henry A. Wallace, the young Iowa geneticist, would become one of their leading lights. He was from a Republican farming clan that had worked the land since frontier days. His father, Harry, had served presidents Warren Harding and Calvin Coolidge as secretary of agriculture.

Roosevelt told Wallace to take whatever actions were necessary to repair the nation's devastated rural sector. His solutions were controversial—to stop overproduction, he paid farmers to destroy 25 percent of the cotton crop that was in the ground. He also ordered the slaughter of 6 million baby pigs. Although he made sure the Agriculture Department distributed much of the pork, lard, and soap to needy Americans, furious farmers attacked him. He took to the radio to defend his program. Calling it "A Declaration of Interdependence," he laid out his philosophy: "The ungoverned push of rugged individualism perhaps had an economic justification in the days when we had all the West to surge upon and conquer; but this country has filled up now, and grown up. There are no more Indians to fight. . . . We must blaze new trails in the direction of a controlled economy, common sense, and social decency."

In the end, Wallace's plan worked brilliantly. Cotton prices doubled. Farm income jumped 65 percent from 1932 to 1936. Corn, wheat, and pig prices stabilized. And the farmers became Wallace's staunchest supporters.

For a man who had spent years perfecting a strain of hybrid corn and who believed that abundant food supplies were essential for a peaceful world, Wallace was horrified by the unfortunate message such policies sent: "The plowing under of 10 million acres of cotton and the slaughter of 6 million little pigs in September 1933 were not acts of idealism in any sane society. They were emergency acts made necessary by the almost insane lack of world statesmanship during the period from 1920 to 1932."

The public, which blamed business for causing the Depression, welcomed Roosevelt with great enthusiasm, hoping he could spark a recovery. But he was an enigma, campaigning at times as a big-government liberal spinning out one new government program after another, and at other times as a budget-balancing conservative. Some thought him a socialist in the Eugene Debs/Norman Thomas tradition. Others thought him a fascist or corporatist, supporting the merger of state and corporate power. His industrial recovery program, the NRA, regulated production, competition, and minimum wage rates, some of which smacked of Italian Fascism.

(ABOVE) *Civilian Conservation Corps (CCC) crew at work in Idaho's Boise national forest. (BELOW) Public Works Administration (PWA) hod carriers carry bricks for the construction of a high school in New Jersey. The PWA and CCC were part of Roosevelt's ambitious recovery plan laid out during his first one hundred days in office.*

In reality, Roosevelt was more pragmatic than ideological. Nonetheless, he was misunderstood by big business. Openly opposing Wall Street made for smart politics, but it won the everlasting enmity of conservative Republicans who attacked his inflationary policies as unconstitutional. "Printing-press money," they called it. And worse yet, FDR took the U.S. off the gold standard. He sacrificed foreign trade and its profits in order to stimulate domestic recovery. He also took steps to reduce the country's small 140,000-man army.

In 1934, retired general Smedley Butler re-entered the picture, presenting shocking information to the House Special Committee on Un-American Activities.

Butler charged the anti-Roosevelt oligarchs, including J. P. Morgan's son Jack and the wealthy du Pont business clan, with trying to recruit him to lead an uprising of desperate veterans to force Roosevelt from office.

The press dismissed it as "The Business Plot"—a paranoid conspiracy. Henry Luce's *Time* magazine led the charge. But after hearing the testimony, the House committee, chaired by future Speaker of the House John McCormack of Massachusetts, reported that it had been able to verify all the pertinent statements made by General Butler and concluded that attempts to establish a fascist organization in the United States "were discussed, were planned, and might have been placed in execution when and if the financial backers deemed it expedient."

The committee, strangely, chose not to call many of those implicated to testify, including failed 1928 presidential candidate Al Smith, Thomas Lamont of Morgan, army general Douglas MacArthur, and various high-placed corporate executives, as well as the former American Legion commander and the head of the NRA. The tumultuous, frightening prospect of a fascist coup was popularized in the best-selling novel by Nobel Prize winner Sinclair Lewis, *It Can't Happen Here*, which depicted a series of events similar to those alleged by Butler.

And later, a similar plot emerged in the very popular Frank Capra film *Meet John Doe*.

Al Smith, who became a spokesman for the right-wing American Liberty League, scorched Roosevelt. "There can be only one capital, Washington or Moscow. . . . There can be only the clear, pure, fresh air of free

America, or the foul breath of Communistic Russia. There can be only one flag, the Stars and Stripes, or the flag of the godless Union of the Soviets."

Although the Smedley Butler hearings could be soft-pedaled by the media, the House of Morgan and the four du Pont brothers were actually called to testify at one of the most remarkable congressional hearings in U.S. history—that of the Senate committee investigating the munitions industry under North Dakota's Gerald Nye, a progressive Republican. The target: war profiteering on an unimaginable scale and collusion with the German enemy in World War I.

Nye, sensing another war was coming, supported nationalizing the arms industry and increasing taxes on incomes over ten thousand dollars to 98 percent on the day a war began. The investigations reached their zenith in early 1936, when the House of Morgan and other Wall Street firms were called in.

Was it true that Morgan and other firms had pushed the U.S. to war in order to recoup the enormous sums they'd lent the Allies? Morgan Jr. along with Thomas Lamont and other partners dismissed this as a fantastic theory, claiming there was no material advantage to having the U.S. enter World War I, because the U.S. businesses were already thriving from supplying the Allies.

One skeptical senator asked the bankers, "Do you think Great Britain would have paid her debts if she had lost the war?" A banker replied, "Yes, even had she lost the war she would have paid." But we must ask, would a broken and bankrupt Britain really have repaid those debts?

Although Nye and his committee failed to stop war profiteering, they did succeed in educating the public and also raised another disturbing issue that continues to rankle historians—what to say about U.S. businesses' contributions to German economic and military revitalization.

World War II continues to be one of the most heroic periods in American history and myth. A modern media industry of books, television shows, and movies, like *Saving Private Ryan*, have applauded America's contribution to the defeat of Hitler's Nazi regime. But they ignore, forget, or overlook the fact that many prominent American businessmen and citizens—driven by greed, but sometimes by fascist sympathies—knowingly aided the Third Reich.

Republican Senator Gerald Nye of North Dakota led the 1934 hearings on the U.S. arms industry that revealed the nefarious practices and enormous wartime profits of American munitions companies. "The committee listened daily to men striving to defend acts which found them nothing more than international racketeers, bent upon gaining profit through a game of arming the world to fight itself," he said. Among the more damning details brought to light by the hearings was that U.S. arms companies were rearming Nazi Germany.

IBM, headed by Thomas Watson, had purchased a controlling interest in the German firm Dehomag in the early 1920s and held on once the Nazis seized power.

On his seventy-fifth birthday in 1937, Watson accepted the Grand Cross of the German Eagle given him for the assistance IBM's German subsidiary provided the government in tabulating its census with its punch card machines. This technology later proved very effective in, among other things, identifying Jews, and, later still, in helping make the trains to Auschwitz run on time.

On an even larger scale, General Motors' Alfred Sloan, through his German subsidiary Adam Opel, built cars and transport vehicles for the German army. Sloan, on the eve of Germany's invasion of Poland, said his company was too big to be affected by a "petty international squabble."

Henry Ford's German subsidiary manufactured a fleet of military vehicles throughout the war with the consent of the parent company in Michigan. Henry Ford himself had earlier published a series of articles, later a book, titled *The International Jew: The World's Foremost Problem.*

A German edition of Henry Ford's The International Jew, *a collection of anti-Semitic articles that was widely read by future Nazi leaders.*

Hitler hung a portrait of Ford in his Munich office and told the *Detroit News* in 1931, "I regard Heinrich Ford as my inspiration."

When the European war was declared in 1939, Ford and GM, despite subsequent disclaimers, refused to divest themselves of their German holdings and even complied with German government orders to retool for war production, while resisting similar demands from the U.S. government.

Ford, GM, Standard Oil, Alcoa, ITT, General Electric, the munitions maker Du Pont, Eastman Kodak, Westinghouse, Pratt & Whitney, Douglas Aircraft, United Fruit, Singer, and International Harvester continued to trade with Germany up to 1941.

Although the United States declared many of these business activities illegal under the Trading with the Enemy Act, several corporations still received special licenses to continue operations in Germany. Profits piled up in blocked bank accounts as Americans were dying on the battlefield.

Another to profit off ties to German business was Prescott Bush, father of future president George H. W. Bush and grandfather of George W. and Jeb Bush, five of whose accounts were seized by the U.S. government in 1942.

By 1943, half of the German workforce was slave labor or, as the Nazis called them, "foreign workers." Despite having lost direct control, Ford profited from these people, earning millions in sequestered funds after the war.

Ford also benefited from its alliance with I.G. Farben, a chemical cartel that built the Buna rubber plant at Auschwitz, which manufactured Zyklon B, the poison gas that killed so many. Farben employed eighty-three thousand forced laborers from Auschwitz and held a 15 percent share of the subsidiary Ford-Werke.

American authorities knew of the death camps by August 1942, but said nothing to the public. Rabbi Stephen Wise finally broke the silence in late 1942. The story was carried on page ten in the *New York Times* and not much was made of it.

After the war, IBM fought for and succeeded in recovering all of its sequestered profits. And Ford and GM both reabsorbed their German subsidiaries, even having the audacity to sue and win reparations for those European factories that had been destroyed or damaged in Allied bombing raids—up to $33 million in the case of GM.

These corporations took steps to obscure their involvement. Documents were burned or suddenly went missing, especially in former Nazi-occupied areas. The subject of collaboration remains highly taboo. To facilitate such dealings, banks and law firms were needed.

The corporate powerhouse law firm Sullivan and Cromwell, whose managing director was future secretary of state John Foster Dulles, with his brother Allen Dulles, the future CIA chief, as a partner, had as clients many of these powerful institutions, including the very important Bank for International Settlements (BIS), which was set up in Switzerland in 1930 to channel World War I reparations between the U.S. and Germany.

After war was declared, the bank continued to offer financial services to the Third Reich. The majority of gold looted during the Nazi conquests of Europe ended up in BIS vaults, which allowed the Nazis access to money that would normally have been trapped in blocked accounts. Several Nazis and supporters were involved at high levels, including Hjalmar Schacht and Walther Funk, who both ended up in the dock at the Nuremberg trials, though Schacht was acquitted. American lawyer and chairman of the bank Thomas McKittrick, claiming "neutrality" in Switzerland, managed this process.

Roosevelt's secretary of the Treasury Henry Morgenthau tried unsuccessfully to close the bank down after the war, claiming it had acted as an agent of the Nazis. The Chase Bank continued to work with Vichy France, a client state and intermediary of the Third Reich. Its deposits doubled during the war years.

In 1998, the bank was sued by Holocaust survivors, who claimed it held blocked accounts from this era. Morgan Bank, Chase Bank, Union Banking Corporation, and BIS were the four dominant banks that succeeded in obfuscating their collaborations with the Nazis.

William Randolph Hearst, the newspaper baron, who was proud to have provoked the Spanish-American War, was still alive and went to Germany to meet with Hitler, whom he admired. Throughout the thirties, his papers demonized the Soviet Union, while running stories depicting the Nazis in a "friendly light."

American hero Charles Lindbergh, one of the most celebrated Americans of the 1920s, alongside Jack Dempsey, Babe Ruth, and Charlie Chaplin, became the poster boy for the America First movement.

After Hitler had just smashed France, Lindbergh feared Germany's ultimate defeat and implored the American public: "Hitler's destruction would lay Europe open to the rape, loot, and barbarism of Soviet Russia's forces, causing possibly the fatal wounding of Western civilization."

Lindbergh was enthralled with Hitler and almost moved to Germany. Roosevelt suspected a darker reality than simple pacifism, and remarked in 1940, "If I should die tomorrow, I want you to know this, I am absolutely convinced Lindbergh is a Nazi."

Most American abhorred fascism and repudiated Lindbergh's right-wing views, but they remembered the horrors of World War I and wanted the U.S. to keep out of Europe's wars.

Even General Smedley Butler joined the ranks of the isolationists, although he would die in 1940 before the U.S. entered the war.

From the American point of view, in the heart of the 1930s Depression, in a time of great moral confusion, when the world was upside down, and even a maverick like Smedley Butler would become isolationist, when American business was not to be trusted by the workers, there was a gigantic, unseen global struggle going on. It was essentially between the left and the right. Between communism at one extreme and fascism at the other. Between these poles, America was a baby giant—a nascent empire going through birthing pains—confused, anxious, scared. What would America become?

It could be argued in hindsight that the nonintervention of the United States in the Spanish Civil War, which Roosevelt later characterized as a "grave mistake," set the course for a numb neutrality between fascism and communism that would seriously confuse the stakes for the American public.

We've described the lurch toward fascism that would end with World War II, but the wrestling match with communism would continue to haunt the American imagination for decades to come. In 1931, as U.S. unemployment approached 25 percent, desperate Americans stampeded Soviet offices in the U.S. looking for jobs.

In the eyes of the poor, there was this great hope that the world would be a better place. The combination of a left-leaning Congress, an energized progressive populace, and a responsive president in Roosevelt now made possible the greatest period of social experimentation in American history. It's there to be seen in the passionate works of Dos Passos and Clifford Odets, in the iconic photos of Dorothea Lange, in the riveting message of *Mr. Smith Goes to Washington*, written by Sidney Buchman, who was a Communist Party member, in the lyrics of Yip Harburg's "Over the Rainbow" and Woody Guthrie's "This Land Is Your Land," and in one of the greatest novels of that era, *The Grapes of Wrath* by Nobel Prize–winning John Steinbeck, in which can be found the dark optimism of the ordinary American.

Hundreds of thousands of people either joined the Communist Party itself or passed through the popular front groups during the period from 1935 to 1939, when the party appealed to progressive Democrats, including Roosevelt, to unite with the Soviet Union against fascist aggression.

Not only did the communists lead the fight against fascism, they provided the foot soldiers to build the great industrial unions of the CIO and they battled for African-American civil rights, decades ahead of their time. To many, they seemed to represent the moral conscience of the nation.

Communist sympathizers included some of the nation's greatest writers, such as Sherwood Anderson, James Farrell, Richard Wright, Odets, Hughes, Hemingway, Dos Passos, Steinbeck, and Lewis. Renowned

ABOVE: *Unemployed march, Camden, New Jersey. The year 1934 saw major strikes in Toledo, Minneapolis, and San Francisco, as well as a national textile strike, as workers turned to radical groups for leadership. Unemployed Councils and Unemployed Leagues brought in unemployed workers to support the strikes rather than take jobs as strikebreakers.*

BELOW: *Evicted sharecroppers along Highway 60, New Madrid County, Missouri. During the Depression, African Americans' economic hardship was exacerbated by racism and discrimination.*

writer and critic Edmund Wilson visited Russia, saying he felt as if he were "at the moral top of the universe where the light never really goes out." He wrote in 1932, "To the writers and artists of my generation who had grown up in the Big Business era and had always resented its barbarism . . . these years were not depressing but stimulating. One couldn't help being exhilarated at the sudden and unexpected collapse of the stupid gigantic fraud. It gave us a new sense of freedom and it gave us a new sense of power to find ourselves still carrying on while the bankers, for a change, were taking a beating."

Was communism the answer for America? The popular perception of Russia was still a forbidding one.

Henry Wallace, a symbol of the New Deal's new "caring capitalism," professed himself an admirer of Soviet social programs that offered citizens universal health care, free public education, and subsidized housing. Roosevelt's Republican opponents, however, were horrified. Things grew worse when Wallace hit the cover of *Time* magazine in 1938 as Roosevelt's logical successor. Wallace, like many Americans, was focusing more on the Soviet Union's achievements than on the ugly and still largely hidden brutality of Stalinist repression, which he would later discover and renounce.

What they saw in the USSR was a thriving, state-run, full employment economy. It was based, starting in 1928, on a five-year plan, which was building big, highly visible projects—dams, steel mills, canals—by unleashing science and technology. Progressives had long favored this kind of intelligent planning over the dog-eat-dog ethic of capitalism in which individuals made decisions based on maximizing individual profit.

In the late 1920s, a former Bolshevik enforcer, Joseph Stalin, had risen to prominence through a calculated course of murder and ruthlessness. Some called him the "Red Tsar." In another century, Stalin would simply have declared himself divine, as a king would, and ruled without protest. In fact, he often behaved more like a traditional tsar, using communism as a blunt instrument with which to rule.

During the 1930s, controversial reports, often disbelieved by American progressives, filtered out of the USSR, telling of famines and starvation, political trials and repression, secret police, brutal prisons, and ideological orthodoxy. More than 13 million lives were terminated under Stalin's despotic regime. Kulaks were slaughtered or allowed to starve for resisting forced collectivization of agriculture. Organized religion was stifled. Scientists were arrested. Military leaders loyal to the Russian Revolution of 1917 were purged in huge phony showcase trials. It was a backward police state, having nothing in common with Karl Marx's vision.

Stalin believed that the West would ultimately combine to try to crush revolutionary Russia as it had in 1918. But, although he defended Soviet interests abroad, he was primarily concerned with maintaining control at home. His war was not with the world but with his own people.

Unlike Hitler, who was devoted mystically to his Nazi ideology, the highly paranoid Stalin was in comparison a poor student of the communism preached by Marx and Lenin and that of his implacable enemy, whom he exiled in 1929, Leon Trotsky. Trotsky felt that the Soviet Union, with its vast peasantry and small industrial base, was much too backward economically and could not stand on its own, especially when surrounded by hostile powers. He called for a worldwide permanent revolution to realize the Bolsheviks' vision of transformation.

But Stalin's response was "socialism in one country," by which he meant the USSR. And when Stalin finally had the outspoken, idealistic Trotsky silenced once and for all with a pickaxe in his skull by agents in Mexico City in 1940, few in the West understood that this murder signified the end truly, not the beginning—the end of a revolutionary movement toward international communism.

Stalin, unlike Trotsky or Lenin, was finally no more a true communist than Mao Zedong would ultimately become in China. In pursuit of his nationalistic goal, Stalin, encircled by hostile capitalist nations and fearing this new war with Germany, concluded the nonaggression pact with Hitler after desperately trying to forge an alliance to stop Hitler. In hindsight, it was Stalin who was right about Germany, not the United States. He had to get ready for the bloodiest war in human history.

The West not only painted Stalin as a monster, which he was, but added the fundamentally tragic misperception that Russia itself and Stalin's victims, the almost 200 million Soviet people, were indeed an equally implacable monster bent upon global conquest.

But the facts reveal that during the 1930s, it was the anticommunist fascists who were spreading the world revolution we so feared, not Stalin, who was turning backward Russia into an industrial giant, at great human cost, so it could stand up to the Nazis on its own. And out of this confusion and suspicion grew the basis of a severe and grievous future misunderstanding between the West, particularly the United States, and the USSR, which would result, once World War II ended, in the equally dangerous Cold War.

In the cross-currents of the 1930s, the U.S. stumbled between isolationism and engagement, and between hatred and fear of communist Russia and friendship and alliance with it. But then the curtain of hatred and fear descended once again.

And with the great brutality and soon-to-be discovered horrors of World War II, a new pessimism was about to enter the human consciousness. With his hopes ground once more to dust under the boot of fascism, war, and big business, the common man would have to find his own one-eyed way to survive in the kingdom of the blind.

CHAPTER
THREE

*T*he Sangre de Cristo, or "blood of Christ," mountain range is one of the United States' most remote and most primitive landscapes. On July 16, 1945, in an isolated ranch house, the world's top scientists, many of them European, gathered nervously in the chill morning air. Nearby in the darkness, something hung atop a steel tower. A bomb.

After three years, they were finally ready to test it. The test was codenamed TRINITY. The inspiration—John Donne—Robert Oppenheimer's favorite poet. One of the premier scientists of his age, Oppenheimer loved literature and the desert of the Southwest. He was a peaceful man, who just happened to have coordinated creation of the most destructive weapon in all history.

Only a few miles away waited the project's military commander, Brigadier General Leslie Groves, the man responsible for building the War Department's gigantic new headquarters in Virginia, known as the Pentagon. He didn't like relying on unreliable civilian scientists. His career was on the line.

In the last few minutes, general silence prevailed as the countdown began . . . 10, 9, 8, 7, 6, 5, 4, 3, 2, 1. At 5:29 and 45 seconds, the bomb detonated. The light was brighter than the sun. Observing the explosion, Oppenheimer recalled a line from the Hindu scripture, the Bhagavad Gita: "Now I am become death, the destroyer of worlds." This terrifying weapon would launch the United States on a journey—turning the refuge of the Founding Fathers into a militarized state.

Generations of Americans have been taught that the United States reluctantly dropped atomic bombs at the end of World War II to save the lives of hundreds of thousands of young men poised to die in an invasion of Japan. But the story is really more complicated, more interesting, and much more disturbing.

Many Americans view World War II nostalgically as the "Good War" in which the United States and its allies triumphed over German Nazism, Italian Fascism, and Japanese militarism. Others, not so blessed, remember World War II as the bloodiest war in human history.

By the time it was over, 60 to 65 million people lay dead, including an estimated 27 million Soviets, between 10 and 20 million Chinese, 6 million Jews, over 6 million Germans, 3 million non-Jewish Poles, 2.5 million Japanese, and 1.5 million Yugoslavs. Austria, Britain, France, Italy, Hungary, Romania, and the United States each counted between a quarter million and a half million dead.

Unlike World War I, World War II began slowly and incrementally. The opening shots were fired in 1931 when Japan, rapidly industrializing, launched its Kwantung Army into Manchuria, overwhelming Chinese forces.

In Europe, Germany, under Nazi leader Adolf Hitler, seeking to avenge its own devastating defeat in World War I, was building up the war machine.

Hitler's ally, Italian Fascist leader Benito Mussolini, invaded Ethiopia in October 1935. But the United States, Britain, and France did little to protest. And as a result, Hitler concluded that the major Western nations had no real stomach for war.

In March 1936, German troops occupied the demilitarized Rhineland. It was Hitler's biggest gamble to date and it worked. "The forty-eight hours after the march were the most nerve-wracking in my life," he said. "The military resources at our disposal would have been wholly inadequate for even a moderate resistance. If the French had marched into the Rhineland, we would have had to withdraw with our tails between our legs."

The feeble international response to the Spanish Civil War was even more disheartening. Fighting erupted in July 1936 when General Francisco Franco's forces set out to topple the elected Spanish republic and establish a fascist regime. The republic had made enemies among U.S. officials and corporate leaders with its progressive policies and tight regulation of business.

Many American Catholics rallied to Franco's support, as did Hitler and Mussolini, who sent abundant aid and thousands of troops. Hitler supplied his feared air force Condor Legion, whose bombing of Guernica was depicted by Pablo Picasso in his famous mural.

Soviet leader Joseph Stalin sent arms and advisors to assist the loyalists. But France, England, and the United States did nothing to help. The U.S., under President Franklin Delano Roosevelt, banned the shipment of weapons to either side, which weakened the outgunned government forces. But Ford, General Motors, Firestone, and other U.S. businesses provided the fascists with trucks, tires, and machine tools.

Texaco Oil Company, headed by a profascist, promised Franco all the oil he needed on credit. Roosevelt was furious and threatened an oil embargo and slapped Texaco with a fine. But Texaco persisted, undeterred, and also supplied oil to Hitler.

The fighting dragged on for three years. Some twenty-eight hundred brave Americans snuck into Spain to battle the fascists, most joining the communist-backed Abraham Lincoln Brigade. Almost one thousand did not return.

But Franco triumphed and the republic fell in the spring of 1939, burying with it not only over one hundred thousand Republican soldiers and five thousand foreign volunteers but the hopes and dreams of progressives worldwide.

By 1939, Roosevelt told his cabinet that his policies in Spain had been a grave mistake and warned that they all soon would pay the price. But that policy convinced Stalin that the Western powers had no real interest in collective action to slow the Nazi advance.

For years, the Soviet dictator had implored the West to unite against Hitler and Mussolini, even joining the League of Nations in 1934. But Soviet pleas were repeatedly ignored.

And then, in 1937, full-scale war erupted in China as the powerful Japanese army captured city after city. With Jiang Jieshi's nationalist forces fleeing in retreat, Japanese soldiers brutalized the citizens of Nanjing in December 1937, killing between two hundred thousand and three hundred thousand civilians and raping tens of thousands of women. Japan soon controlled the east coast of China with its population of 200 million.

The international situation deteriorated further in 1938 with German annexation of Austria and the British and French capitulation to Hitler at Munich, dismembering Czechoslovakia and giving Germany the Czech Sudetenland. British prime minister Neville Chamberlain infamously proclaimed that the settlement had brought "peace in our time."

Nor did the U.S. and its allies officially do much to help Germany's desperate Jewish community, when in late 1938 an orgy of violence was let loose on Kristallnacht, and rape and murder of the ancient Jewish population escalated. As in Europe, the U.S. did little to help, admitting only approximately two hundred thousand Jews between 1933 and 1945. Emboldened, Hitler struck again in March 1939, breaking his promise and invading the rest of Czechoslovakia.

Stalin recognized the truth; his country was facing its most deadly enemy alone. He needed to buy time, and fearing a German-Polish alliance to attack the USSR, he shocked the West when he signed a nonaggression pact with Hitler, dividing Eastern Europe between them.

Stalin's primary concern was the security of his own nation. In fact, the Soviet dictator had proposed the same alliance with Britain and France, but neither would accept Stalin's demand to place Soviet troops on Polish soil as a way of blocking the Germans.

Less than two weeks after the pact was signed, Hitler invaded Poland from the west. Britain and France, allied with Poland, finally stood up to Hitler and declared war. Two weeks later, on September 17, Stalin also invaded Poland.

The Soviets soon thereafter asserted control over the Baltic states of Estonia, Latvia, and Lithuania and invaded Finland. The world was at war once again.

In rapid succession, the invincible German army conquered Denmark, Norway, Holland, and Belgium. The once-great French army,

Hitler and Mussolini formed the Axis in 1936 and began a campaign of aggression in Ethiopia and Spain. Initially, the Western democracies did little to stop them.

which had been decimated in the slaughter of World War I, collapsed in June 1940 after only six weeks of fighting. The bulk of its ruling class, conservative and anti-Semitic to the core, opted for collaboration. Hitler now turned his attention to England and launched a punishing air assault as precursor to a cross-Channel invasion.

But a new war leader, Winston Churchill, rallied the nation behind him. And in what seemed a miracle, the battered air force held the Germans at bay in the historic Battle of Britain. Churchill called it their finest hour. And, leading the British people, Churchill became a living legend.

Although most Americans wanted Britain and France to win the war, according to a Gallup poll in October 1939, 95 percent wanted the U.S. to stay out, fearing essentially that Britain was again, as in 1917, drawing the U.S. into a futile world war.

Roosevelt promised in the 1940 election that "no American boys would go to a foreign war." Yet he now believed that Hitler was intent on world domination.

And with neutrality legislation on the books and military preparedness at a low level, Roosevelt nonetheless made several bold moves. Bending the rules, he unilaterally sent fifty old destroyers to Britain. And in order to drive Japan out of China, he imposed select embargoes on the flow of vital raw materials, critical to the Japanese war machine.

In September 1940, Japan retaliated and established, with Germany and Italy and others, the Tripartite Pact. With war clouds growing darker, Roosevelt now made his boldest move yet. Breaking the famous precedent of George Washington, he declared he was running for a third term in 1940.

The stakes have rarely been higher in a presidential election, and Roosevelt, in this spirit, now chose his controversial secretary of agriculture, Henry A. Wallace, as his running mate. Wallace had been at the nerve center of Roosevelt's successes in overcoming the perils of the Great Depression, easing the way with government subsidies for farmers to stay in business by cutting back on production. For the urban poor, Wallace had provided food stamps and school lunches. He instituted programs for land-use planning and soil conservation. Considered the scientific community's best ally, Wallace spoke out strongly against the building up of false racial theories in rebuke of Hitler's policies in Germany.

He cited the example of pioneering botanist George Washington Carver to refute the still-pervasive assumptions of racial hierarchy: "George Carver, born into slavery, now a chemist at Tuskegee University, specializing in botany, first introduced me to the mysteries of plant fertilization. I spent a good many years breeding corn because this scientist deepened my appreciation of plants in a way I could never forget. Superior ability is not the exclusive possession of any one race or any one class, provided men are given the right opportunities."

Democratic Party bosses feared Wallace's progressive views, and it looked as if the Wallace nomination would go up in flames, when Roosevelt, angry and frustrated, wrote a remarkable letter to the assembled delegates in which he flatly turned down the presidential nomination. "The Democratic Party," he explained, ". . . has failed . . . when . . . it has fallen into the control of those [who] think in terms of dollars instead of . . . human values. . . . Until the Democratic Party . . . shakes off all the shackles of control fastened upon it by the forces of conservatism, reaction, and appeasement . . . it will not continue its march to victory . . . the Democratic Party . . . cannot face in both directions at the same time. [Therefore, I] declin[e] the honor of the nomination for the Presidency."

His wife, Eleanor Roosevelt, saved the day. The first president's wife ever to address a convention, she told disgruntled delegates that "We face now a grave situation."

The party bosses buckled and put Wallace on the ticket. They would, however, come back for their revenge.

But the crisis over Wallace never went away. Previous vice president "Cactus Jack" Garner, an affable, outgoing Texan, had said: "This job ain't worth a barrel of warm piss."

Wallace stuck out like a sore thumb on Capitol Hill. He was a spiritual man, fascinated by Navajo tribal religion. He studied Buddhism and Zoroastrianism. The Washington scene with its cocktail parties and smoky members' clubs didn't suit him. He didn't drink or smoke. He preferred to play tennis and box. He liked to spend evenings reading and throwing boomerangs on the Potomac.

In a sign of his great confidence, Roosevelt made Wallace chairman of both the Supply Priorities and Allocations Board and the Board of Economic Warfare, effectively putting him in charge of the national economy. Wallace was at the zenith of his influence in Washington.

The year 1941 would be one of epic change. The fuehrer of Germany had fulfilled his promise to the German people and reversed the shame of World War I. The Germans now were at their height. With foodstuffs from France, Holland, Denmark, and Norway, luxury goods, and thriving industries, the Thousand Year Reich of the future looked like it might come true after all.

But, as history repeatedly shows, the fatal flaw arises not from without, but from within. And Hitler, at the acme of his arrogance, attacked the Soviet Union. The concept of *lebensraum*—or "living space"—was described first by him in his 1925–26 two-volume autobiography, *Mein Kampf (My Fight)*. He stated that the future of the German peoples lay in the East and would need to be carved out of the USSR. And it was going to be the Slavic and Jewish peoples who were going to be eliminated to make room for the ascendant German race.

The clash between Germans and Slavs over Eastern Europe dated back to the Baltic crusades of the thirteenth century, in which German knights had fought the Russians, and later intensified with the rise of nation-states. Now Hitler was prepared to finish the job, believing that racially pure Germany was destined to vanquish the decadent, racially mixed Slavs.

Racial mixing, he reasoned, caused the collapse of civilization. He had witnessed it firsthand in his native country in the multinational city of Vienna before World War I and now saw it also occurring in a decadent Britain and the United States.

With England no longer a serious threat in the West, Hitler was now ready to go after the biggest prize of all. Less than two years after he had signed the peace pact with Stalin, he attacked.

He sent three million men in a blitzkrieg movement cutting deep into Soviet territory along a two-thousand-mile front, from the Arctic all the way down to the Black Sea. The Germans quickly destroyed two-thirds of the Soviet Air Force. With the added loss of tanks and artillery, Stalin's massive post-1939 buildup had been rendered useless. Fearing that Britain was planting disinformation to incite war between Germany and the USSR, Stalin disbelieved his own intelligence reports about the imminence of the invasion. In the 1930s purges, Stalin had killed or imprisoned most of the Soviet high command—some forty-three thousand officers—because of their alleged loyalty to Red Army founder Leon Trotsky, whom Stalin had had assassinated the year before in his exile in Mexico City.

Stalin was equally paranoid, and rightly so, about the loyalty of local Soviet populations that he'd brutalized in the prewar years.

But Hitler, instead of seeking the alliance of this restive population, was even more ruthless than Stalin, intending the annihilation of the Soviets on a scale far larger than his war in the West or even against the Jews. Ukraine fell in the summer of 1941, and the battle for Kiev, the oldest major city in the Soviet Union, cost half a million Soviet lives.

Civilians were either executed or condemned to slave labor ranks, and with the fall of Ukraine came the loss of the Soviet industrial heartland. The coal, the steel, the gas, and the mineral ores of the Soviet Union were stolen by the Germans, who were moving toward Moscow in the fall of 1941. American and British military leaders estimated the USSR would hold on for no more than three months and might even fold in four weeks. They feared that Stalin would conclude a separate peace.

The prospects were so devastating that Churchill swallowed his long-standing loathing of communism and pledged support for the Soviet Union.

Stalin begged Britain to supply military matériel and to land immediately in Europe and engage Hitler on a second front. And for the West, it was now crucial to keep the Soviet Union in the war to absorb the main thrust of the Nazi war machine.

In August, Roosevelt ordered delivery of the first one hundred fighter planes to the USSR. But American military leaders, intent upon building up U.S. defenses, impeded Roosevelt's efforts, and the British, reinforcing Stalin's mistrust, also objected to diversion of their supplies. There were still many in the West who were glad to see the Soviet Union finally on her knees.

Missouri senator Harry Truman declared on the floor of the Senate in 1941: "If we see that Germany is winning we ought to help Russia, and if Russia is winning we ought to help Germany, and that way, let them kill as many as possible."

Ignoring such advice, Roosevelt, in November 1941, announced that the U.S. would extend aid to the Soviets. In March of that year, Roosevelt had managed to get a Lend-Lease Act through a reluctant Congress. He then sent the first $7 billion of what would eventually become $32 billion to Britain. The Soviets, in the end, would receive $11 billion.

In August 1941, Roosevelt met secretly with Churchill in Newfoundland. A ship came out of the mist, mooring side by side with the *Augusta*. It was the HMS *Prince of Wales*. The prime minister had come solely to convince the United States to join the war now.

Elliott Roosevelt, one of Franklin's sons, who was there as a military attaché, described in his book *As He Saw It* a late-night encounter during which Churchill made a naked appeal: "It's your only chance," he said. "You've got to come in beside us."

Elliott later helped his father on his leg braces walk to his cabin. The president said of Churchill, "A real old Tory, isn't he? . . . He's a perfect wartime prime minister. His one big job is to see that Britain survives this war. But Winston Churchill lead England after the war? . . . It'd never work."

"The British Empire is at stake here," Roosevelt had told his son. "It's something that's not generally known, but British bankers and German bankers have had world trade pretty well sewn up in their pockets for a long time. . . . We've got to make clear to the British from the very outset that we don't intend to be simply a good-time Charlie who can be used to help the British Empire out of a tight spot, and then be forgotten forever."

Roosevelt began to spell out his vision for a new world: "I think I speak as America's President when I say that America won't help England in this war simply so that she will be able to continue to ride roughshod over colonial peoples."

At the heart of Roosevelt's vision was that political freedom meant economic freedom, which was in sharp contrast to the British Empire's rationale that kept the colonies poor and dependent on London. Roosevelt's global New Deal would create a financial credit system that would allow the colonies to develop.

Roosevelt reminded Churchill that the U.S.'s colonial relationship with the Philippines was to be terminated in 1946 and urged the British to do the same with their empire, which offended many American sensibilities.

Churchill realized that there were limits to Roosevelt's generosity and that the price of American aid would be the world after the peace.

In his January 1941 State of the Union Address, Roosevelt articulated his commitment to the four freedoms that would constitute America's war aims: freedom of speech, freedom of worship, freedom from want, and freedom from fear. At his meeting with Churchill in August, the two leaders went even further in drafting the Atlantic Charter, which included eight "common principles" that the two nations would support in the postwar world. These were big hopes, but the Atlantic Charter was a truly visionary document that later became the guiding manifesto of the United Nations—a universal statement of a kind rarely heard since the French or Russian revolutions on the rights of men and women everywhere.

Fearing Roosevelt's proposed wording, Churchill added a clause stipulating that equal access to international wealth would be guaranteed "only

Churchill and Roosevelt aboard the Prince of Wales *during the Atlantic Charter conference in August 1941. The Charter renounced a number of imperialist practices and proclaimed such themes as self-government and disarmament. But, afraid that Roosevelt's wording could eliminate Britain's colonial sphere, Churchill added the condition that equal access to international wealth would be guaranteed only "with due respect for existing obligations."*

with due respect for existing obligations." But, as Elliott Roosevelt wrote: "Gradually, very gradually, and very quietly, the mantle of leadership was slipping from British shoulders to American." The next day, the *Prince of Wales* headed "back to the wars"—the two statesmen parting ways for now. Churchill later told his cabinet that Roosevelt said he would wage war but not declare it. Everything was to be done to force an incident.

Neither man would have then predicted this path to war would lead through Japan, not Germany. Japan had avoided the Nazi war against its old Russian antagonists and in fact had been alienated from Berlin by the Soviet-German alliance of 1939. In his arrogance, Hitler, who considered the Japanese racially inferior, had made no attempt whatever to confide his Soviet invasion plans to them or offer any new territory for their support in the Far East. In hindsight, this had enormous consequences for the fate of the world. If the Japanese had entered the war against Stalin, it is almost certain the Soviet Union would have been crushed.

But Japan wanted, like Britain, Germany, and Italy, a colonial empire of its own, and taking advantage of the vacuum created by the German conquest of France and Holland, and the neutralization of British power, it drove south into Indochina in July 1941, seeking resources and military bases. The United States, which now produced half of the oil supplies of the world, responded by completely embargoing all trade to Japan, including oil. Its supplies dwindling fast, Japan determined to secure its oil from the Dutch East Indies, but the American fleet at Pearl Harbor could significantly interfere with those plans. Thus, the Japanese launched an all-out surprise attack on the U.S. naval base at Pearl Harbor, Hawaii, leaving almost twenty-five hundred dead and disabling much of the American fleet. The Americans knew an attack was coming, but most thought it would be in the Philippines.

The next day, the U.S. and Britain declared war on Japan. Although he had not even been told about Pearl Harbor by his Japanese allies, Hitler now unnecessarily declared war on the United States, a mistake nearly equivalent to invading the Soviet Union. Roosevelt could declare a popular war on Japan but was now relieved of the enormous burden of breaking his word to the American electorate. He could finally declare war on Germany. The chaos was now global.

The U.S. strategy was to build up and advance gradually in the Pacific, while focusing its major effort against the Germans. Defeating Japan, Roosevelt reasoned, would not defeat Germany, but the defeat of Germany would mean the defeat of Japan.

And with the U.S. focused on Europe, the Japanese conquest proceeded largely unimpeded. Japan captured one-sixth of the earth's surface in only six months—Thailand, Malaya, Java, Borneo, the Philippines, Hong Kong, Indonesia, Burma. Citizens of those countries often greeted the Japanese as liberators from European colonial oppressors, a judgment that would prove short-lived. President Roosevelt said privately: "Don't think for a minute that Americans would be dying in the

The U.S. naval base at Pearl Harbor during the Japanese bombardment on December 7, 1941.

Pacific . . . if it hadn't been for the short-sighted greed of the French and the British and the Dutch."

In another great blow to the Allied cause, Japan stunned the British at Singapore in early 1942. The British had more troops defending Singapore than defending England itself. Eighty thousand Commonwealth soldiers—many of them Australian—were taken prisoner. But in a sign of the true feelings of colonized peoples, of the fifty-five thousand British Indian troops taken prisoner by the Japanese, forty thousand changed sides to fight for the Japanese. If the Japanese had attacked eastern India and coordinated that with the German advances in the Middle East before Germany's invasion of the Soviet Union, the British Empire would have been severely threatened in India. But Japan and Germany, throughout the war, never behaved as if close allies.

Japan crucially failed to deliver the knockout blow at Pearl Harbor, and the Allies began a counteroffensive led by General Douglas MacArthur and Admiral Chester Nimitz. In June 1942, U.S. forces defeated the Japanese navy at Midway and began an island-hopping strategy that would continue for more than three years.

The Japanese would fight fiercely, ensuring that victory would come at a great cost to American soldiers. But by 1943, the U.S. was churning out almost one hundred thousand planes a year, dwarfing the seventy thousand Japan produced for the entire war. By the summer of 1944, the U.S. had deployed almost one hundred aircraft carriers in the Pacific, far more than Japan's total of twenty-five.

Allied scientific advances figured prominently on every front. Development of radar and the proximity fuse contributed to victory. But it was the atomic bomb that would change the course of history.

In December 1938, two German physicists stunned the scientific world by splitting the uranium atom, making development of atomic bombs a theoretical possibility. Those in the U.S. most alarmed by this development were the scientists who had escaped from Nazi-occupied Europe, many of them Jewish, who feared the consequences should Hitler get his hands on such a weapon. The émigré scientists had tried, but failed, to arouse interest on the part of American authorities.

Desperate, in July 1939, Leo Szilard solicited the help of Albert Einstein, who agreed to write to President Roosevelt urging him to authorize a U.S. atomic research program. Einstein later said, "I made one great mistake in my life—when I signed the letter to President Roosevelt recommending that the atom bombs be made."

At first the project was small, but, in September 1942, the "Manhattan Project" was turned over to the military. General Groves's superiors told him to get results. Vice President Wallace, who tracked scientific developments closely, had a low opinion of Groves, believing him a "slightly pathological," anti-Semitic "Roosevelt-hater" and outright fascist. Amazingly, to head up the Project's Los Alamos lab, the man Groves chose, Robert Oppenheimer, was an unapologetic leftist, who admitted to having been a member of every Communist Party front organization on the West Coast—at one point giving 10 percent of his monthly salary to support the Republican forces in Spain.

Though completely opposite in temperament, Groves, with Oppenheimer's help, assembled an incredible coterie of international scientists—including Enrico Fermi and Leo Szilard---who achieved the first nuclear chain reaction in an atomic pile, constructed in a University of Chicago squash court.

Scientists worked long hours in the desert, fearing a last-minute German victory in the atomic race. The truth came out in late 1944 that Germany had actually abandoned the bomb research in 1942, opting instead to throw its scientists and resources into developing V1 and V2 rocketry—but America's scientists continued.

In the east, the Soviet Union lay on the brink of catastrophe, the Nazis threatening to take Moscow. In September 1941, Stalin pleaded with the British to send twenty-five to thirty divisions to the Motherland and once again pressed for a second front in northern France.

The following May, Roosevelt acknowledged that "the Russian armies are killing more Axis personnel and destroying more Axis materiel than all the other twenty-five United Nations put together." He publicly announced the U.S. would open a second front in Europe by the end of 1942, and Army Chief of Staff George Marshall instructed his European commander, General Dwight Eisenhower, to draw up plans for an invasion of Europe. The Soviets were elated.

But Churchill was facing a huge crisis in North Africa—thirty thousand British troops had just surrendered humiliatingly to a Nazi force half their size. Fearing a bloodbath on the shores of France, Churchill said that the British could not muster enough ships to transport invading forces across the Channel and convinced Roosevelt to postpone the second front and instead mount an invasion of North Africa. When the U.S. agreed to this, Eisenhower predicted that this would be the blackest day in history; he had said previously, "We should not forget that the prize we seek is to keep 8 million Russians in the war."

To George Marshall, who dismissed the invasion of Africa as "periphery pecking," it appeared that the British, unlike the Soviets, were afraid to take on the Germans. The shadows of World War I still hung too heavily over the imagination of Churchill's government.

But the British had a different strategy. Relying on sea power and attacking Hitler's softer southern front in Italy, Churchill wanted to avoid directly engaging the German war machine, instead seeking to secure

North Africa and the Mediterranean around Gibraltar, and then the Middle East, in order to hold on to their oil reserves, as well as maintaining access to India and the rest of their Eastern empire through the Suez Canal.

The resulting paranoia of the Soviets cannot be underestimated. Britain and Russia had been rivals since the nineteenth century. Stalin especially mistrusted the British, but he was also wary of the Americans because of their intervention against the communists twenty years earlier in the Russian Civil War.

Churchill had then promised to "strangle Bolshevism in its cradle." And up until his nonaggression pact with Hitler, Stalin even harbored the fear that Churchill and the British Empire might ally with Nazi Germany and launch a grand crusade against the Soviet Union.

Yet, against all odds and to the shock of much of the world, it was to be the Red Army itself that would reverse the course of the war. It would need a Tolstoy to describe the heroic endurance of Soviet men and women who made this possible. Few fully appreciated its meaning then, but, as had happened to Napoleon in the winter of 1812 at Moscow, the crack German war machine was, for the very first time, stopped.

But because the Japanese had marched south, Stalin was able to bring back Marshal Gyorgi Zhukov's forty Siberian divisions to Moscow. Zhukov made the difference. German losses that winter were around four hundred thousand. Meanwhile, at the capital of Leningrad, once called St. Petersburg, the Germans besieged the city over nine hundred consecutive days that included the two winters of 1941 and 1942. The population of the city in 1941 was 2.5 million people. One out of three would die.

The incessant bombing, the cold, starvation, eating soups made of glue from wallpaper, or rats, or fellow human beings—this went on to a far greater extent than has ever been officially admitted. Such was their pride that many civilians refused to evacuate the city when given the chance. Composer Dmitri Shostakovich wrote his great Seventh Symphony in honor of this sacrifice.

The orchestra continued to play throughout the siege, until most of its members had dropped from starvation. The Germans never took Leningrad. Soviet losses were over a million. Much of the art collection from

American observers took special notice of the "heroic" struggle to repel the Nazi invaders by both the Red Army and Soviet civilians. Clockwise from top: A group of women and elderly men dig a trap to halt the German advance on Moscow; a group of distraught women in Kiev, Ukraine, gather during a Nazi attack; frightened children look up from a bunker in Kiev during a German air raid; Red Army soldiers in the Soviet Union.

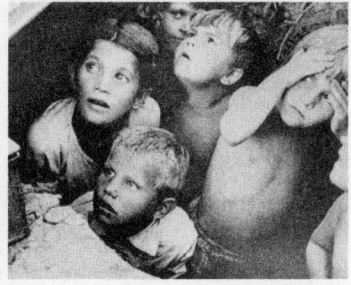

the famous Hermitage was shipped to the Ural Mountains. The Soviets were salvaging what they could. Much was burned to deny the Germans anything.

Not relying on the West to open a second front or to send much more in aid, Stalin now began the greatest forced migration in human history—evacuating some 10 million people to the east of the Ural Mountains in Central Asia and Siberia and to the south to Kazakhstan, to rebuild the USSR in a second industrial revolution that matched that of the 1920s and 1930s.

To fight the German war machine, almost two thousand new factories were built—housing followed. The transfer of the greatest part of the Soviet economy was accomplished in two incredible years, and, by 1943, the USSR was the equal of any industrial power in Europe and was now able to outproduce Germany itself.

Forty thousand T-34 tanks—superior to the German Panzers—were built. Fifty thousand Ilyushin planes, the famous IL-2, were superior in fact to those of the German Luftwaffe. The steel, wheat, and ores that were lost in Ukraine in 1941 were gradually replaced. An entire society made up mostly of women and children labored twelve- to eighteen-hour shifts to survive. All was for Mother Russia.

The patriotism of the people was extraordinary. They gave their personal treasures to finance the war—heirlooms, jewelry, everything. An entire society facing extermination by Hitler had no choice but to fight, with every last drop of blood, for their own lives and for their country.

By late 1942, the United States was, despite early setbacks, coming through with Lend-Lease—almost 2 million tons of supplies, approximately 400,000 trucks, 52,000 jeeps, 7,000 tanks, artillery, combat vehicles, 15,000 aircraft, 18,000 antiaircraft guns, 8,000 railway cars, and food.

Behind German lines, Russian, Ukrainian, and Belorussian partisans were attacking from forests and caves, blowing up trains, interfering with transportation, and in any way possible tampering with the German war machine. They engaged up to 10 percent of the German occupation forces. The partisans became an indispensable factor in the ultimate victory of the Soviet troops.

But the consequences were devastating. The Germans responded

American-made howitzers ready for transport to Great Britain in 1941 as part of the Lend-Lease program to aid the British war effort. Lend-Lease deepened United States involvement in the European war, outraging isolationist Republicans in Congress.

with more and more terrorism, hanging partisans and innocents alike. No one knows how many, but estimates range from 4 to 8 million Ukrainians died in the war. And Belorussia may have lost a quarter of its population—more than 2.5 million dead.

Approximately 200 cities and 9,000 villages were burned to the ground. At least 100,000 partisans were killed or missing.

Hitler's generals warned him that a longer war of attrition was now a reality. The Soviets seemed able to withstand huge losses. The only victory for Hitler lay not in wiping out the Slavs but in acquiring the resources of the Soviet Union.

Thus, the Germans, under General Friedrich Paulus, now drove south toward the oil-rich port of Baku. The Soviets, under Marshal Zhukov, were determined to stop them at all costs. Without oil, the Soviet army would not be able to fight. The loss of Baku would force Stalin to surrender.

One city barred the road to Baku—Stalingrad. And in the winter of 1942, the German army finally met its match.

*German cavalry leave a Russian village in flames during Operation Barbarossa,
the full-scale German invasion of the Soviet Union in June 1941.*

In the single greatest battle in history, the Soviets lost more men than
the British or Americans in the entire war. An estimated half million
men were killed. The Germans lost at least 200,000 of their best troops,
but likely far more. The civilian dead, unknown. Germans could destroy
Stalingrad, but they could never take it. Under Stalin's strict orders, anyone retreating or surrendering was to be treated as a traitor—his family
subject to imprisonment. It was his feared "Not One Step Back" policy.
At Stalingrad, more than 13,000 Soviet soldiers were shot by their own
side. During the course of the war, 135,000 were killed in this manner.
Four hundred thousand served in punishment battalions. In that year,
there were still 4 million prisoners in gulags. Nonetheless, with motives
ranging from patriotism to terror, Soviet soldiers, with their backs against
the Volga River, fought from street corner to street corner in that cruelest of winters. By January 1943, the end finally came when General
Paulus surrendered the remainder of his Sixth Army. He had started
with 300,000 men, and 91,000 now surrendered, of whom approximately

9,000 returned alive after the war to Germany. Hitler reportedly lamented, "The god of war has gone over to the other side."

And with their resources kicking in—new aircraft, new artillery—the Soviets now took the offensive. At Kursk, the greatest tank battle in history, they beat the Germans again—70,000 German dead and several times that number Soviet dead. After their colossal defeat, the German army began a full-scale retreat on the eastern front.

Throughout these pivotal years, the Soviets regularly battled more than two hundred German divisions. In contrast, the Americans and British fighting in the Mediterranean rarely confronted more than ten German divisions. Germany lost over 6 million men fighting the Soviets and approximately one million fighting on the western front.

Though the myth lives on that the United States won World War II, serious historians agree that it was the Soviet Union and its entire society, including its brutal dictator Joseph Stalin, who through sheer desperation and incredibly stoic heroism forged the great narrative of World War II—the defeat of the monster German war machine.

CHAPTER FOUR

*I*n January 1943, just days before the final German surrender at Stalingrad, Roosevelt and Churchill met at Casablanca in French Morocco. Stalin was not in attendance. He'd withdrawn his ambassadors from London and Washington. The alliance was in crisis. The Red Army was moving west against the Germans. The momentum had shifted.

But appreciation of the Soviet sacrifice was finally growing in the U.S. Even fervent anticommunist media baron Henry Luce made Stalin *Time* magazine's "Man of the Year" in 1942, praising his industrialization, stating: "Stalin's methods were tough, but they paid off." Another Luce magazine, *Life*, painted the Soviet Union as a quasi-America with its citizens "one hell of a people who to a remarkable degree look like Americans, dress like Americans, and think like Americans." His ruthless secret police was even described as a national police similar to the FBI.

Roosevelt felt he had to take action or risk the breakup of the alliance. Both he and Churchill feared Stalin might indeed make a deal with Hitler—to save the Soviet Union further destruction. After all, he'd done it before. But on many issues, Roosevelt saw eye to eye with Stalin. Both wanted a weakened, pastoralized postwar Germany without industry. It was Germany's militarism that had been the cause of such unrest in Europe. "We either have to castrate the German people," Roosevelt cautioned, "or you have got to treat them in such a manner so that they can't just go on reproducing people who want to continue the way they have in the past."

At Casablanca, the president announced a policy of "unconditional surrender." He wanted to send a message to Stalin that the U.S. would not rest until Hitler's Germany had been destroyed.

"Unconditional surrender" was a declaration of war, not merely on the enemy governments, but on the German and Japanese people themselves, which, in its unintended way, would lead to terror bombing of civilian populations, harden the resistance of those populations, and result in the most controversial decision of the war—the dropping of the atomic bomb on Japan.

In hindsight, one might argue that the declaration of "unconditional surrender" was one of Roosevelt's greatest blunders. To make matters worse, Roosevelt and Churchill confirmed at Casablanca the Allied decision to land in Sicily after North Africa, again postponing the second front in Europe and relegating their nations to further irrelevance in determining the outcome of the war. This would lead to the disastrous Italian campaign of 1943–45 that achieved little but a fierce bloodletting of Allied troops in Sicily and at slaughterhouses like the beachhead at Anzio and the four battles for Monte Casino, which did little damage to the Nazis.

With the Allies bogged down in Italy and the Soviets increasingly suspicious of British intentions, Roosevelt and Stalin met ten months after Casablanca for the very first time in Tehran, in Iran, in November 1943.

After trying unsuccessfully to exclude Churchill from the meeting, Roosevelt accepted Stalin's offer to stay in the Soviet embassy. But Roosevelt found Stalin cold and aloof during the first three days of meetings and feared he would not succeed. Then on the fourth day, after Roosevelt had teased Churchill in front of Stalin about his Britishness and about his cigars, Churchill, according to Roosevelt, grew red and scowled, and the more he did, the more Stalin smiled. Until finally Stalin broke out into a deep, hearty guffaw, at the expense of Churchill, and, before long, Roosevelt was calling him "Uncle Joe." The ice had been broken, and Roosevelt felt that he and Stalin were now talking like men and brothers.

Roosevelt reiterated to the Soviet leader that he would open the long-delayed second front the following spring. Churchill was forced to commit but still argued that the landing should be made to the east through the Balkans, heading off the advancing Soviets. Roosevelt accurately gauged Britain's concerns: "The P.M. is thinking too much of the post-war, and where England will be. He's scared of letting the Russians get too strong."

Roosevelt clearly indicated that he would allow the Soviets considerable latitude in shaping the future of Eastern Europe and the Baltic states, requesting only that Stalin implement changes judiciously and not offend world opinion. Roosevelt had written Stalin a personal note promising "the United States will never lend its support in any way to any provisional government in Poland that would be inimical to your interests."

Crucially, Roosevelt made important headway when he got Stalin to agree to enter the war against Japan after the war against Germany was concluded. Exhausted, Roosevelt wrote of the Tehran conference, "We made great progress."

The Soviet war continued with a bloody campaign in Belorussia, followed by Soviet entry into Poland—Russia's ancient border enemy—in January 1944. The retaking of Poland and particularly Warsaw is a tragic and bloody story. Few suffered as much as the Poles in this long war. Six million were killed, 3 million of them Jewish. But the USSR, too, paid a stiff price to free Poland. Six hundred thousand Soviets perished. It was here that the first death camps were actually found in 1944 by Soviet troops, revealing unquestionably to the world pictures of the true insanity of Hitler's regime.

The Soviets quickly set up a friendly government in Lublin that cracked down on the opposition, triggering a civil war. They had excluded the fiercely anticommunist representatives of the Polish exile government that had been set up in London. The Westerners thought of them as democrats, but Stalin said they were terrorists—descendants of the White Russians who had fought against the revolution in the Russian Civil War of 1919–22.

No stranger himself to terrorist tactics, Stalin, in order to prevail against the hated anticommunist Poles in London, committed the dual atrocities of killing thousands of Polish army officers in the Katyn Forest in 1940, and then, in 1944, he ordered the Red Army to halt outside the capital, while the Germans crushed the native Warsaw uprising. Soviet defenders argued that the Red Army had exhausted itself in a grueling forty-five-day, 450-mile advance against tough German troops, overstretching their supply and communication lines—that they needed to stand down.

Differences over Poland would become the single greatest source of distrust between the U.S., Britain, and the Soviet Union during and after the war. But, to be fair, many Westerners did not understand that anti-Semitism had long been common among a significant portion of Polish Catholics or that to Stalin, Poland was a matter of life and death for the Soviet Union, because the Polish territories were the corridor through which the hated Germans had twice passed into Russia in the twentieth century. For these reasons, Stalin demanded and enforced a friendly government on his border. It was no less an issue to him than hostile regimes in Canada or Mexico would have been for the United States.

Through 1944 and 1945, the Soviets continued to advance, taking Romania, Bulgaria, Hungary, Czechoslovakia, and, with the significant help of partisan guerillas, Yugoslavia. Mile by mile, across Eastern and Southeastern Europe, the Germans fought to the last man. Cities became fortresses and were reduced to rubble. Warsaw, Budapest, Vienna—an estimated 1 million Soviet troops perished liberating these areas.

And as the Soviets fought their way to Berlin from several directions, in the west, on June 6, 1944, the long-delayed second front was finally opened, one and a half years after Roosevelt first promised it to Stalin.

It was the largest armada the world had ever seen, involving 11,000 planes and some 4,000 ships. Over 100,000 Allied troops and 30,000 vehicles landed on the French beaches in Normandy. An estimated three thousand men died in this landing.

Allied forces were now approaching Germany from both east and west. Victory was inevitable.

A month later, in July 1944, a key event in the future of the world was taking shape. The Democratic Party convention opened in Chicago. Despite his clearly failing health, Roosevelt easily secured the nomination for an unprecedented fourth term. Henry Wallace, his vice president, was probably the second most popular man in America, the people's

Echoing Americans across the country, twenty-five thousand rallied in New York's Union Square on September 24, 1942, to demand that the United States open a second front in the war in Western Europe to relieve some of the tremendous pressure on Russia in its fight against Germany.

choice to be his running mate. But he had made many enemies over the years. In May 1942, Wallace had given his acclaimed "Century of the Common Man" speech in which he challenged publishing magnate Henry Luce's vision of U.S. global domination and said, "Some have spoken of the American century. I say the century on which we are entering, the century which will come out of this war, can be and must be the Century of the Common Man. . . . There must be neither military nor economic imperialism. The march of freedom of the past 150 years has been a great revolution of the people. There were the American Revolution . . . the French Revolution . . . the Latin American revolutions . . . the Russian Revolution. Each spoke for the common man. Some went to excess, but people broke their way to the light."

Wallace called for a worldwide people's revolution and an end to colonialism. His speech was received coldly across the Atlantic. Churchill charged his secret agents in the U.S. to spy on Wallace. It was clear

Wallace detested the British Empire. Wallace described an encounter with Churchill: "I said bluntly that I thought the notion of Anglo-Saxon superiority, inherent in Churchill's approach, would be offensive to many . . . Churchill had had quite a bit of whiskey . . . said why be apologetic about Anglo-Saxon superiority, that we were superior, that we had the common heritage which had been worked out over the centuries in England and had been perfected by our constitution."

Wallace's hatred of imperialism was universally known and widely acclaimed. In March 1943, Roosevelt sent him to Latin America on a goodwill tour—secretly charging him to recruit nations for the Allied cause. Sixty-five thousand people greeted him in Costa Rica, 15 percent of the population. More than one million cheered as his motorcade moved down the streets of Santiago, Chile.

The vice president returned with a dozen countries declaring war on Germany. It was more than anyone had imagined possible.

Back home, in a Gallup poll, Wallace was the choice of 57 percent of Democratic voters to succeed Roosevelt. But opposition to him from inside the party was enormous.

Wallace got into a brouhaha over economic policy with Jesse Jones, who was allied to a powerful group of Democratic Party bosses, led by party treasurer and oil millionaire Edwin Pauley, who admitted that he'd gone into politics when he realized it was cheaper to elect a new Congress than to buy up the old one. United by their hatred of Wallace, their champion was a man known to many as the "Assistant President." James Byrnes had been raised in the hothouse politics of sultry South Carolina, an environment where white superiority and segregation trumped all other issues. He was a driving force behind blocking a federal antilynching bill in 1938. After making his name smashing trade unions in the South, Byrnes became a powerful U.S. senator. If you wanted something done on Capitol Hill—you saw Jimmy Byrnes.

By 1943, the mood in Washington had shifted. It was no longer the "New Deal," and Roosevelt removed Wallace from the Bureau of Economic Warfare and put Byrnes in charge of the new Office of War Mobilization. But Wallace still had a powerful supporter—the American working man.

Today, few remember that despite unions' no-strike pledges, World

War II witnessed an enormous number of strikes. In 1944 alone, one million workers were on strike at one time or another. The war had rejuvenated American capitalism. Corporate profits rose from $6.4 billion in 1940 to $10.8 billion in 1944. Put simply, the war was good business. But, in the face of rising corporate profits, workers' wages were frozen, leading to sharp worker discontent and a wave of strikes that rocked the nation.

Detroit was the key city in Roosevelt's "arsenal of democracy." Many African-American families migrated north in search of work in the armaments factories. Racial tensions soon escalated. One demonstrator jeered: "I'd rather see Hitler and Hirohito win than work beside a nigger on the assembly line."

In June, violence exploded, exacerbated by the city's nearly all-white police force. Federal troops arrived to restore order—with live ammunition. Thirty-four were killed in the riots—twenty-five of them black.

Wallace went to Detroit to survey the damage. He was appalled. "We cannot fight to crush Nazi brutality abroad," he said, "and condone race riots at home."

Years later, this remark would be echoed by civil rights leader Martin Luther King, Jr., in reference to the Vietnam War.

By 1944, powerful labor leaders Sidney Hillman and Scotsman Phil Murray, expressing complete confidence in Wallace, had taken a dislike to the new men like Byrnes taking power in Washington. But the anti-Wallace forces told the president that renominating Wallace as vice president would split the party. The president did not answer their ultimatum; he stalled for time.

Eleanor Roosevelt reminded him that Wallace had been there with him since the beginning, a fellow visionary. But the president's attitude toward Wallace remained a puzzle, encouraging the conservative bosses to continue their campaign.

Roosevelt sent Wallace to evaluate the war's forgotten front—in China. U.S. ally Jiang Jieshi had been fighting Japan since the early 1930s and with his wife, the powerful, American-educated Madame Jiang, had strong ties to U.S. conservatives.

Wallace, however, saw the growing power of Mao Zedong's

communist army and was unsure of Jiang's future. His final report, considered too controversial, was suppressed.

On his return, Wallace was summoned immediately to meet the president. The ticket would be the subject of discussion. It was the moment Wallace had been dreading. Wallace recalled, "His affection for me seemed to be completely undimmed, because I can remember him pulling me down so his mouth was next to my ear and saying, 'Henry, I hope it will be the same old team.'"

When the convention opened, Wallace was waiting for that support. But, increasingly weak and ill and therefore dependent on the bosses to run his campaign, the president, staying in San Diego, only sent a note that said, "If I were a delegate to this convention, I would vote for Henry Wallace.'"

Despite these words, it was a cruel blow. The president was not willing to fight for his vice president.

But Wallace remained the favorite. Labor told the president that the strikebreaking Jimmy Byrnes was not acceptable. He was out. Desperate, the party bosses, led by Edwin Pauley, party chairman Robert Hannegan, Ed Flynn, Ed Kelley, and others, needed an eleventh-hour substitute. And they settled on Missouri senator Harry Truman, a man of limited qualifications, but one with few enemies.

A high school graduate, Truman had been involved in three failed businesses. He'd served honorably in World War I. His most ambitious business venture, a haberdashery, went belly up in 1922, and in 1933 he wrote: "Tomorrow I'll be 49, but for all the good I have done, the 40 might as well be left off."

A year later, Kansas City political boss Tom Pendergast, after having been turned down by his first four choices, picked the fifty-year-old Truman to run for the Senate. When asked why by a reporter, Pendergast replied, "I wanted to demonstrate that a well-oiled machine could send an office boy to the Senate."

Shunned by most senators, who dismissed him as the "senator from Pendergast," and failing to gain Roosevelt's endorsement in his reelection bid, Truman worked hard to achieve respectability in his second Senate term.

But a Gallup poll on the opening day of the 1944 convention showed 65 percent supporting Wallace as vice president—Jimmy Byrnes had 3 percent of the vote, and Truman came in eighth with 2 percent. As Wallace arrived at the convention, labor leaders Hillman and Murray had delivered. Wallace supporters were there by the thousands. Murray, in a thick Scottish accent, shouted to his men: "Wallace—that's it! Just keep pounding!"

Wallace seconded Roosevelt's nomination. He boldly declared, "The future must bring equal wages for equal work—regardless of sex or race." He was constantly interrupted by applause. A chant of "WE WANT WALLACE" filled the hall. Someone hijacked the loudspeakers and played Wallace's campaign song with its chorus "Iowa, Iowa, that's where the tall corn grows!"

Furious, Ed Pauley threatened to cut the sound to the amplifiers.

A victorious vote was almost a foregone conclusion—a Wallace victory was certain. Florida senator Claude Pepper realized that if he got Wallace's name in nomination that night, Wallace would sweep the convention. Pepper fought his way through the crowd to get to the microphone. Seeing this, the bosses demanded that session chair Samuel Jackson immediately adjourn. This chaos was a fire hazard, they screamed. Not knowing what to do, Jackson called the vote for adjournment. A few said "aye," but the overwhelming majority boomed "nay" and, yet, Jackson had the gall to announce that the vote to adjourn had passed.

It was outrageous. Confusion filled the hall. Pepper had reached the first step of the stage—only five feet—probably nine seconds—from the microphone, before the bosses forced adjournment against the will of the delegates. If he could have nominated Wallace in those moments, there is no doubt Henry Wallace would have been overwhelmingly returned as vice president. "What I understood," Pepper wrote, "was that for better or worse, history was turned topsy turvy that night in Chicago." Samuel Jackson apologized to Pepper the next day, and Pepper wrote in his autobiography that Jackson said: "I had strict instructions from Hannegan not to let the convention nominate the vice president last night."

Hillman and Murray rallied the same troops to return the next day and see it through to victory. But, over that night, Edwin Pauley and the anti-Wallace forces united behind Harry Truman. Deals were cut. Jobs offered. Ambassadorships. Postmaster positions. Cash payoffs. Bosses called every state chairman, telling them that Roosevelt wanted the Missouri senator as his running mate.

Bob Hannegan managed to put up sixteen "favorite son" nominees to draw votes away from Wallace, and then channeled those votes to Truman.

Even so, the next day, when voting began, things started to swing Wallace's way again. When the first ballot ended, it was Wallace's 429 to Truman's 319. Then a second ballot got under way—and now the deals the bosses had made kicked into action.

Jackson announced that the second ballot would begin at once—therefore, no new convention tickets would be honored. Chicago mayor Edward Kelly's police barred thousands more of Wallace's supporters from the hall. But those inside began chanting as before—attempting to drown out the proceedings.

Wallace started the second ballot firmly in the lead, but gradually he lost ground to Truman, as the nominees put up by Hannegan signed over their votes to Truman, one by one. Truman prevailed. It was over. It was what Jefferson Smith, played by Jimmy Stewart in the powerful 1939 movie *Mr. Smith Goes to Washington*, realizing he'd been defeated by corrupt Washington insiders, called "another lost cause."

But lacking the Hollywood ending that Frank Capra inserted over the objections of screenwriter Sidney Buchman, Henry Wallace accepted his defeat and pledged his loyalty to the Roosevelt/Truman ticket. Upon Roosevelt's urging, he agreed to remain in the cabinet as secretary of commerce.

Today, buried by the traditional tale of World War II, the events of the 1944 Democratic convention have been largely forgotten. They would, however, change the course of history. The man who might have been president could now only watch from the sidelines as events unfolded.

There were other deals going on behind the scenes in this critical year. Mistrusting Roosevelt's optimism in Europe, Churchill flew to Moscow in October 1944 to meet alone with Stalin. Based on the previous experience of U.S. isolationism after World War I, neither leader seriously believed that American troops would remain in Europe after the war. Therefore, it was vital to Churchill that he shore up the British position as strongly as possible.

During a secret meeting in Moscow in October 1944, Churchill and Stalin outlined an agreement for British and Soviet spheres of influence in postwar Europe on this scrap of paper.

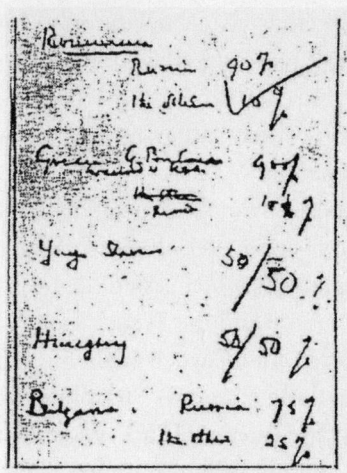

On the back of a scrap of paper, Churchill proposed the share of influence each nation would exert in postwar Europe. The USSR would get 90 percent in Romania, 75 percent in Hungary and Bulgaria. Yugoslavia would be split 50/50, but Britain would get 90 percent in Greece. Greece was vital to the British position in the Mediterranean, close to Egypt and the strategic Suez Canal, through which flowed the trade that kept the empire alive, from Eastern Africa, through the Middle East, the Near East, and at the heart of this empire—India, the crown jewel—and beyond it, the Far East, where Singapore was now British again.

Although Churchill wanted a noncommunist Poland, the truth was that Poland was simply off the agenda and Churchill was more concerned with safeguarding British power. Stalin took the paper and made a large check with a blue pencil before handing it back. Churchill remarked, "Might it not be thought rather cynical if it seemed we had disposed of these issues so fateful to millions of people, in such an offhand manner? Let us burn the paper."

But Stalin urged Churchill to hold on to the historic scrap of paper, which Churchill called a "naughty document."

This was exactly the kind of secret deal that Roosevelt had set out to prevent. He mistrusted British machinations. At a press conference in 1944, he'd said of British Gambia in West Africa, which he had visited the previous year, "It's the most horrible thing I have ever seen in my life. The natives are five thousand years back of us. . . . The British have been there for two hundred years—for every dollar that the British have put into Gambia, they have taken out ten. It's just plain exploitation of these people."

Roosevelt spoke repeatedly about a postwar trusteeship system that would prepare the colonies for independence. One of these would be Indochina, which he insisted not be given back to the French after the war, as Churchill and the French exiled leader Charles De Gaulle demanded. Roosevelt told Cordell Hull, his secretary of state in 1944, that "France has had the country—30 million inhabitants—for nearly one hundred years, and the people are worse off than they were at the beginning."

Churchill told his number two, Anthony Eden, in late 1944, "There must be no question of our being hustled or seduced into declarations affecting British sovereignty in any of the Dominions or Colonies . . . 'Hands off the British Empire' is our maxim, and it must not be weakened or smirched to please sob-stuff merchants at home or foreigners of any hue."

Churchill sent British troops into Athens to repress the left-wing and communist partisans who had led the underground resistance to the Nazis and were now battling for power against reactionary forces who wanted to restore the king. But the Greek people did not want to exchange the Nazis for the old monarch. Street fighting raged through the Greek capital. Churchill ordered his men to treat Athens as a conquered city. British general Ronald MacKenzie Scobie called in dive bombers. Stalin, however, refused to back the partisans, delivering on his bargain to Churchill. Roosevelt deplored British actions: "Greece. British troops. Fighting against the guerrillas who fought the Nazis for the last four years. How the British can dare such a thing! The lengths to which they will go to hang on to the past!"

With the approach of victory in Europe, Roosevelt, Stalin, and Churchill met for the second and last time at Yalta on the Black Sea in early February. The Soviet Union was preoccupied with its security. Britain was preserving its empire. The U.S. wanted Soviet assistance in ending the Pacific war and support for a world economy open to U.S. trade and investment and for establishing a United Nations to preserve the new peace.

The Big Three at Yalta, February 1945, where they overcame serious differences over the future of Poland and the rest of Europe to reach a series of agreements, igniting optimism in both the U.S. and the Soviet Union.

Roosevelt's doctors had begged him not to go to Yalta. The president was weakening daily, but his vast spirit kept him going. "It's been a global war," he said. "And we've already started making it a global peace."

There was little time to waste. And though they didn't see eye to eye on Germany, the Big Three agreed to a complete disarmament, demilitarization, and dismemberment of Germany. They would divide the conquered nation into four military zones, with one controlled by France.

The U.S. still had one major card to play—postwar economic assistance to help the Soviets rebuild their shattered nation. A reparations commission was established based on a projected figure of $20 billion, with half going to the Soviet Union. This was the carrot.

Poland was the focus of seven of Yalta's eight sessions. Ultimately, the three leaders compromised on a Polish Provisional Government of National Unity, which was admittedly vague, intended to include democratic leaders from outside Poland.

Naval Chief of Staff William Leahy, a veteran of the Spanish-American and First World Wars, warned Roosevelt, "This is so elastic that the Russians can stretch it all the way from Yalta to Washington without technically breaking it." Roosevelt agreed. "I know, Bill—I know it. But it's the best I can do for Poland at this time."

In truth, the United States and Britain had lost their leverage by failing to open up the second front until very late in the war. So, at the end of the day, Roosevelt didn't give away anything at Yalta that Stalin didn't already have. On the other hand, Stalin was in no rush to institute revolutionary change, if he was planning to do so at all. As in Greece, he recognized that the communists, although they'd often played a leading role in anti-Nazi resistance movements, represented a minority element in most of these liberated nations. Never having shared Trotsky's zeal for international communism, he once remarked that communism fit Poland like a saddle fit a cow.

It was these conflicts, primarily over Poland, that would eventually tear the alliance apart. But, most importantly to Roosevelt, Stalin definitely committed the USSR to join the war against Japan three months after the close of the European war. There were still close to 2 million Japanese soldiers in China. Without Soviet aid, the war could drag on indefinitely. In return, Roosevelt reached a secret agreement with Stalin, initially without Churchill's knowledge, that promised territorial and economic inducements for entering the war against Japan.

Additionally, the Big Three reached some agreements on the United Nations, which was set to convene in April of 1945, and on a system of trusteeships to deal with the liberated colonial territories. There were many ambiguities left when it came to the British and French empires in Indochina, Africa, and Asia.

News of Yalta ignited a kind of optimism that hadn't been seen for decades. Former president Herbert Hoover called the conference a "great hope to the world." CBS war correspondent William Shirer, who later authored the renowned bestseller *The Rise and Fall of the Third Reich*, declared it a "landmark in human history." Roosevelt returned in triumph. Addressing Congress for the first time without standing on his braces, he called for acceptance of the results "as the beginning of a permanent structure of peace upon which we can begin to build, under God, that better

Harry S. Truman taking the oath of office at the White House following Roosevelt's death. The new president was shockingly unprepared for the moment.

world in which our children and grandchildren, yours and mine, the children and grandchildren of the whole world, must live and can live."

For Franklin Delano Roosevelt, it was an amazing conclusion to an amazing life. The Yalta agreement would forever be controversial, and Roosevelt would be unfairly attacked for capitulating to Stalin. And, in the weeks to follow, disagreements with the Soviets would surface over Poland and other issues. But Roosevelt never lost hope, and in his last cable to Churchill he wrote: "I would minimize the Soviet problem as much as possible, because these problems in one form or another seem to arise every day and most of them straighten out."

Roosevelt truly thought he would live to enforce the peace. But, less than two months later, after twelve years in office, his great, great heart finally gave out and he died of a massive stroke. The longest-serving president in American history, Franklin Roosevelt had seen the country through its hardest times—the Great Depression and the Great War. Without him, the postwar peace that was achieved at Yalta between the British and American and Soviet empires could not be maintained.

Between these giants, America's new president was a shadow of his predecessor, and he openly admitted it.

On his first day in office, a group of reporters asked how the job was going and Truman replied, "Boys, if you ever pray, pray for me now. I don't know whether you fellows ever had a load of hay fall on you, but when they told me yesterday what happened, I felt like the moon, the stars and all the planets had fallen on me. I've got the most terribly responsible job a man ever had."

When a reporter yelled out, "Good luck, Mr. President," Truman responded, "I wish you didn't have to call me that." This was not false humility on Truman's part. He'd been vice president for eighty-two days and had spoken to Roosevelt only twice. But neither Roosevelt nor anyone else had ever bothered to inform the lightly regarded vice president that the United States was building the most powerful weapon in history.

On April 15, Truman and Wallace, who was now secretary of commerce, met the funeral train at Washington's Union Station. There was another man with them—Jimmy Byrnes, Truman's old mentor from his Senate days, who had befriended the Missourian at a time when most senators avoided him as a Pendergast hack.

Impressed with the fact that Byrnes had accompanied Roosevelt to Yalta, although he found out later that Byrnes had left the conference early and was not in on the important discussions, Truman came to rely on Byrnes above all others for advice. Byrnes gave Truman his first real briefing about the atomic bomb, which he described as "an explosive great enough to destroy the whole world" that "might well put us in a position to dictate our own terms at the end of the war." He did not specify exactly to whom the U.S. would be dictating those terms.

This turns out to be a crucial moment in the history of the world, and much of it has been forgotten, but it is well worth revisiting.

The first to see Truman on April 13, his first full day in office, was Secretary of State Edward Stettinius. The former U.S. Steel chairman of the board had had very little influence with Roosevelt. But, for Truman, Stettinius painted a picture of Soviet deception and perfidy, saying that Britain's Churchill felt even more strongly, and Churchill wasted little

Truman with James Byrnes (left) and Henry Wallace at Roosevelt's funeral. Having been Truman's mentor as a senator, Byrnes became the new president's closest advisor on foreign policy. He would later help convince Truman to fire Wallace from his cabinet.

time confirming that view both in cables and in a hurried visit to Washington by his foreign secretary, Anthony Eden.

The British ambassador to the U.S., Lord Halifax, sized Truman up, saying the new president was "an honest and diligent mediocrity . . . a bungling, if well-meaning amateur," surrounded by "Missouri county courthouse caliber" friends.

That afternoon Truman met with Jimmy Byrnes. Admitting his abject ignorance, he implored Byrnes to tell him about everything "from Teheran to Yalta" and "everything else under the sun." Byrnes gladly accommodated. In a series of meetings, Byrnes reinforced Stettinius's message that the Soviets were breaking their Yalta agreements and urged Truman to be, above all, uncompromising with them. Truman made clear his intention to make Byrnes secretary of state as soon as Stettinius had gotten the United Nations off the ground.

In this atmosphere, the ambassador to the Soviet Union, Averill Harriman, having rushed back from Moscow, warned that the U.S. was facing a "barbarian invasion of Europe" and urged Truman to stand firm and tell Foreign Minister Molotov, who was en route to Washington, that "we would not stand for any pushing around on the Polish question." As soon as the Russians had control over a country, Harriman said, the secret police moved in and wiped out free speech. But he clarified that the Soviets would not risk a break with the U.S. because they desperately sought the postwar reconstruction aid that Roosevelt had promised them.

Truman masked his limited understanding of the issues with bluster and bravado, telling Harriman that he didn't expect to get 100 percent of what he wanted from the Russians, but he did expect to get 85 percent.

It is important to note that many of the most vociferous critics of the Soviet Union shared a similar class background and a deep hatred for anything that smacked of socialism. Harriman was the son of a railroad tycoon who had founded Brown Brothers Harriman. James Forrestal had made a fortune on Wall Street. Stettinius had been chairman of the board of the nation's largest corporation. They were joined by enormously wealthy international bankers, Wall Street and Washington lawyers, and corporate executives, who had mostly inherited or made their fortunes during the interwar years.

These men would come to shape postwar U.S. policy and included Dean Acheson, Robert Lovett, John McCloy, John Foster and Allen Dulles, Nelson Rockefeller, Paul Nitze, and General Motors president Charles Wilson, who, as head of the War Production Board, had said that the United States needed "a permanent war economy." Although they had served Roosevelt, they had in fact had little influence on him.

Opposed to this antagonistic point of view toward the Soviets were the veterans—Secretary of War Henry Stimson, Army Chief of Staff General George Marshall, and former vice president Henry Wallace. Admiral William Leahy again noted the elasticity of the Yalta agreement and the difficulty of alleging bad faith on that basis. In fact, he said, after Yalta, he would have been surprised had the Soviets behaved differently than they had.

Marshall, whom *Time* magazine had named "Man of the Year" for 1943, contended that a break with the Soviets would be disastrous given U.S. dependence on them to help defeat the Japanese. The conservative secretary of war, Henry Stimson, who had fought the Ute Indians in the nineteenth century, and still liked to be called "the Colonel," was long practiced in the ways of the world. When confronted by the issues of acquisition by force, he explained that the USSR had been a trustworthy ally, often delivering even more than it had promised, especially in military matters.

He reminded the president of Poland's importance to Russia, explaining, "The Russians perhaps were being more realistic than we were in regard to their own security." He had previously noted that Russia "prior to 1914 had owned the whole of Poland including Warsaw and running as far as Germany and that she was not asking for restitution of that." He added that outside the U.S. and Britain, very few countries shared the Western understanding of free elections.

Nonetheless, in his first meeting with Soviet foreign minister Molotov on April 23, eleven days after Roosevelt's death, Truman wasted little time accusing the Soviets of having broken their Yalta agreement, particularly in Poland. When Molotov tried to explain the Yalta Polish agreement through Stalin's eyes, Truman dismissed his clarifications. When Molotov raised other issues, Truman snapped, "That will be all, Mr. Molotov. I would appreciate it if you would transmit my views to Marshal Stalin." Stunned, Molotov replied, "I've never been talked to like that in my life." "Carry out your agreements and you won't get talked to like that," Truman shot back. Molotov stormed out of the room. After the meeting, Truman boasted, "I gave it to him straight. I let him have it. It was the straight one-two to the jaw."

His bullying of the Soviet foreign minister probably conjured up images of five-foot-four John "Peanuts" Truman, the five-foot-eight-inch president's father, who, back in Missouri, would pick fights with men a foot taller to show how tough he was. He wanted that same toughness in his sons and found it in Harry's younger brother Vivian. Harry, however, was diagnosed with flat eyeballs and forced to wear Coke bottle–thick glasses. He could not play sports and he was bullied by the other boys, who called him "four-eyes" and "sissy" and chased him home after school. When he arrived home trembling, his mother would comfort him by telling him not to worry because he was meant to be a girl anyway.

Gender issues plagued him for years. He would often refer to his feminine features and attributes. Economic hardship added to his woes. No sissy anymore, he now proved he could stand up to leaders of the second most powerful nation in the world. His father, whose approval he struggled unsuccessfully to win when he was alive, would have been proud of him now!

Stalin, feeling betrayed, wasted no time cabling Truman the following day, insisting that Roosevelt had agreed that the pro-Soviet Polish government would form the kernel of the new government. He added that he didn't know if the governments of Belgium or Greece were really democratic, but he wouldn't make a stink because they were vital to British interests.

These were strong words. And where the opening of the United Nations in San Francisco two days later on April 25 should have been an occasion to celebrate a new era in international peace, it was instead ruined by tension between the allies. The Russian request to have the pro-Soviet government seated to represent Poland was rejected. After that, relations continued to deteriorate rapidly.

Realizing that his get-tough tactics had not produced the desired results, Truman met twice with Joseph Davies, the former ambassador to the Soviet Union. A conservative corporate attorney, Davies had surprised liberal critics by sympathizing with the Soviet experiment. Davies counseled Truman that the Soviets had always been "sticklers for reciprocity . . . between allies." So they accepted British-imposed governments in Africa, Italy, and Greece, even though they did not represent the antifascist forces in those countries, because they understood these were "vital interests" to America and Britain. And they expected similar consideration for their vital security interests in Poland.

Davies noted how fundamentally the relationship had changed in the last six weeks, with the British acting as instigators. He warned that if the Russians decided the U.S. and Britain were "ganging up on them," they would respond by out-toughing the West as they had done in concluding the 1939 pact with Hitler when it became clear that the West would not help them stop the Nazis. But he assured Truman that "when approached with generosity and friendliness, the Soviets respond with even greater generosity." Davies agreed to set up a meeting between Truman and Stalin.

In that same crucial month, a few days after Roosevelt's death, the Soviets had amassed three armies of 2.5 million men to take Berlin and end forever Hitler's "One Thousand Year Reich." But, incredibly, the Germans were still able, with all their losses, to muster an enormous defense of 1 million men with fortified bunkers, air, and artillery. Their most fanatical recruits in this terrible Götterdämmerung: child soldiers.

It was the Third Reich's last stand. The battle was bloody. Eighty thousand Russian troops were killed, at least three hundred thousand wounded, fighting street to street. Berlin fell in four days. Hitler and his long-term mistress, Eva Braun, married and the next day committed suicide.

Seeking revenge for the German rape of the USSR and further fueled by what they had witnessed liberating the concentration camps of Majdanek, Sobibor, Treblinka, and Auschwitz, en route to Berlin, the Soviet soldiers behaved brutally toward the vanquished Germans. Stalin did nothing to stop it.

But when reports began to fill the world's airwaves of vast hordes of Soviet soldiers raping their way through Germany, orders came from above to cease, and the rapes stopped. The stories continued—up to 2 million women, some claimed, were raped. In just a few weeks, more than one hundred thousand did seek medical care for rape.

As part of the intended Roosevelt-Stalin plan for the pastoralization of Germany, Soviet officials, in the first few months, shipped one hundred thousand rail cars of construction materials and personal goods back to Russia—some to help rebuild the shattered economy and some, like furs, paintings, gold, and jewels, for purely monetary purposes. But, as a result, the worldwide perception of the Soviet Union endured that it was a barbaric and brutal semi-Asian nation invading what had once been civilized Europe.

The dictionary definition of "empathy" is "the imaginative projection or capacity for participating in another's feelings or ideas." But Truman did not seem capable of comprehending the pain and suffering of the Soviet people or their motives. Roosevelt, a man who had suffered from polio in his life, had understood that the war had been won by Soviet sacrifice and that peace now depended on mutual respect.

Even Churchill had admitted the Soviet army "tore the guts out of" the German military machine. Stalin was a tyrant, absolutely—a ruthless, paranoid dictator who disdained the U.S. concept of democracy. But he was also in the tradition of the cruelest tsars. He had clearly gotten along with Roosevelt, and had, with very few exceptions, delivered on his promises. He desperately wanted friendly relations with the U.S. to continue. But, as the Cold War descended, the laurels of the USSR's victory over Nazi Germany were stolen—or rather, forgotten.

It would take twenty years for another U.S. president and veteran, John Fitzgerald Kennedy, who had lived his entire life in some degree of pain and had faced the prospect of death, to pay homage to the Soviet contribution in World War II. "No nation in the history of battle ever suffered more than the Soviet Union in the Second World War," Kennedy reminded graduating seniors at American University. "At least 20 million lost their lives. Countless millions of homes and families were burned or sacked. A third of the nation's territory, including two-thirds of its industrial base, was turned into a wasteland—a loss equivalent to the destruction of this country east of Chicago."

Germany officially surrendered on May 7.

As V-E Day was celebrated around the world, it also meant that the Soviets, as agreed at Yalta, would enter the Pacific war around August 8—almost three months before the November 1 start date for the planned Allied invasion of mainland Japan. When Truman and Byrnes, now secretary of state, met with Stalin and Churchill in the most important conference of World War II at Potsdam, in a suburb of Berlin, they were waiting for news of the secret atomic test in the desert of Alamogordo.

Truman had pushed the start of the summit back two weeks to mid-July and hoped the bomb would be tested before negotiations with Stalin began. In the desert, Robert Oppenheimer said, "We were under incredible pressure to get it done before the Potsdam meeting." It turned out, from Truman's perspective, to be worth the wait.

On July 16, while Truman was touring bombed-out Berlin and preparing for the next day's meeting with Stalin, scientists exploded the first atomic bomb. It exceeded all expectations. Some scientists even feared they had indeed set the atmosphere on fire.

Groves cabled the preliminary results to Stimson, who rushed to brief Truman and Byrnes. They were elated. They knew that they had a date with destiny.

CHAPTER FIVE

On August 6, 1945, President Truman addressed the nation. "A short time ago, an American airplane dropped one bomb on Hiroshima and destroyed its usefulness to the enemy. . . . The Japanese began the war from the air at Pearl Harbor. They have been repaid many fold. And the end is not yet. . . . It is an atomic bomb. It is a harnessing of the basic power of the universe. . . . We shall destroy their docks, their factories, and their communications. Let there be no mistake—we shall completely destroy Japan's power to make war."

The war in Europe had ended close to three months before on May 7. Looming on November 1 was Operation Downfall, the invasion of the Japanese Islands, overseen by General Douglas MacArthur. Many feared a bloodbath, as Americans confronted what some leaders considered a fanatically hostile civilian population as well as the remaining Japanese imperial armed forces.

The climate for the war on Japan was shaped by the profound hatred Americans felt toward the Japanese. Pulitzer Prize–winning historian Allan Nevins wrote after the war, "Probably in all our history, no foe has been so detested as were the Japanese."

Admiral William "Bull" Halsey, Commander of the South Pacific Force, was notorious in this regard, urging his men to kill the "yellow monkeys" and "get some more monkey meat." *Time* magazine wrote: "The ordinary, unreasoning Jap is ignorant. Perhaps he is human. Nothing . . . indicates it."

The British embassy in Washington reported back to London that the Americans viewed the Japanese as a "nameless mass of vermin." When popular war correspondent Ernie Pyle was transferred from Europe to the Pacific in February 1945, he observed: "In Europe we felt that our enemies, horrible and deadly as they were, were still people. But out here I soon gathered that the Japanese were looked upon as something subhuman and repulsive; the way some people feel about cockroaches or mice."

Some of this sentiment can be attributed certainly to racism, but American rancor toward Japan soared with the "sneak attack" at Pearl Harbor. And in early 1944, the government released information about the sadistic treatment of U.S. and Filipino prisoners during the Bataan Death March two years earlier. Reports of unspeakable Japanese cruelty—torture, crucifixion, castration, dismemberment, beheading, burning and burying alive, vivisection, nailing prisoners to trees and using them for bayonet practice—flooded the media.

President Truman's bigotry long antedated reports of Japanese savagery. As a young man courting his future wife, he wrote: "I think one man is as good as another so long as he's honest and decent and not a nigger or a Chinaman. Uncle Will says that the Lord made a white man of dust, a nigger from mud, then threw up what was left and it came down a Chinaman. He does hate Chinese and Japs. So do I."

To be fair, Truman was a product of his time and place. His biographer, Merle Miller, reported, "Privately Mr. Truman always said 'nigger'; at least he always did when I talked to him."

This racism prevailed when President Roosevelt, in February 1942, signed an Executive Order calling for the evacuation of more than 110,000 Japanese and Japanese-Americans from California, Oregon, and Washington on the grounds that they represented a threat to national security. Seventy percent of them were American citizens.

But still, with few defending these citizens' constitutional rights, they were eventually placed in ten different camps, often referred to at the time as "concentration camps." Conditions there were deplorable, lacking running water, bathroom facilities, decent schools, insulated cabins, and proper roofs. They worked under scorching desert sun for minuscule pay.

Americans felt a profound hatred toward the Japanese. As Newsweek reported in January 1945, "Never before has the nation fought a war in which our troops so hate the enemy and want to kill him." Whereas American wartime propaganda took pains to differentiate between evil Nazi leaders and "good Germans," no such distinction was made among the Japanese, who were portrayed as vermin, cockroaches, rattlesnakes, and rats. Simian imagery also abounded.

Despite the fact that there was no evidence of Japanese-American sabotage, on February 19, 1942, Roosevelt signed Executive Order 9066, which laid the groundwork for the evacuation and incarceration of Japanese and Japanese-Americans from California, Oregon, and Washington, two-thirds of whom were U.S. citizens by birth. Although the executive order made no explicit mention of race or ethnicity, its intended target population was unmistakable.

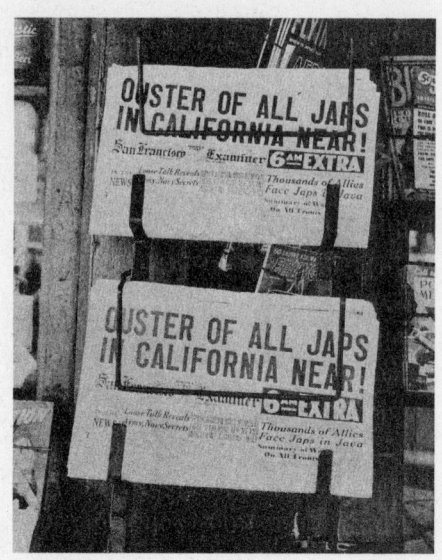

Evacuees were only allowed to bring what they could carry. And some greedy westerners used the opportunity to seize their neighbors' properties at a fraction of their real value. The Japanese lost an estimated $400 million in personal property—worth more than $5 billion today.

Japanese resoluteness in the face of defeat was legendary. In February and March of 1945, after five weeks of combat at Iwo Jima, almost 7,000 American sailors and marines were killed and more than 18,000 wounded. Even Hollywood movie star John Wayne would fall victim in the movie *The Sands of Iwo Jima.*

At Okinawa, the bloodiest battle of the Pacific, more than 12,000 Americans were killed or missing and more than 36,000 wounded. One hundred thousand Japanese soldiers were killed as were an equivalent number of Okinawan civilians—some of whom committed suicide.

Americans were especially shocked by the 1,900 kamikaze attacks that sank 30 and damaged some 360 naval vessels. Japanese soldiers fought for the emperor, whom many worshipped as a god. They believed that surrender would shame their families but that death on the battlefield would bring the highest honor.

All military planners agreed that an invasion would be costly. But

ABOVE: *Japanese-Americans arrive at the Santa Anita Assembly Center from San Pedro, California, where they were housed in horse stables before being moved to more permanent relocation centers.*

BELOW: *Inside relocation centers, Japanese toiled under scorching desert sun in Arizona and California, swamplike conditions in Arkansas, and bitter cold in Wyoming, Idaho, and Utah and were paid minuscule wages for their efforts.*

the debate over just how costly has raged for decades. General George Marshall told Truman on June 18 that he expected no more than 31,000 casualties, which would have meant more than 6,000 dead, in the first thirty-day period.

America's moral threshold would be dramatically lowered by World War II. Urban area bombing had begun before, during World War I, when the Europeans had bombed one another's cities. And to its credit, the U.S. had strongly condemned Japanese bombing of Chinese cities in 1937. When the war began in 1939, Roosevelt implored combatants to refrain from the "inhuman barbarism" involved in bombing defenseless cities.

But by the mid-1940s, great cities such as Barcelona, Madrid, Shanghai, Beijing, Nanjing, Warsaw, London, Rotterdam, Moscow, Leningrad, Budapest, Vienna, Cologne, Berlin, and many others had been severely bombed. Germany had begun with deadly raids on British cities, and the British responded with thousand-plane formations over urban targets in Germany.

When U.S. Air Force general Curtis LeMay arrived in England in 1942, air force strategy involved targeting Germany with precision bombing of key industries and transportation networks in vast daylight raids. But the crews were being shot to pieces. Terrified for their lives, many pilots simply aborted their missions and returned to base. Morale was at the point of collapse. LeMay issued a severe order to his flyers: "Our abort rate is too high and the cause of it is fear. Therefore, I will be on the lead plane in these missions, and any crew that takes off, and that doesn't get to the target, will be court-martialed."

The abort rate dropped off to nothing. But, even then, LeMay looked to overhaul strategy, frustrated with the limitations of conventional bombing. His inspiration came from the British and especially the notorious Sir Arthur "Bomber" Harris, who made no distinction between military and civilian targets. It was Harris, in February 1942, who masterminded the shift from precise, but dangerous, daytime bombing to notoriously imprecise nighttime area bombing raids that indiscriminately targeted civilians. The U.S. balked at such slaughter. Round-the-clock bombing ensued—the British at night, the Americans by day.

In July 1943, British bombers, including Harris, destroyed the German city of Hamburg, creating fires higher than the Empire State

Building. LeMay felt he could do even better, and, in November of 1943, the U.S. Air Force destroyed Munster. It was the beginning of a new war.

On the night of February 13, 1945, the beautiful baroque city of Dresden on the Elbe River, packed with refugees fleeing the Red Army, disappeared from the face of the earth. Twenty-five thousand were killed by British bombers at night, followed by the U.S. Air Force the next morning. The city had little military value. The cost of Allied area bombing in Europe was vast in terms of men and material, representing almost a quarter of the entire British war effort and much of the American. But was it worth it?

The bombing slowed the rate of increase in German armaments production and took its toll on civilian morale, killing more than an estimated half million German, Italian, and French civilians. And it forced the Luftwaffe to divert forces to defend the mainland, making them unavailable for the Soviet front. But defending itself and repairing damage may have cost the Germans less than the Allies spent to wreak such damage. More than seventy-nine thousand U.S. and an equal number of British air crew members were killed in action. Even Churchill wondered out loud in 1943, "Are we beasts? Are we taking this too far?"

By mid-April, there was simply nothing worthwhile left to destroy in Germany. LeMay argued, "You've got to kill people and when you kill enough of them, they stop fighting."

In late 1944, the man the Japanese came to know as "Demon" LeMay was transferred to the Pacific, where he bombed Japanese civilians with a ferocity never before witnessed in the annals of war. More explicit than the British area bombing, LeMay called it "Terror Bombing."

In that year, the U.S. was capturing more and more Japanese-occupied territories, bringing Japan itself within range of U.S. bombers. And on the night of March 9–10, 1945, LeMay sent 334 planes over Tokyo, the imperial capital—carrying incendiary bombs, consisting of napalm, thermite, white phosphorus, and almost every kind of inflammable material designed expressly to kill civilians.

Tokyo was a thousand-year-old concentration of bamboo and wood. It was called a paper city. B-29s destroyed sixteen square miles, killing more than eighty thousand civilians and leaving an estimated one million

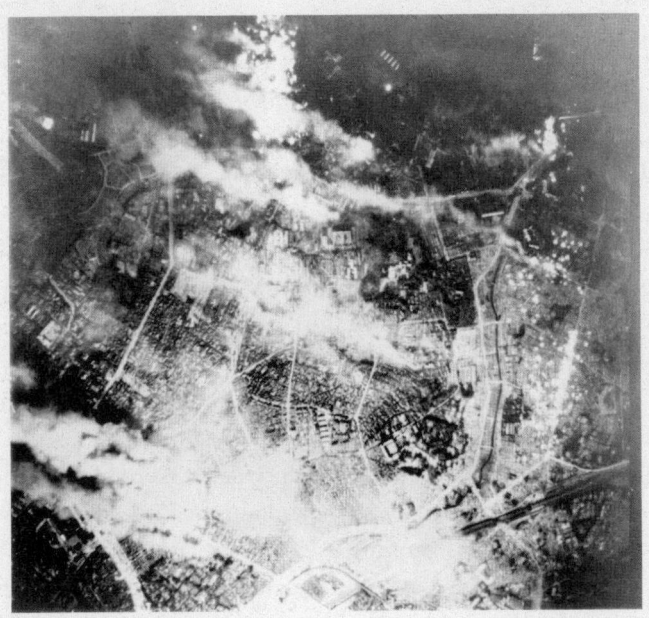

ABOVE AND OPPOSITE: *On the night of March 9–10, 1945, General Curtis LeMay sent 334 planes to attack Tokyo with incendiary bombs consisting of napalm, thermite, white phosphorus, and other inflammable materials. The bombs destroyed 16 square miles, killing more than 80,000 and injuring close to a million. The scalding inferno caused canals to boil, metal to melt, and people to burst spontaneously into flames. The victims, LeMay reported, were "scorched and boiled and baked to death."*

homeless. The scalding inferno caused canals to boil, metal to melt, and people to burst spontaneously into flames. The stench of burning flesh was so powerful that crew members vomited in their planes. The Tokyo raid was to be known as LeMay's masterpiece.

The U.S. Air Force actually firebombed more than one hundred Japanese cities—some of no military significance—taking more than an estimated half million lives. Almost no one objected to the slaughter bombing of Japanese civilians. It was, as Brigadier General Bonner Fellers lamented, "one of the most ruthless and barbaric killings of noncombatants in all history."

Destruction reached 99.5 percent in the city of Toyama. Secretary of War Henry Stimson told Truman he "did not want to have the U.S. get the reputation of outdoing Hitler in atrocities." And future defense secretary Robert McNamara, who was on LeMay's staff in 1945, agreed with his boss's comment that if the United States lost the war, they'd all be tried as war criminals and, McNamara felt, deserved to be convicted.

Seen through the prism of the terrible destruction being wrought by LeMay's "Terror Bombing," the atomic bomb can be viewed as a chilling, if logical, next step. But, as it crept closer, many scientists began to squirm. Leo Szilard and others understood that this bomb they were building was a primitive prototype for what was to follow. Szilard, Nobel Prize–winning chemist Harold Urey, and astronomer Walter Bartky attempted to see Truman to caution against use of the bomb. But they were rerouted to South Carolina to speak with Jimmy Byrnes, whose response appalled Szilard. He later wrote, "Mr. Byrnes . . . knew at that time, as the rest of the government knew, that Japan was essentially defeated. . . . Byrnes was much concerned about the spreading of Russian influence in Europe; [insisting] that our possessing and demonstrating the bomb would make Russia more manageable in Europe."

Brigadier General Leslie Groves also admitted that, in his mind, Russia had always been the enemy: "There was never from about two weeks from the time I took charge of this Project any illusion on my part that Russia was our enemy, and the Project was conducted on that basis."

In June, scientists at Chicago's Met Lab drafted a report warning that a nuclear attack on Japan would not only destroy America's moral position, but instigate a nuclear arms race with Russia spurred by the threat of "total mutual destruction." The report also noted that because there was no secret to the bomb, Russia would soon catch up.

When security officers banned its circulation, Szilard drafted a petition to Truman signed by 155 project scientists. But Robert Oppenheimer barred the petition's circulation at Los Alamos and alerted Groves, who made sure that Szilard's petition did not reach Stimson or Truman. Groves's security agents had been conducting extensive surveillance of Szilard throughout the war. And at one point, Groves had labeled Szilard an "enemy alien" and requested that he "be interned for the duration of the war."

In May 1945, General Marshall supported Oppenheimer's suggestion to share information with Soviet scientists, suggesting that they invite Soviet observers to the test, but Byrnes vetoed the whole idea. The bomb's use now seemed inexorable, unstoppable. And the issue came to an apocalyptic head in Potsdam in July, where the Big Three were discussing the shape of the postwar world. It was the perfect place to reveal the existence of the bomb.

The conference setting was strange and otherworldly. Soviet troops occupied the wrecked capital of Berlin. Truman had said his primary reason for going to Potsdam was to ensure the Soviet entry into the

Groves and Oppenheimer at ground zero of the Trinity test. The two leaders of the Manhattan Project were opposites in every imaginable way— in stature, religion, taste in foods, smoking and drinking habits, and especially politics. The two were also opposites in temperament. Whereas Oppenheimer was beloved by most who knew him, Groves was universally despised. But Groves's gruff, bullying, take-no-prisoners style actually complemented Oppenheimer's ability to inspire and get the most out of his colleagues in driving the project forward to completion.

Pacific war, an assurance that Stalin was ready to give again. Truman wrote in his diary: "He'll be in the Jap War on August 15. Fini Japs when that comes about."

Allied intelligence concurred, reporting: "An entry of the Soviet Union into the war would finally convince the Japanese of the inevitability of complete defeat." In May, Japan's Supreme War Council drew a similar conclusion: "At the present moment, when Japan is waging a life-or-death struggle against the U.S. and Britain, Soviet entry into the war will deal a death blow to the Empire."

Yet, it was clear to most that the Japanese were already finished. By the end of 1944, the Japanese navy had been decimated; the air force was badly weakened; the railroad transit system was in tatters; food supplies had shrunk, and public morale was plummeting. Upon Germany's defeat, the Soviet army began gathering in Siberia in enormous numbers, preparing to invade Japanese-occupied Manchuria in early August 1945.

In February of that year, Prince Konoe, the former prime minister, had written to the emperor, "I regret to say that Japan's defeat is inevitable." What was essential, he averred, was to avoid a communist revolution in its wake.

In May, Japan's Supreme War Council decided to feel out the Soviets. They wanted not only to keep the USSR out of their war but also to see if the Soviets could help secure better surrender terms from the Americans. This was a delicate negotiation. But American intelligence had been intercepting Japanese cables since the start of the war, and a July 18 cable from Tokyo to the Japanese ambassador in Moscow seeking surrender terms said unequivocally: "Unconditional surrender is the only obstacle to peace." Truman unambiguously characterized this as "the telegram from the Jap emperor asking for peace."

Forrestal noted "evidence of a Japanese desire to get out of the war." Stimson described "Japanese maneuverings for peace." Byrnes pointed to "Japanese peace feelers." They all knew the Japanese were finished. The end was near. And several of Truman's close advisors urged him to modify the demand for "unconditional surrender" to signal that Japan could keep its emperor and speed the end of the war.

To the people, the emperor was a sacred figure and the center of their Shinto religion. To see him hanged like Mussolini in Italy or humiliated in a war trial would be more than they could bear. MacArthur's command reported, "The hanging of the Emperor to them would be comparable to the crucifixion of Christ to us. All would fight to die like ants."

But Jimmy Byrnes told Truman that he would be "crucified" politically if the imperial system was retained. Once again, his advice prevailed. Truman and Byrnes believed they had a way to speed Japanese surrender on American terms without Soviet help, thereby denying the USSR the territorial and economic concessions promised by Roosevelt.

Truman had delayed the start of Potsdam for two weeks, giving the scientists time to ready the bomb test. It worked. Stimson gave him the news. The conference began the very next day. He later read the full report. The test was terrifying—almost beyond comprehension. Truman's demeanor changed completely. Churchill was stunned by the transformation. "I couldn't understand it. When he got to the meeting after having read this report he was a changed man. He told the Russians just where they got on and off and generally bossed the whole meeting."

Stalin and Truman with Secretary of State James Byrnes and Soviet Foreign Minister Vyacheslav Molotov at the Potsdam Conference in July 1945. While at Potsdam, Truman and his advisors learned of the successful Trinity test of the atomic bomb. Now armed with the new weapon and hoping to deny the Soviets promised territorial and economic concessions, Truman, Byrnes, and Secretary of War Henry Stimson no longer welcomed the Soviet Union's entry into the war in the Pacific.

On the twenty-fourth of July, Truman informed Stalin that the United States was in possession of "a new weapon of unusual destructive force." Truman was surprised by Stalin's disinterested response and wondered if Stalin had grasped what he was telling him.

But Truman was naive in this matter. Klaus Fuchs, a man of ideological conviction who was part of the British scientific mission at Alamogordo, had delivered technical information relating to the bomb to his Soviet handlers. Stalin already knew when the test had been scheduled and now was being told it had succeeded.

Anthony Eden, the British foreign secretary, noted Stalin's response to Truman was a nod and a muttered "thank you." Apparently, once he stepped away from the conference, Stalin called his secret police chief,

Beria, and scolded him for not having told him of the success of the test before Truman.

Foreign Minister Andrei Gromyko reported that when Stalin returned to his villa he remarked that the Americans would use their atomic monopoly now to dictate terms in Europe but that he wouldn't give in to that blackmail. He ordered Soviet military forces to speed their entry into the Asian war, and he ordered Soviet scientists to pick up the pace of their research.

Truman's behavior at Potsdam reinforced Stalin's belief that the U.S. intended to end the war quickly and renege on its promised concessions in the Pacific.

On July 25, Truman approved a directive signed by Stimson and Marshall ordering the atomic bomb to be used against Japan as soon after August 3 as the weather permitted. He and Byrnes fully expected the Japanese government to reject the Potsdam Declaration, which failed to give any reassurances about the emperor. The U.S. even vetoed Stalin's wish to sign the declaration. Adding Stalin's signature would have signaled the Japanese that the Soviet Union was about to come into the war. It was incredibly underhanded behavior by the U.S.— toward both the Japanese and the USSR.

While the hours were ticking off until the atomic bomb was ready to use, the absence of a Soviet signature was encouraging the Japanese to continue their futile diplomatic efforts since May of that year to keep the Soviets out of the war, knowing that the entry of their giant army would crush the Japanese Empire. Stimson, who had serious misgivings about using the bomb, referring to it as "the dreadful," "the terrible," "the diabolical," repeatedly tried to convince Truman and Byrnes to assure the Japanese about the emperor, but it was an exercise in futility. When Stimson complained to Truman about being ignored, Truman told his elderly, frail secretary of war that if he didn't like it, he could pack his bags and go home.

Though Truman always, somewhat proudly, accepted responsibility for his decision, Groves, who drafted the final order to drop the bomb, contended that Truman didn't really decide. "As far as I was concerned, his decision was one of noninterference—basically, a decision not to upset

General Douglas MacArthur with Emperor Hirohito. In what many consider a cruel irony, the United States allowed Japan to keep the emperor, whose retention, most experts believed, was essential to postwar social stability. Contrary to Byrnes's admonitions, Truman suffered no political repercussions from this decision.

the existing plans . . . Truman did not so much say 'yes' as not say 'no.'" Groves described Truman scornfully as "a little boy on a toboggan."

Truman's attitude in all this was puzzling. Though at times treating the bomb as a poker hand to hold over Stalin's head, he also understood that it was really a sword of Damocles hanging over all humanity. He wrote in his Potsdam diary: "We have discovered the most terrible bomb in the history of the world. It may be the fire destruction prophesied in the Euphrates Valley Era, after Noah and his fabulous Ark."

Six of America's seven five-star officers who received their final star in World War II—Generals MacArthur, Eisenhower, Arnold, and Admirals Leahy, King, and Nimitz—declared the bomb morally reprehensible, militarily unnecessary, or both.

Eisenhower said, "So then [Stimson] told me they were going to drop it on the Japanese. Well, I listened, and I didn't volunteer anything because, after all, my war was over in Europe and it wasn't up to me. But I was getting more and more depressed just thinking about it. Then he asked for my opinion, so I told him I was against it on two counts. First, the Japanese were ready to surrender and it wasn't necessary to hit them with that awful thing. Second, I hated to see our country be the first to use such a weapon."

General MacArthur, supreme commander of Allied forces in the Pacific, considered the bomb "completely unnecessary from a military point of view." He later said that the Japanese would have surrendered in May if the U.S. had told them they could keep the emperor.

Opposition to dropping the bomb was sufficiently known that Groves imposed a requirement that U.S. commanders in the field clear all statements on the bombings with the War Department. "We didn't want MacArthur and others saying the war could have been won without the bomb," he later admitted.

Shortly after the war was over, General Curtis "Demon" LeMay declared, "Even without the atomic bomb and the Russian entry into the war, Japan would have surrendered in two weeks. The atomic bomb had nothing to do with the end of the war."

The target committee had selected a number of sites on the Japanese mainland. Stimson removed Kyoto, the ancient cultural capital, which was spared its fate over the strong opposition of Groves. It was the city of Hiroshima that was decided upon. It had been deliberately left undamaged by LeMay's bombers. Here the U.S. could showcase its new weapon.

On August 6, at 2:45 a.m., three B-29s took off from the island of Tinian for Japan. The lead plane, the *Enola Gay*, carried the uranium bomb, "Little Boy." Pilot Paul Tibbets named the plane after his mother. Six and a half hours later, the *Enola Gay* came into sight of its target. The doomed city lay quiet in flooding early morning sunshine.

Hiroshima's 300,000 civilians, 43,000 soldiers, and 45,000 Korean slave laborers were just beginning their day. The target was a bridge near the center of the city. At 8:15, right on schedule, the giant plane went into its bombing run at 31,000 feet, speed 330 miles per hour.

As the bomb was released, the plane twisted violently to get as far as possible from the blast. At the last minute, a gust of wind blew the bomb, carrying it toward Shima Hospital at one end of the bridge. The bomb fell almost five miles to 2,000 feet, and then the two masses of uranium came together at lightning speed and turned to energy.

Pilot Paul Tibbets (center with pipe) with his crew and the Enola Gay.

The plane, now nine miles away, was battered by the shockwave. The fireball expanded outward, enveloping the densely populated center of the city, its intense heat and blast driving outward to shatter buildings and ignite all debris. The bomb totally destroyed an area extending approximately 1.2 miles in all directions. An hour and a half later, from almost 400 miles away, the crew could look back and still see the mushroom cloud rearing up to 40,000 feet or more.

At the hypocenter, where temperatures reached 5,400 degrees Fahrenheit, the fireball roasted people "to bundles of smoking black char in a fraction of a second as their internal organs boiled away." Tens of thousands were killed instantly. An estimated 140,000 were dead by the end of the year and 200,000 by 1950. The U.S. officially reported only 3,243 Japanese troops killed. Among the casualties were 23 American prisoners of war, some of whom lived through the blast only to be beaten to death by bomb survivors.

When he got news that the bomb had exploded at Hiroshima, Truman, aboard the *Augusta*, had gone from one crew member to another

A mushroom cloud rises over the Japanese city of Hiroshima following the atomic bombing on August 6, 1945. The view from the ground was very different and far more harrowing. At the hypocenter, where temperatures reached 5,400 degrees F, the fireball roasted people "to bundles of smoking black char in a fraction of a second as their internal organs boiled away."

telling them the great news like a town crier. "This is the greatest thing in history," he said. Responding to this, Catholic lay worker and pacifist Dorothy Day wrote: "We have killed 318,000 Japanese. . . . Mr. Truman was jubilant. President Truman. True man; what a strange name, come to think of it. We refer to Jesus Christ as true God and true Man. Truman is a true man of his time in that he was jubilant."

But the Japanese did not surrender. Stalin, honoring his pledge to Roosevelt, and having now moved 1.5 million men to the eastern front, attacked Japan on August 9 on three fronts in Manchuria. The fighting was bloody.

The Kwantung Army was practically obliterated. Estimates range up to 700,000 Japanese killed, wounded, and captured. Soviet troops also attacked in Korea and in the Kuril Islands and Sakhalin Island. This enormous event has been mostly forgotten to history because, later that morning on August 9, before Japan had time to react to the Soviet invasion, the United States dropped its second bomb—an implosive plutonium bomb, nicknamed "Fat Man," on the city of Nagasaki.

It exploded, ironically, over the largest Catholic cathedral in Asia with a force of twenty-two kilotons; 40,000 died immediately. Of them, 250 were soldiers.

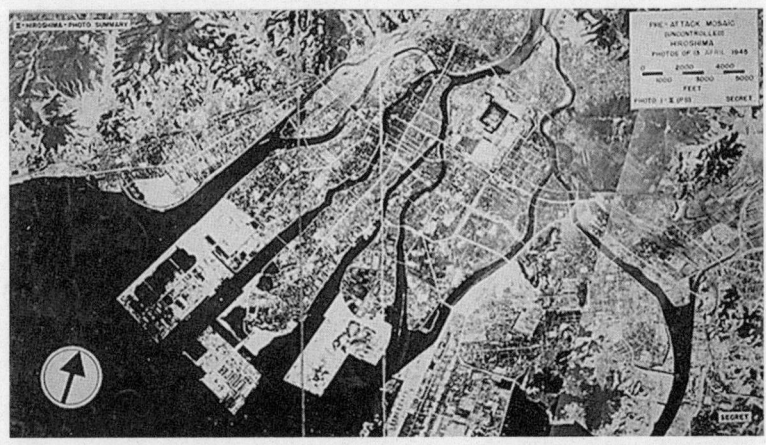

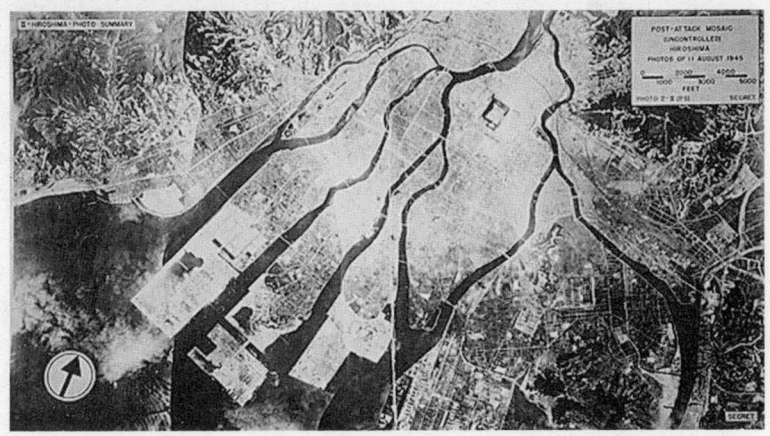

These before and after photos from the U.S. Strategic Bombing Survey help demonstrate the magnitude of destruction leveled on the city of Hiroshima by the atomic bomb.

Henry Wallace wrote of Truman and Byrnes in his diary on August 10, one day after Nagasaki: "It is obvious that the attitude of Truman, Byrnes and both the war and navy departments . . . will make for war eventually."

Yet, neither the announcement of Nagasaki nor army minister Anami's fallacious report that the U.S. had one hundred more atomic bombs moved Tokyo any closer to surrendering unconditionally. After all, Japanese cities were being wiped out all through 1945.

Two hundred planes and thousands of bombs or one plane and one bomb didn't seem to make a noticeable difference. For Japanese leaders, the devastating news on August 9 was the Soviet invasion. Nagasaki was just one more city that was destroyed. But the Red Army easily overwhelming Japanese forces in their richest colony, the puppet state of Manchukuo, was cause for alarm. General Kawabe, the army deputy chief of staff, explained, "It was only in a gradual manner that the horrible wreckage which had been made of Hiroshima became known. . . . In comparison, the Soviet entry into the war was a great shock when it actually came. Reports reaching Tokyo described Russian forces as 'invading in swarms.' It gave us all the more severe shock because we had been in constant fear of it with a vivid imagination that 'the vast Red Army forces in Europe were now being turned against us.'"

Prime Minister Suzuki said Japan must surrender immediately or "the Soviet Union will take not only Manchuria, Korea, Karafuto, but also Hokkaido. This would destroy the foundation of Japan. We must end the war when we can deal with the United States."

A top secret study done in January 1946 by the intelligence staff of the War Department's operations division concluded: "There was little mention in the Japanese cabinet of the use of the atomic bomb by the U.S. The dropping of the bomb was the pretext seized upon . . . as a reason for ending the war. But . . . it [is] almost a certainty that the Japanese would have capitulated upon the entry of Russia into the war."

Not only would the Soviets destroy Japan's empire, but they would have no qualms about destroying the emperor himself. After all, they'd murdered their own emperor in 1918.

On August 14, five days after the U.S. dropped the second bomb at Nagasaki, and with desperate fighting still raging against the Soviets, Emperor Hirohito exerted his personal power. For centuries, the Japanese emperors had lived without contact with their people, revered as divine beings. But now, Hirohito, speaking to the Japanese people directly, ordered surrender over the radio. It was the first time most of them had heard the voice of God.

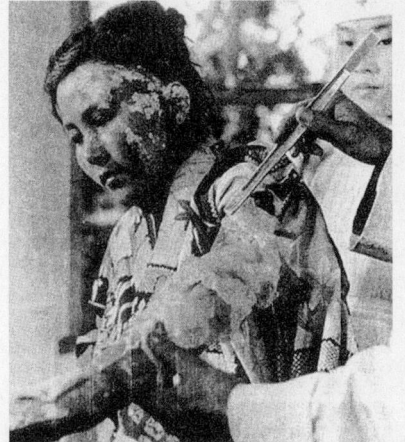
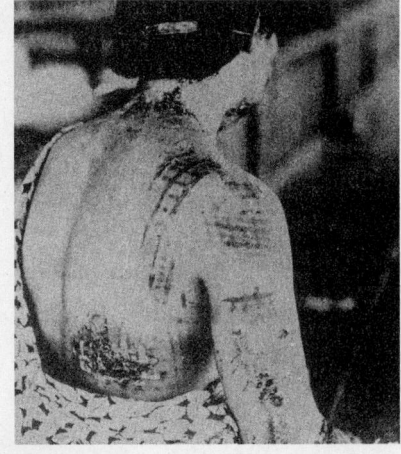
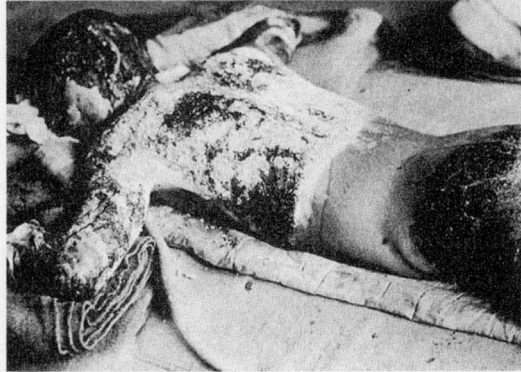

Injured and burned survivors suffered immensely. Hibakusha (bomb-affected persons) described it as walking through Hell.

The horrors and bloodshed of World War II coarsened many people to the suffering of others. Freeman Dyson, the future renowned physicist, who was part of the Tiger Force fleet of three hundred British bombers, explained, "I found this continuing slaughter of defenseless Japanese even more sickening than the slaughter of well-defended Germans. But still I did not quit. By that time I had been at war so long that I could hardly remember peace. No living poet had words to describe that emptiness of the soul which allowed me to go on killing without hatred and without remorse. But Shakespeare understood it, and he gave Macbeth the words: ' . . . I am in blood/Stepp'd in so that, should I wade no more,/ Returning were as tedious as going o'er.'"

Ruins in Nagasaki, where 40,000 people died immediately during the atomic bombing; 70,000 died by the end of 1945 and 140,000 in five years. Telford Taylor, the chief prosecutor at the Nuremberg trials, observed, "The rights and wrongs of Hiroshima are debatable, but I have never heard a plausible justification of Nagasaki."

In that spirit, 85 percent of the American public, convinced that the bombs had ended the war, applauded their use. Almost 23 percent said they wished the Japanese had not surrendered so quickly, so that the U.S. could have dropped more bombs on them.

Truman's estimates of American casualties kept climbing as the years went by, the number of projected deaths jumping from "thousands" shortly after the bombing to a half million a decade later. Almost fifty years later, in 1991, President George H. W. Bush praised "Truman's tough, calculating decision [which] spared millions of American lives."

Controversy over the atomic bombings continued to roil American society. Protests by the American Legion, the Air Force Association, and congressional conservatives forced the Smithsonian Air and Space Museum to cancel a 1995 exhibit on the bombings.

Young second lieutenant Paul Fussell, who was in the Pacific at the time of the bombing, published "Thank God for the Atom Bomb" in 1988, in which he wrote, "For all the fake manliness of our facades, we cried with relief and joy. We were going to live. We were going to grow up to adulthood after all."

Like millions of others of his generation, and millions since, Fussell was convinced that Truman and the bomb saved them from invading Japan. But attributing victory to the bomb, in a sense, insults the memory of the many men and women who gave their lives to defeat the Japanese, year by grinding year.

Robert Oppenheimer met with Henry Wallace shortly after the war, deeply worried about "the eventual slaughter of tens of millions." Earlier that year, he'd informed top military and civilian leaders that within three years the U.S. would likely have weapons up to seven thousand times as powerful as the bomb that would destroy Hiroshima. He proposed international control of the atomic technology to assuage Soviet fears over U.S. intentions. Wallace wrote in his diary: "The guilt consciousness of atomic scientists is one of the most astounding things I have ever seen."

He agreed with Oppenheimer. What was needed was an olive branch, and it came from the most unexpected quarter. Henry Stimson, "the Colonel," was a true old soldier, but he was terrified by the forces he'd helped unleash and now wanted to put the genie back in the bottle. In early September, Stimson sent a memo to Truman explaining that "our . . . relations with Russia [are] . . . virtually dominated by the problem of the atomic bomb." The Soviets, he advised, should be treated as allies: "If we . . . hav[e] this weapon rather ostentatiously on our hip, their suspicions and their distrust of our purposes and motives will increase. . . . The chief lesson that I have learned in a long life is the only way you can make a man trustworthy is to trust him; and the surest way to make him untrustworthy is to distrust him and show your distrust."

He proposed that the U.S. dismantle its atomic bombs if the Soviets agreed that both countries would ban atomic weapons research and thus submit to an international system of control. Truman devoted the historic September 21, 1945, cabinet meeting—Stimson's last—to discussing his proposal.

Wallace allied himself with Stimson, indicating the absurdity of trying to keep an atomic "monopoly." "I then went at some length into the whole scientific background, describing how foreign Jewish scientists had in the first place sold the President in the fall of 1939. I indicated the degree to which the whole approach had originated in Europe and that it was impossible to bottle the thing up no matter how much we tried."

With Byrnes away in London, navy secretary James Forrestal argued that the Soviets could not be trusted. "The Russians," he said, "like the Japanese, are essentially oriental in their thinking." The cabinet split sharply over Stimson's proposal, which would have put the United States squarely on the side of wanting world peace. But Truman vacillated and ultimately yielded to the Byrnes/Forrestal hardline faction. The feared, and potentially suicidal, arms race would escalate.

When Truman finally met with Robert Oppenheimer in October 1945, he asked him to guess when the Russians would develop their own atomic bomb. Oppenheimer did not know. Truman responded that he knew the answer. "Never." Clearly surprised by the president's truculent ignorance and frustrated that he did not understand the seriousness of the evolving crisis, Oppenheimer blurted out: "Mr. President, I feel I have blood on my hands." Truman responded with anger. "I told him the blood was on my hands and to let me worry about that."

Afterward, Truman told Dean Acheson, "I don't want to see that son of a bitch in this office ever again."

Oppenheimer was later attacked by right-wing conservatives as an agent of the Soviet Union and subjected to numerous investigations by the FBI.

In 1954 his security clearance was revoked. His real crime in the eyes of American authorities was opposing building the new hydrogen bomb, which he considered a weapon of genocide.

Contrary to the belief of Truman's inner circle, the dropping of the atomic bombs on Hiroshima and Nagasaki did not make the Soviet Union any more pliable. Soviet forces occupied the northern half of the Korean Peninsula, left face to face with U.S. forces in the south. Korea would later become a major flashpoint in the Cold War that would engulf the world for another fifty years.

But on a far larger scale, the bombing haunted the Soviet imagination. Future foreign minister Andrei Gromyko's son Anatoly recalled his father telling him that Hiroshima "set the heads of the Soviet military spinning. The mood in the Kremlin in the General Staff was neurotic, the mistrust toward the Allies grew quickly. Opinions floated around to preserve a large land army, to establish control over extended territories to lessen potential losses from atomic bombings."

And, in what many consider a cruel irony, the Japanese were allowed, after all, to keep the emperor, whose retention most experts believed essential to postwar stability in Japan. Truman suffered no political repercussions from this decision.

As Truman anticipated, the process he unleashed did indeed threaten the future existence of life on this planet. Even pugnacious Winston Churchill had moral qualms. He visited Truman toward the end of his presidency. Margaret, the president's daughter, described the scene. "Everyone was in an ebullient mood, especially Dad. Without warning, Mr. Churchill turned to him and said, 'Mr. President, I hope you have your answer ready for that hour when you and I stand before Saint Peter and he says, "I understand you two are responsible for putting off those atomic bombs. What have you got to say for yourselves?"'"

Although Harry Truman left office with approval ratings so low that only George W. Bush has come close since, he is now widely viewed as a near-great president and routinely showered with praise by Republicans and Democrats alike. Former national security advisor and secretary of state Condoleezza Rice, whom George Bush credited with telling "me everything I know about the Soviet Union," named Truman her "Man of the Century" to *Time* magazine.

David McCullough's 1993 biography of Truman won him a wide readership and a Pulitzer Prize, followed by an Emmy-awarded Best TV Movie on the cable network HBO in 1995, seen by millions.

In the myth the film creates, Henry Stimson and General George Marshall are portrayed as looking down on the underdog, little man, Truman, who is following his moral conscience. But their real positions on the bomb and Japan are misrepresented.

In the film, the Soviet point of view is entirely ignored, and the characters of Henry Wallace and Jimmy Byrnes are omitted. But the real Harry Truman is far darker than McCullough's heroic underdog. Despite Truman's denials, his flawed and tragic decision to use the bomb against Japan was meant instead as a ruthless and deeply unnecessary warning that the United States could be unrestrained by humanitarian considerations in using these same bombs against the Soviet Union, if it continued to interfere in Europe or Asia. However, on a larger moral scale, Truman *knew* he was beginning a process that could end life on the planet, as he said explicitly on at least *three* occasions—and forged ahead recklessly nonetheless. Unnecessarily killing people is a war crime. Threatening human extinction goes far, far beyond that.

This is what Henry Wallace understood more deeply than any other government official. The man who did his utmost to end the U.S. monopoly of the atomic bomb has been largely lost to history.

After leaving government in 1946, Wallace ran for president in 1948 as the candidate of the newly formed Progressive Party. His message of peace in a time of rising tensions was not heard. Repeatedly attacked by Truman and the press as a communist sympathizer, Wallace garnered less than 3 percent of the vote. Following the election, he retired from politics. Increasingly accused of sheltering communists during his campaign, he compromised himself under the pressures of the Korean War and the McCarthy period, loudly condemning the Soviets. But he clung to his progressive ideals and decried later U.S. involvement in Vietnam. He lived quietly on his farm in upstate New York, where he died in 1965.

In an irony that only an American capitalism could embrace, the Hi-Bred corn company that Wallace founded in 1926 was sold in the late 1990s to the Du Pont corporation for more than $9 billion—a bittersweet reminder to those who repeatedly denigrated *Mr. Smith Goes to Washington* as naive and communist.

He remains one of the unsung heroes of World War II, showing the world a kinder America. Though his vision was opposed at every step, it did not die. Following in the footsteps of others before him, Henry Wallace continued to lay the foundations—and others followed.

Franklin Roosevelt said, "No man was more of the American soil than Wallace."

But few now remember how close Wallace came to getting the vice presidential nomination on that steamy Chicago night in July 1944.

It was here that Roosevelt committed the greatest blunder of his splendid career—acceding to the party bosses' choice of Harry Truman. He could have resisted and, with the people's backing, had Wallace back as his vice president. But he was tired of defending his vision for world peace—very tired and near death. This sad moment points most clearly to the fallibility of all human history. To fail is not tragic. To be human is. What might this country have become had Wallace succeeded Roosevelt in April 1945 instead of Truman? Would no atomic bombs have been used in World War II? Could we have avoided the nuclear arms race and the Cold War? Would civil rights and women's rights have triumphed in the immediate postwar years? Might colonialism have ended decades earlier and the fruits of science and industry been spread more equitably around the globe? We'll never know.

CHAPTER SIX

As World War II came to a close, U.S. and Soviet soldiers celebrated together at the River Elbe with little thought that their countries would soon be bitter enemies.

There was a brief moment in time when the United States, alone among the victors, was on top of the world. Its death toll was 405,000, compared to the Soviet Union's 27 million. The economy was booming. Exports more than doubled prewar levels. Industrial production had grown 15 percent annually. The U.S. held two-thirds of the world's gold reserves and three-fourths of its invested capital. It was producing an incredible 50 percent of the world's goods and services.

In 1945 at Bretton Woods, New Hampshire, the U.S. established the two new major economic institutions of capitalism—the World Bank and the International Monetary Fund—each budgeted at $7 billion to $8 billion.

President Harry Truman, who had made his name investigating excess spending in the Senate, was overseeing a gigantic demobilization.

And yet, there was a lingering unease in this new society where the home front had prospered while the servicemen were away.

World War II left as many as 70 million people dead in Europe and Asia—two-thirds of them civilians. Hiroshima was an ominous forewarning. The Depression was over, but America's business and social planners feared a relapse and fretted over the consequences of worldwide poverty, with populations uprooted, homeless, and unemployed. Would revolution sweep the globe? What would happen to American trade and investment?

In France, the Communist Party, which had half a million members and fought bravely in the resistance to the Nazis, won 26 percent of the vote in 1945. In Italy, 1.7 million people joined the party.

Even in Britain, the people, exhausted and broke from two world wars, were uncharacteristically turning to the state to make their lives tolerable.

And fortune, which had made Winston Churchill one of the most respected statesmen of his era, now cast him aside with a reversal befitting Greek tragedy.

His successor as prime minister, Clement Attlee, embodied the new socialist European, promising to build a free health care system for all, and advocating the complete nationalization of many of Britain's oldest industries—a man preoccupied not with empire but with a massive social welfare state. By contrast, Churchill was offering empire. He had said in late 1942, at a time when England's very existence was threatened, "I have not become the king's first minister to preside over the liquidation of the British Empire."

But dismemberment is exactly what he would live to see. Attlee would administer the independence of India, Pakistan, Burma, Sri Lanka, Jordan, and Palestine. Attlee understood that there was a new American world order. The U.S. extended an almost $4 billion loan to Britain, not to be repaid for fifty years, and was now leasing military bases on English soil. Britain, in essence, was to become a new client state of the U.S.

Franklin Roosevelt, who had always disliked the concept of king and empire, and voiced the American disapproval of Britain's repressive policies in India, Greece, and elsewhere around the world, had successfully steered a middle course between Great Britain and the Soviet Union. The prospect of a large American credit to help the Soviets rebuild had been encouraged and discussed openly during the war. But Harry Truman showed none of Roosevelt's dexterity, as he tacked, at a time of maximum U.S. strength, increasingly toward the British camp. When the Soviets did not receive anything close to the aid package given the British, they were greatly disappointed. They already sensed the wartime alliance would be the first casualty of the postwar era.

In mid-September 1945, at a foreign ministers' meeting in London, Secretary of State Jimmy Byrnes berated Foreign Minister Molotov about Soviet policies in Eastern Europe. Molotov pointed in response to exclusionary U.S. policies in Italy, Greece, and Japan and, tired of Byrnes's belligerence, asked if he was hiding an atomic bomb in his pocket. Byrnes replied: "You don't know southerners. We carry our artillery in our pocket. If you don't cut out all this stalling and let us get down to work, I'm going to pull an atomic bomb out of my pocket and let you have it."

In December, Secretary of Commerce Henry Wallace pressed Truman to take control of America's atomic weapons away from Soviet-hater Leslie Groves, who still had unilateral control over them. Groves had advocated a preemptive attack against any potential rival trying "to make or possess atomic weapons."

The Soviet Union, having played the leading role in the antifascist effort and now possessing the largest army in the world, sent shivers down the spines of some U.S. officials.

In early 1946, a Gallup poll found that 26 percent of Americans thought the Soviets sought world domination. Thirteen percent thought the British did.

The Soviets, though aware of the rightward shift in the Truman administration, were hoping still to maintain the wartime alliance, and actually went out of their way to restrain their frustrated communist allies in China, Italy, France, and Greece. Stalin, whose major foreign policy goal was to make certain Germany and Japan never again posed a threat to his country, had enormous problems at home. His nation was in the grip of a crushing poverty, engaged still in extensive, continuing partisan warfare in its western sectors, particularly Ukraine, which would soon be racked with famine. The Soviets were isolated at the UN and the U.S. had a monopoly on the bomb. Yet, the U.S. was creating an image of the Soviet Union as being out to conquer the world.

In Germany, the two systems were already at odds. Roosevelt had once spoken about pastoralizing Germany, but the U.S. decided to revitalize the German economy as a key to overall European recovery. This was not in itself a bad decision, given what happened to West Germany in later years, but, at the time, it was highly insensitive to the concerns of a country that had been twice overrun, within recent memory, by German invaders. It was in fact a profound conflict of interest, and the image of the Soviets stripping the eastern zone of everything to ship back to their own impoverished land struck many Americans as looting.

As far back as the nineteenth century, the precommunist Russian Empire had been in conflict with the British Empire, both seeking influence in Turkey and Iran. Russia had repeatedly sought access to the warm-water ports of the Mediterranean.

During the 1917 Russian Revolution, Churchill, as first lord of the admiralty, had been a fierce foe of communism, which he proclaimed ought to be "strangled in its cradle." He'd wanted to draw the United States into a military engagement with the new communist regime, and in the fierce counter-revolution against it, forty thousand British and fifteen thousand American troops actually participated, poisoning relations from the start. It had been Roosevelt who finally recognized the Soviet Union in 1933.

Churchill, out of office and favor, was now itching for a confrontation. It would happen, not unsurprisingly, in the Middle East. Great Britain controlled 72 percent of Middle Eastern oil; the U.S. had 10 percent and wanted a bigger share. The Soviet Union wanted a piece, too. Having stationed troops during the war across its border in northern Iran, to keep oil supplies out of Nazi hands, the Soviets now came into conflict with Britain in the south.

Churchill additionally expressed concern about Soviet probes in Turkey threatening Britain's sphere of interest in the Middle East.

The exposure of a Soviet espionage ring in Canada in early February 1946 added credibility to his warnings. And a speech by Stalin, in which he proclaimed a new postwar Five Year Plan to rebuild the Soviet Union, was misunderstood as incendiary and wrongly interpreted as declaring that war between the two systems was inevitable. It was in this context, in early March 1946, that Winston Churchill would remind the world that he was still a power to be reckoned with. He traveled to Fulton, Missouri, not far from Truman's home, to make one of the most consequential speeches of the Cold War—words that would condemn forever, in the minds of many, the Soviet Union.

Truman and Churchill gesture from a train en route to Fulton, Missouri, where Churchill would deliver his bellicose "Iron Curtain" speech in early March 1946.

Truman introduced Churchill as "one of the great men of the age." "He's a great Englishman, but he's half-American," Truman noted.

From the podium at Westminster College, Churchill intoned: "From Stettin in the Baltic to Trieste in the Adriatic, an iron curtain has descended across the continent . . . in a great number of countries . . . the Communist parties or fifth columns constitute a growing challenge and peril to Christian civilization. . . . I do not believe that Soviet Russia desires war. What they desire is the fruits of war and the indefinite expansion of their power and doctrines."

This was a quantum leap in belligerence toward the Soviet Union.

The *New York Times* applauded the speech, saying it was spoken "with the force of the prophet proved right before."

Visibly upset, Stalin accused Churchill of being in bed with the "warmongers" who followed the "racial theory" that only English speakers could "decide the fate of the whole world."

The *Chicago Tribune*, although agreeing with his assessment of Eastern Europe, sharply questioned Churchill's "begging assistance for that old and evil empire . . . to maintain British tyranny thruout the world. We cannot become partners in slave holding."

Florida's Senator Claude Pepper observed that Churchill was "as much opposed to Russia as to a labor government in his own country." Pepper told reporters, "It is shocking to see Mr. Churchill . . . align himself with the old Chamberlain Tories who strengthened the Nazis as part of their anti-Soviet crusade."

Eleanor Roosevelt deplored Churchill's inflammatory remarks and James Roosevelt, Eleanor and Franklin's oldest son, urged Truman to fly Henry Wallace to Moscow to meet with Stalin and ease tensions.

The following month, on the first anniversary of Roosevelt's death, Wallace offered a different vision: "The only way to defeat Communism in the world is to do a better and smoother job of maximum production and optimum distribution. . . . Let's make it a clean race, a determined race but above all a peaceful race in the service of humanity. . . . The source of all our mistakes is fear. . . . Russia fears Anglo-Saxon encirclement. We fear Communist penetration. If these fears continue, the day will come when our sons and grandsons will pay for these fears with rivers of blood. . . . Out of fear great nations have been acting like cornered beasts, thinking only of survival. . . . A month ago Mr. Churchill came out for the Anglo Saxon century. Four years ago I repudiated the American century. Today I repudiate the Anglo Saxon century with even greater vigor. The common people of the world will not tolerate a recrudescence of imperialism even under enlightened Anglo-Saxon, atomic bomb auspices. The destiny of the English speaking people is to serve the world, not dominate it."

Following Churchill's speech, conditions deteriorated rapidly. When Soviet troops stayed in northern Iran beyond their March deadline, Truman threatened war. He wrote, "If the Russians were to control Iran's oil, either directly or indirectly . . . it would be a serious loss for the economy of the western world."

Truman later privately claimed to Senator Henry "Scoop" Jackson that he summoned Soviet ambassador Andrei Gromyko to the White House and warned him that if Soviet troops were not out in forty-eight hours, "We're going to drop it on you." They were out, he claimed, in twenty-four. The Soviets did withdraw, but probably for reasons other than atomic blackmail. Less than two months later, the U.S. cut off desperately needed reparation payments from West Germany to the Soviet Union.

And in July of 1946, sending another chilling message about its intentions, the U.S. decided to proceed with an atomic bomb test in the Marshall Islands.

That September, in front of twenty thousand people at New York's Madison Square Garden, Henry Wallace tried to put a stop to the growing madness, warning: "The tougher we get, the tougher the Russians will get. . . . I believe that we can get cooperation once Russia understands that our primary objective is neither saving the British Empire nor purchasing oil in the Near East with the lives of American soldiers. . . . Under friendly peaceful competition the Russian world and the American world will gradually become more alike. The Russians will be forced to grant more and more of the personal freedoms and we shall become more and more absorbed with the problems of social-economic justice." But, he warned, "He who trusts in the atom bomb will sooner or later perish by the atom bomb."

The speech became world news, deeply embarrassing to Secretary of State Jimmy Byrnes, who told Truman either he or Wallace had to go.

Support for Wallace, the last remaining New Dealer in the Truman administration, poured in throughout the ensuing controversy from people such as Eleanor Roosevelt and Albert Einstein but not from Truman's closest advisors.

James Forrestal regarded Wallace as at best a security risk and secretly had his naval intelligence unit monitoring the secretary of commerce. He shared information with the FBI's J. Edgar Hoover, who harbored deep suspicions about Wallace's loyalties. Wallace, in turn, considered Hoover an "American Himmler."

Truman at first acknowledged and then later tried to deny that he had read and approved the entire speech in advance. Caught in his own web of deceit, he vented in his diary: Wallace is "a pacifist one hundred percent. He wants us to disband our armed forces, give Russia our atomic

Secretary of Commerce Henry Wallace arrives at the White House for a cabinet meeting. After his call for a more conciliatory approach to dealing with the Soviet Union in his September 12, 1946, speech at Madison Square Garden, Truman fired him. Cold War hardliners such as James Byrnes helped convince Truman that Wallace had to go.

secrets and trust a bunch of adventurers in the Kremlin Politbureau. I do not understand a 'dreamer' like that."

Truman fired Wallace, and, with his departure, the chances of averting a nuclear arms race disappeared. The year 1947 would be the turning point, as the U.S. plunged headlong into the Cold War at home and abroad.

Behind the liberation movements in places such as British Malaya, French Indochina, and Dutch Indonesia, U.S. leaders painted a dire picture of Stalin spreading world revolution. They ruled out negotiations with their former ally and ignored any grays in their black-and-white conclusions.

In Greece, the British army toppled the popular leftist National Liberation Front and restored the monarchy and right-wing dictatorship, sparking a communist-led uprising.

Following the severe winter of 1946–47, the financially strapped British could not control the revolt and asked the United States to take the lead in defeating the Greek insurgents and modernizing the Turkish army.

One State Department official later summed it up: "Great Britain had within the hour handed the job of world leadership . . . to the United States."

A war-weary public had no appetite for costly initiatives, but Truman, addressing both houses of Congress, appealed for $400 million, laying out a new vision for America as the world's policeman: "The very existence of the Greek state is today threatened by the terrorist activities of several thousand armed men, led by communists. . . . At the present moment in world history, nearly every nation must choose between alternative ways of life. . . . I believe that it must be the policy of the United States to support free peoples who are resisting attempted subjugation by armed minorities or outside pressure."

Truman, in not distinguishing vital threats from peripheral ones and by linking the fate of people all over the world to the security of the United States, was making a momentous statement. These words could in fact be transposed to Korea, Vietnam, Iraq, and Afghanistan. After a heated debate, Congress fell into line.

Moscow was stunned by this warlike language and accused the U.S. of imperialist expansion under the guise of charity and trying to extend the Monroe Doctrine to the Old World.

From outside the government, Henry Wallace led the opposition, decrying the "utter nonsense" of describing the Turkish or Greek governments as democratic and accusing Truman of "betraying" Roosevelt's vision for world peace. "When President Truman proclaims the world-wide conflict between east and west, he is telling the Soviet leaders that we are preparing for eventual war." "President Truman," he admonished, "cannot prevent change in the world any more than he can prevent the tide from coming in or the sun from setting. But once America stands for opposition to change, we are lost. America will become the most hated nation in the world." Anticipating that the Soviets would reply in kind, he warned: "Truman's policy will spread communism in Europe and Asia."

Two months later, the Soviets sponsored a communist coup overthrowing the democratically elected government of Hungary. The *New York Times* wrote: "The coup in Hungary is Russia's answer to our action in Greece and Turkey." And it clearly contributed to the Soviet decision to impose a new, stricter order across Eastern Europe.

The Greek civil war grew bloody and U.S. personnel, identified as "advisors," arrived in the war zone in June of 1947. The United States amply armed the right-wing monarchy and tolerated its client's mass political arrests and executions. It was an especially savage conflict, with tactics, some old, some new, that previewed those later used in Vietnam—such as mass deportations to concentration camps, mass imprisonment of wives and children of subversives, executions, destruction of unions, torture, and napalming villages. Greece was kept in the hands of wealthy businessmen, many of them Nazi collaborators; the victims were primarily workers and peasants who'd resisted the Nazis.

The Soviet Union temporarily assisted the left-wing forces. But in February 1948, Stalin ordered Yugoslavia's Josip Tito, as well as neighboring Albania and Bulgaria, to stop supporting the guerilla movement. "What do you think," he berated Tito, "that . . . the United States, the most powerful nation in the world—will permit you to break their line of communication in the Mediterranean Sea! Nonsense. And we have no navy. The uprising in Greece must be stopped, and as quickly as possible."

The tough Tito, who'd fought his own grueling war against the Nazis and had no fear of Stalin's assassins, refused, and Stalin excommunicated him from the international communist movement, antagonizing uncompromising allies like Mao in China. The State Department reported: "For the first time in history we may now have within the international community a communist state . . . independent of Moscow. . . . A new factor of fundamental and profound significance has been introduced into the world communist movement by the demonstration that the Kremlin can be successfully defied by one of its own minions." But, despite providing covert support for Tito, the United States never adjusted its rhetoric to reflect the fact that communism was not monolithic. In public statements by American leaders, the Soviet Union remained at the center of a communist conspiracy to dominate the world.

But the truth was not so simple. In 1956, out of office a second time and in retirement, the old lion Churchill confirmed in an interview, "Stalin never broke his word to me. We agreed on the Balkans. I said he could have Romania and Bulgaria and he said we could have Greece. . . . He signed a slip of paper and he never broke his word. We saved Greece that way."

Stalin's lack of support for the Greek uprising doomed the rebels, and the war ended with victory in 1949 for the national government. Though

U.S. officials cheered the victory, the Greek people weren't so sure. More than one hundred thousand died and eight hundred thousand became refugees. Successive Greek governments would use the state apparatus—the police, the military, and intelligence operatives—to brutally rule the country.

Domestically, pressured by the Republican right, Truman decided to appease the public's growing unease with communism even though, as Clark Clifford later admitted, "the President didn't attach fundamental importance to the so-called Communist scare. He thought it was a lot of baloney." Truman mandated loyalty checks on all government employees to root out "subversives." Having the wrong views on religion, sexual behavior, foreign policy, or race could make one suspect. Through 1952, loyalty boards reviewed more than twenty-two thousand cases and more than four thousand employees were fired or resigned.

In October 1947, the House Un-American Activities Committee held highly publicized hearings on communist influence in Hollywood. It was an easy target.

Hollywood studio executives shamefully denounced those accused and pledged not to hire anyone with suspect affiliations. Although a great number of Hollywood stars publicly criticized the witch-hunts, the "blacklist" gave way to the "graylist," and hundreds more were denied work. Among the friendly witnesses who testified were Screen Actors Guild president Ronald Reagan, actors Robert Taylor and Gary Cooper, and studio executive Walt Disney.

From 1948 through 1954, more than forty strongly anticommunist motion pictures were made, not including terrifying science fiction parables like H. G. Wells's *The War of the Worlds*, which implied the threat of communism.

The FBI, under publicity-conscious J. Edgar Hoover, whose single greatest obsession in life was communism, conducted most of the investigations into its existence in America. Those accused could not know the basis of the accusations. In his paranoia, Hoover distrusted even the White House, the Pentagon, and the Justice Department and hid what he did—both inside and outside the law—drawing up plans for mass detentions of communists in the event of an anticipated Soviet attack.

In July 1947, Truman pushed through the National Security Act, which created a vast new bureaucracy, headed by the fiercely anti-Soviet James Forrestal as this country's first secretary of defense. The act also created the Central Intelligence Agency, which was given four functions—three of them dealing with the collection, analysis, and dissemination of intelligence. It was the fourth function that would prove the most dangerous—a vaguely worded passage that allowed the CIA to perform "other functions and duties related to intelligence affecting the national security," as the president saw fit.

The CIA would use that vague wording to conduct hundreds of covert operations around the world, including more than eighty during Truman's second term. Its earliest success was to subvert Italy's 1948 election to ensure victory over the Communist Party. Democracy was apparently a virtue only when it served U.S. interests. Sometimes referred to as "capitalism's invisible army," the CIA was truly the beginning of a new America, built upon a secret state that would grow exponentially over the following decades.

Despite his public face, Truman had feared from the start that the CIA could turn into a "Gestapo" or "military dictatorship." And in 1963, shortly after John Kennedy had been assassinated, Truman, surprisingly but explicitly, called for the CIA to end operations and simply gather intelligence. His op-ed appeared in the *Washington Post* but strangely generated little discussion in other media outlets and disappeared from public attention.

General George Marshall, having led the Allied armies to victory in World War II, was named "Man of the Year" again by *Time* in January 1948 and planned a quiet retirement. But Truman, who had had more than enough of Byrnes, forced his resignation and made Marshall his new secretary of state.

Privately believing that Truman's descriptions of a communist threat were exaggerated, Marshall's common sense dictated that the best way to win a war was to prevent it from occurring. What was needed in a ruined and destitute Europe was not a military response but a humanitarian one. In that spirit, at Harvard University's graduation ceremony in June 1947, America's most prestigious general invited European leaders

A man labors in West Berlin on a Marshall Plan–funded project (as indicated by the sign in the background) in June 1948. The United States spent $13 billion on European recovery between 1948 and 1952. With Britain, France, and Germany as its largest recipients, the plan exacerbated Soviet fears of both a rearmed Germany and capitalist encirclement.

to submit a plan for economic recovery. Out of this was born the Marshall Plan. Marshall explained, "Our policy is directed not against any country or doctrine but against hunger, poverty, desperation, and chaos."

What the United States did after World War II was rare in imperial history. It restored its old rivals Germany and Japan and made them economically powerful satellites of the United States. "It is a difficult program," Marshall continued. "And you know, far better than I do, the political difficulties involved in this program. But there's no doubt whatever in my mind, that if we decide to do this thing, we can do it successfully."

The U.S. eventually spent $13 billion between 1948 and 1952, with Britain, France, and Germany being the largest recipients, adding greatly to Soviet fears of restored German power. The Soviets turned down an offer to join the plan, as it called for too much American control over the Soviet economy.

When Czechoslovakia's freely elected coalition government, headed interestingly enough by the Communist Party, accepted Marshall's offer of aid, that went too far for the mistrustful Stalin, who demanded the Czechs reject the plan. In February 1948, a Stalinist regime was imposed on Czechoslovakia. Liberals in the U.S. and Europe were shocked. Actor James Cagney voiced the Western point of view: "Subversion is of course an important technique of communist conquest. Czechoslovakia in 1948 is an established democracy in Eastern Europe. Suddenly a rash of strikes. Conservative elements return from the capital. But Jan Masaryk, son of the country's greatest hero, will not go along and remains in the foreign office. Two weeks later his dead body is discovered. Whether he was murdered or killed himself is not known to this day."

Masaryk's manner of death—falling out of his bathroom window—would come to particularly haunt Forrestal and vindicated the darkest view of Soviet intentions.

Marshall, however, had told a cabinet meeting the previous November that the Soviets would soon clamp down on Czechoslovakia as a "purely defensive move," but Truman seized on the outrage to speed the Marshall Plan through Congress, as well as a rearmament program the Pentagon had long been pushing. The U.S., also at this point, made the fateful decision to press for an independent West German state.

Truman described the Marshall Plan and the Truman Doctrine as "two halves of the same walnut." Although the plan fueled European recovery, much of the aid was used to purchase exports from U.S. corporations. Little aid was given to rebuild Europe's own indigenous refining capacity, allowing the American oil majors to dominate the European market.

The plan was secretly generous to the CIA, which diverted large amounts of Marshall aid money for covert operations. In the summer of 1948, following the Czechoslovakian coup, Truman approved a dramatic escalation of global covert action to include guerilla operations in the Soviet Union and Eastern Europe. One project in Ukraine created a guerilla army codenamed Nightingale, which had originally been set up by the Nazis in 1941, made up of ultranationalist Ukrainians. These groups now wreaked havoc in the famine-racked region where Soviet control was loose, carrying out the murder of thousands of Jews, Soviets, and Poles who opposed a separate Ukrainian state.

Beginning in 1949, for five years the CIA parachuted Ukrainian infiltrators back into the region. To the Soviet mind it was as if they had infiltrated guerillas into the Canadian or Mexican border areas of the United

Truman addresses a joint session of Congress in March 1947. The president asked for $4 million to support efforts in Greece and Turkey and, in what came to be known as the "Truman Doctrine," declared that the United States must support "free peoples who are resisting subjugation by armed minorities or outside pressure."

States and signaled the lengths to which the U.S. was willing to go to dislodge Soviet control of their own border areas and sphere of interest.

The CIA was equally active in Germany, taking over the Gehlen organization from the U.S. Army. Gehlen, a former Nazi who'd run intelligence in Eastern Europe and the Soviet Union for Hitler, recruited a network of Nazis and war criminals, drawn in part from the Gestapo and SS. And in the ensuing years, it painted the worst possible picture of Soviet actions. A retired CIA official acknowledged, "He fed us what we wanted to hear. We used his stuff constantly, and we fed it to everyone else: the Pentagon; the White House; the newspapers. They loved it, too. But it was hyped up Russian bogeyman junk, and it did a lot of damage to this country."

When, in June of 1948, the U.S. instituted currency reform in the three western sectors of Berlin, which was one hundred miles inside East Germany, the Soviets saw this as a major step in establishing an independent, remilitarized West German state, as well as a betrayal of the U.S. promise to provide reparations from the inherently more prosperous Western zones. The Soviets cut off rail and road access to Berlin.

Stalin said the Western powers had forfeited their right of access because they were shattering the postwar framework of a unified Germany. The Western media decried the savage cruelty of the Soviets' Berlin blockade, accusing them of trying to starve civilians into submission. But contrary to this widely held view, the Soviets, for all their faults, guaranteed West Berliners access to food and coal from the Eastern zone or from direct Soviet provisions. U.S. military intelligence analysts confirmed this, reporting in October that "road, rail and water blockade of Berlin by no means constitutes a complete economic blockade either by intent or in fact." What most people do remember, however, is that over the next eleven months, in a heroic defensive maneuver against Soviet aggression, the massive Berlin airlift organized by General Curtis LeMay delivered food and fuel to 2.2 million people in a besieged city. Truman, who was willing to approve the use of atomic weapons, wrote in September: "We are very close to war."

France had little enthusiasm for this U.S. initiative, fearing a remilitarized Germany, nor did Britain, but the U.S. gambled that its atomic monopoly would win out, rejecting Soviet attempts to compromise until it achieved both a basic law outlining a West German state and the creation in April 1949 of the North Atlantic Treaty Organization. This, for the first time in its history, committed the United States to a peacetime military alliance with Western Europe.

Its objectives won, the U.S. now agreed to talks on the future of Germany. And it was then that the Soviets lifted the blockade.

Germany was now officially divided, and, in return for its foreign aid, the U.S. would, with NATO, militarize France, England, Italy, and Germany, and later station nuclear weapons on German soil. In effect, the U.S. was declaring Western Europe the first line of defense and potential launching pad for World War III.

As the 1948 election loomed, and the Republicans were heavily favored, Henry Wallace declared himself the Progressive Party's candidate. In his campaign speeches, he stressed, "The bigger the peace vote in 1948, the more definitely the world will know that the United States is not behind the bipartisan reactionary war policy which is dividing the world into two armed camps and making inevitable the day when American soldiers will be lying in their arctic suits in the Russian snow." "The people of the world," he insisted, "must see that there is another America than this Truman-led, Wall Street–dominated, military-backed group that is blackening the name of American democracy all over the world."

Truman's inner circle unleashed a vicious red-baiting campaign using liberals to accuse the former vice president of being a tool of Moscow. Truman announced: "I do not want, and I will not accept, the political support of Henry Wallace and his communists."

Although Wallace repeatedly denied any involvement with communism and warned that red-baiting was being used to undermine American freedoms, mobs broke up his rallies; universities denied him the right to speak on campuses, and his supporters were sometimes fired from their jobs. Wallace's running mate, Idaho senator Glen Taylor, was arrested and beaten up by police in Birmingham, Alabama, for entering the gathering of a Southern Negro Youth Congress through a door marked "Colored." Wallace wired Taylor: "This dramatizes the hypocrisy of spending billions for arms in the name of defending freedom abroad, while freedom is trampled on here at home."

The communist charges and the dismissive treatment of Wallace by the major newspapers took its toll. Wallace's campaign was a disaster. He came in fourth behind a South Carolina segregationist. But much of his progressive agenda on domestic issues, especially civil rights, seems to have influenced Truman. And, ironically, this made a difference, as a last-minute rush to Truman by Democratic voters who now feared a Republican victory allowed Truman to upset heavily favored Thomas Dewey.

Though it was one of the great come-from-behind miracle tales of U.S. politics, Harry Truman, like Churchill, would watch his presidency crumble. In the next four years, he would see his support plummet, leaving office with historically low George W. Bush–level approval ratings.

In September 1949 came the first of three major events—none of which should have been unforeseen. Truman told a shocked nation: "We have evidence that within recent weeks an atomic explosion occurred in the USSR." In 1948, Oppenheimer had said, "Our atomic monopoly is like a cake of ice melting in the sun." As Henry Wallace had warned in 1945, Truman and his group were terribly wrong to assume the U.S. monopoly would endure.

Americans felt more vulnerable than ever, and the nuclear arms race that Wallace and the scientists had so feared now escalated as the United States hastened development of a hydrogen bomb.

As 1949 ended, the world's largest and most populous nation, China, turned communist. When Mao Zedong routed the corrupt nationalist forces of Jiang Jieshi, it was unquestionably the most important revolution since Russia's 1917 overthrow of the tsar. *Time* magazine warned of the "Red tide that threatens to engulf the world." General Douglas MacArthur wrote in *Life* magazine: "The fall of China imperils the United States."

Acting outraged, as if the corrupt Nationalists' loss had not been anticipated, the conservative China lobby in the U.S. blamed not only the Soviet Union, Democrats, and State Department China experts, but also Secretary of State George Marshall. These would prove to be false accusations. In subordinating world revolution to their own immediate security concerns, the Soviets had provided minimal assistance to the revolutionaries and little encouragement. Stalin did finally form an alliance with Mao in February 1950 but urged the radicalized Chinese leader to maintain cordial relations with the U.S. Both sides made exaggerated claims against each other, but China's commitment to revolutionary change and U.S. refusal to acknowledge the legitimacy of the new government with a seat at the United Nations, while recognizing dictator-run countries, doomed any efforts at peace.

In June 1950, North Korea invaded South Korea and the Cold War now turned hot for real.

Both Soviet-installed dictator Kim Il Sung in the north and U.S.-backed dictator Syngman Rhee in the south had been threatening to unify the country by force. Distressed by the U.S. rebuilding of Japan, with which the Soviets had fought two bloody wars, Stalin gave Kim the green light to beat the south to the punch. Stalin told Kim Il Sung that the war was a way to get back at the "dishonest, perfidious, and arrogant behavior of the United States in Europe, the Balkans, the Middle East, and especially its decision to form NATO." On the other hand, knowing the power of the U.S., Stalin did not want a wider war.

The Joint Chiefs and the State Department had openly declared Korea to be outside the U.S. defense perimeter in East Asia. But with communist victory in China and revolutionary forces threatening to overthrow Western-backed regimes in Vietnam, Malaya, and the Philippines, Truman felt he had to make a stand somewhere, and Korea was the newly appointed place. "If we let Korea down, the Soviet will keep right on going and swallow up one piece of Asia after another. If we were to let Asia go, the Near East would collapse and no telling what would happen in Europe."

Despite deploying tens of thousands of troops, Truman refused to call the intervention a "war," labeling it instead a "police action."

Although it was nominally a United Nations effort, the U.S. provided half the ground forces and almost all of the naval and air power. Most of the other ground forces were South Korean. Truman opted as well to bypass congressional authorization, setting the stage for future interventions. The bloody, indecisive three-year war cost Truman dearly.

As for James Forrestal, though his views had helped shape the poisonous anti-Soviet climate in Washington, he'd been on the losing end of several policy battles with Truman and was relieved of duty with a ceremony in March 1949. He was "shattered."

When friend and future CIA director John McCone came to call, Forrestal, becoming increasingly paranoid, pulled down the shades and sat away from the window so as not to give a sniper an easy target. Whether Forrestal was referring to communists or Jewish "Zionist agents," he never specified. Rumors hit the press and went worldwide that Forrestal was discovered in the streets in his pajamas shouting: "The Russians are coming!"

The Pentagon announced that Forrestal had gone for a routine check-up at the Bethesda Naval Hospital in Maryland. He was diagnosed with reactive depression.

Alone in his room on the sixteenth floor, he suffered constant nightmares of persecution. He thought he would suffer the same fate as Czechoslovakian foreign minister Jan Masaryk—to be pushed out of a window. But his condition began to improve and, on the night of May 22, 1949, he stayed up late copying Sophocles's "The Chorus from Ajax," where the hero ponders his fate far from home. At the word "nightingale," he put his pen down. Sixteen floors up, he jumped.

Philosopher and newspaper columnist Walter Lippmann wrote of Forrestal that he was like a doctor who studies a disease and then contracts it himself.

The first U.S. secretary of defense, James Forrestal, suffered a nervous breakdown and, tormented by his own anticommunist paranoia, committed suicide, jumping from his sixteenth-floor room at Bethesda Naval Hospital.

Behind him, Forrestal left a newborn Pentagon establishment, which, faced with those struggling for a different world, saw only communist conspiracies.

There is still today a fundamental misunderstanding that the United States entered the Cold War in response to Soviet aggression worldwide. There is no doubt the Soviet leadership imposed repressive and, when challenged, brutal dictatorships on Poland, Hungary, Romania, Bulgaria, East Germany, Albania, and Czechoslovakia. But it is equally clear that the Soviets were initially willing to accept governments friendly to them in these countries, until the West began to threaten both Soviet ideology and Soviet security.

During this postwar period, it was the United States, with its atomic monopoly, not the Soviet Union, which bore the lion's share of responsibility for starting the Cold War.

Pacifist A. J. Muste wrote in 1941, "The problem after a war is with the victor. He thinks that he has just proved that war and violence pay. Who will now teach him a lesson?"

The U.S. had helped liberate Western Europe, but subsequent developments signaled that the country was gripped, almost paralyzed, by fear and responding with aggression. Among the signs were Truman's bowing to the views of staunch anticommunists who believed the Soviet

Union was bent on global conquest, his repudiation of Roosevelt's understanding with Stalin, his provocative and unnecessary dropping of the atomic bombs, his call for fighting communism in Greece, his deliberate exaggeration of the communist threat both overseas and at home, Churchill's speech at Fulton, the development of NATO, the division and remilitarization of Germany, the continued testing of bigger and bigger atomic and hydrogen bombs, which the U.S. used to threaten the Soviet Union, and U.S. persecution and silencing of those who challenged these distortions.

Why this fear? It has been said that as Americans we are an immigrant people to a new country, people who in one way or another have escaped persecution and poverty and fear, and, though separated by two enormous oceans, are still subject to that incessant fear. It even infects our children and grandchildren. North Americans have been taught and become enamored of the myth of starting over with a new purity in a new land—the myth of American exceptionalism, in a new Jerusalem, a city on a hill. Is it necessary then to exaggerate the fear of persecution, from abroad, from the corrupt foreigner who would always represent all the old and evil ways?

In the early twenty-first century, there would be more than 300 million guns in American homes. We are the most heavily armed nation in the world. But when any nation goes to an extreme degree to protect itself, it is inevitable that that protection will never seem psychologically to be enough. It is also often true that the image of the enemy will grow proportionate to the size of the defense, resulting in an overreaction and accelerated spending of energies in a futile attempt to liquidate that fear, which never seems to erode.

Fear and uncertainty are two inescapable elements in all human life since the beginning of time. They are to be accepted as one accepts birth and death. It was Alexander the Great who reportedly addressed the notion that "if you can conquer your fear, you can conquer death." And in coenduring with and containing our fear and uncertainty, we become naturally stronger. The irony of life—personal and public—is that often with the changing of time the object of fear, the enemy, becomes, to the surprise of former enemies, a friend, often a best friend, or ally.

Clearly, in hindsight, U.S. leaders had exaggerated the threat from an enemy they felt they needed, wanting to frame the world as an existential clash between two antagonistic social systems. Henry Wallace, who warned that the source of all of our mistakes is fear, had said it could be a healthy competition between those systems. But the hardliners among American policymakers felt that this was impossible, and Wallace was dismissed as naive or disloyal. James Forrestal, one of those hardliners, the first secretary of defense, thus ended his life in a violent fashion that would become a strange omen for an American foreign policy that was increasingly terrified of its own shadow.

Fifty years into this century, halfway from 1900 to 2000, the United States had forged the foundation of a new mindset. It had developed into a full-fledged, if unique, kind of empire, economically supreme and massively armed, policing the world while professing liberty and democracy. For a policeman, it's necessary to locate and arrest enemies. Thus, the story of the next sixty years of American history will resemble a pattern that has already occurred, in the shape of increasing covert activities unknown to the people of the empire, more and more regional wars, and a form of control that is imposed over and over again.

CHAPTER SEVEN

*R*epublican Dwight David Eisenhower was elected president in 1952 in a landslide win, carrying thirty-nine states. The hero of World War II, Ike was both gentle and strong. He knew that militarism had its limits and dismissed the continuing Korean War as "useless." As president, he would end it and restore American confidence and optimism, proclaiming, "Now we look forward to the future, with faith in ourselves, in our country, and in the Creator who is father of us all."

He also had faith in the most powerful arsenal ever assembled. And just three days before his election, the U.S. tested its first hydrogen bomb on what had been the Island of Elugelab.

The sixty-five-ton device was too big to drop by plane. Elugelab burned for six hours under a mushroom cloud one hundred miles across and then disappeared forever.

Who was this new American president with a grandfather's face? At Potsdam he had opposed the atomic bombings of Japan. He had pushed hard for a second front to help the Soviets in 1942 and was furious when Churchill convinced Roosevelt to instead invade northern Africa. He had developed a friendly relationship with Soviet general Zhukov. Stalin held him in high regard: "General Eisenhower is a very great man, not only because of his military accomplishments but because of his human, friendly, kind, and frank nature."

He was the first foreigner to ever witness a parade in Red Square from the platform atop Lenin's tomb. And six weeks after his inauguration, in March 1953, a fresh opportunity presented itself. Americans woke to the news that Joseph Stalin was dead. Despite his extraordinary brutality, most Russians revered him for leading the nation to victory over the Nazis and turning a backward Russia into a modern industrial state.

While the public mourned, the new, somewhat uncertain, Soviet leaders, freed of the onerous ghost of a man who'd ruled their lives like an ancient tsar for thirty years, decided to ease tensions with the capitalist West. They wanted, above all, to focus on improving their quality of life at home and called for coexistence and peaceful competition. How would America's new leadership respond?

Winston Churchill, re-elected a second time to office in 1951, had now seen fifty years of international diplomacy—from the golden age of the European empires to the horrifying rise of fascism. But this new nuclear age held a special terror for the old man. He urged Washington to seize this unprecedented opportunity and pressed for an international summit with the new Soviet leaders. He had hopes for Eisenhower. Six weeks went by. Silence. And then Eisenhower eloquently spoke of peace: "Every gun that is made, every warship launched, every rocket fired signifies a theft from those who hunger and are not fed, those who are cold and are not clothed. . . . This is not a way of life at all. . . . Under the cloud of threatening war, it is humanity hanging from a cross of iron."

The Soviets, inspired, reprinted the speech widely, but then, two days later, an answer came back to Moscow from Eisenhower's secretary of state, John Foster Dulles. The Soviet "peace offensive," he charged, was a "peace defensive," taken in response to U.S. strength, and the communists were "endlessly conspir[ing] to overthrow from within, every genuinely free government in the world."

It was insulting, and the Soviets were perplexed, wondering whether it was the moderate Eisenhower or the more extreme Dulles who spoke for this new administration.

The son of a Presbyterian minister, Dulles had made a career on Wall Street in the 1920s and 1930s as a lawyer for the corporate powerhouse Sullivan and Cromwell. Dulles never wavered in his commitment to

Mourners commemorate Stalin's death in Dresden, East Germany.

protecting U.S. business interests or in his hatred of communism. Despite his later vehement denials of any dealings with the Nazis, he worked for corporate and banker clients and helped secure more than a billion dollars in German bond sales in the U.S. He also dealt extensively with the I.G. Farben corporation, a significant contributor to the Hitler regime.

Dulles was set on the idea of an aggressive liberation of citizens under Soviet control.

By the start of the Eisenhower presidency, the Korean police action had become a two-and-a-half-year nightmare, a brutal land war whose casualties and endless maneuvers for useless hillsides were as frustrating as operations in the jungles of South Vietnam would be fifteen years later.

Battling Soviet-trained and -equipped North Koreans, World War II hero General Douglas MacArthur had pushed north toward the Chinese border despite repeated warnings from Beijing. He assured Truman that the Chinese would never enter the war. In the late fall of 1950, hundreds of thousands of Chinese troops streamed across the Yalu River, sending U.S. and allied forces reeling backward in a frantic retreat. *Time*

In 1948, Lieutenant General Curtis LeMay, the mastermind behind the wartime firebombing of Japanese cities, took charge of the U.S. Air Force's Strategic Air Command (SAC) and set out to turn it into a first-rate fighting force that was ready to do battle against the Soviets at a moment's notice.

magazine called it the "worst defeat the U.S. had ever suffered." Truman wrote in his diary, "World War III is here."

MacArthur repeatedly and Truman separately, at a November 1950 press conference, threatened to use the bomb. The public, according to a Gallup poll, approved by a margin of 52 percent to 38 percent. MacArthur submitted a list of twenty-six targets and requested eight additional atomic bombs to drop on invading forces and "critical concentrations of enemy air power."

General Curtis LeMay volunteered to direct the attacks, and, unknown to the public, American and Soviet pilots were engaging in direct air warfare—the only extended combat between the two sides during the Cold War.

With the *New York Times* reporting on the catastrophic loss of American prestige around the world, MacArthur began issuing statements from Tokyo blaming others for the military debacle and pushing for all-out war with China. Knowing that Truman was seeking a cease-fire, MacArthur broadcast his own ultimatum to China. When a critical letter by MacArthur was read to Congress, the Joint Chiefs unanimously

General Douglas MacArthur at Soldier Field in Chicago during his 1951 farewell tour after his dismissal by Truman and the Joint Chiefs of Staff for demanding that the United States attack China.

recommended he be relieved of his command. Truman announced MacArthur's firing.

The drama of Truman firing MacArthur for insubordination and the shock of seeing America's all-powerful military failing to defeat ill-equipped Chinese peasants drove Truman's approval ratings to a record low of 22 percent.

With no victory in sight, month after month, the UN forces pounded the North and the South with massive, unrelenting, conventional air bombing similar to the campaign visited upon Japan five years earlier. The weapon of choice was napalm. Almost every major city in North Korea was burned to the ground, and little was left standing in the South.

Although Mao Zedong was imagining a worldwide conflict, Stalin, in the summer of 1951, pushed the North Koreans to the bargaining table, but negotiations dragged on for two more years.

Despite some progress at the negotiations, and the Soviet peace initiative after the death of Stalin, Eisenhower now threatened to widen the war. He suggested to his commanders that the Kaesong area in North Korea might be a good place to showcase America's new, tactical atomic bombs.

The Joint Chiefs and National Security Council endorsed atomic attacks on China. Eisenhower and Dulles made sure the communist leaders knew of these threats.

The U.S. also began bombing the dams near Pyongyang, North Korea, causing enormous floods and destroying the rice crop. The Nuremberg tribunal had condemned similar Nazi actions in Holland in 1944 as a war crime.

With casualties skyrocketing on both sides, an armistice was finally signed in July 1953, dividing the country exactly where the war had begun three years earlier. The U.S., despite claiming to have stopped communism, was perceived as having lost, because it had not won.

Vice President Richard Nixon would later insist that Eisenhower's nuclear threats had worked brilliantly, teaching Nixon the value of unpredictability and inspiring his own "madman" thesis, which he applied to Vietnam less than twenty years later.

What was clear was the message to Asians who tried to challenge U.S. interests. Some 3 to 4 million Koreans lay dead out of a population of 30 million—10 percent or more—as well as over a million Chinese and more than thirty-seven thousand Americans. China had stood up proudly to the Americans, as the Vietnamese later would, enhancing its international prestige, but America would block China's entry to the United Nations until 1971. The Soviets, by comparison, looked weak, widening their gulf with China. As for the U.S., it was Churchill who grasped the real meaning: "Korea does not really matter now. I'd never heard of the bloody place until I was seventy-four. Its importance lies in the fact that it has led to the rearming of America."

Fed up with the increasingly militaristic bent of U.S. policy, containment policy architect George Kennan resigned as State Department director of policy planning on December 31, 1949. He was replaced by Forrestal protégé and Wall Street insider Paul Nitze. Nitze immediately took the lead in preparing a National Security Council report known as NSC-68, which would fundamentally revamp the nation's defense posture. The report painted so dire a picture of Soviet intentions and so greatly exaggerated Soviet capabilities that it appeared to be dead in the water. The outbreak of war in Korea gave it new life, hastening the U.S. down the road of hypermilitarism.

ABOVE: *A U.S. plane releases napalm over North Korea. Even after peace negotiations began in the spring of 1951, the U.S. air war continued unabated, with napalm as the weapon of choice. Almost every major city in North Korea was burned to the ground.*

BELOW: *Women and children search through the rubble in Seoul. During the war, 3 million to 4 million Koreans died out of a total population of 30 million, as did more than a million Chinese and 37,000 Americans.*

With the approval of NSC-68, the defense budget quadrupled to almost $50 billion. And military spending would hover at more than 50 percent of the U.S. budget for the rest of the 1950s. Under Eisenhower, a permanent war economy was to be achieved. Put another way, it was not just General Motors that was good for America, anticommunism was good for business.

During his presidential campaign, Eisenhower had in fact done little to lower the Cold War temperature, fanning the flames of anti-Sovietism with calls to move beyond the Democrats' "containment" to a Republican "liberation" of the Eastern Bloc.

Although he despised the venomous anticommunist Wisconsin senator Joe McCarthy and privately deplored his tactics, Eisenhower backed down during the campaign from defending his mentor, General George Marshall, whom McCarthy accused of virtual treason for "losing" China as secretary of state. McCarthy called Marshall "a man steeped in falsehood" and demanded his resignation. He declared, "Even if there were only one Communist in the State Department, that would still be one Communist too many."

Marshall refused to respond and told Truman at the time that if at this point in his life he had to explain that he was not a traitor, it was hardly worth the effort. But it wasn't long before he resigned as secretary of defense. Since early 1950 McCarthy had been making headlines, initially claiming on February 9 in Wheeling, West Virginia, "I have here in my hand a list of 205—a list of names that were made known to the Secretary of State as being members of the Communist Party and who nevertheless are still working and shaping policy in the State Department." The next day in another state, he lowered his number to fifty-seven.

Although he'd stayed silent when it mattered, Truman, in one of his finest speeches, a speech that later presidents would be wise to heed, deplored the mood of hysteria that he had done so much to create. "Well, I'm going to tell you how we're not going to fight communism—we're not going to transform our fine FBI into a Gestapo secret police. That's what some people'd like to do. We're not going to try to control what our people read and say and think. We're not going to turn the United States into a right-wing totalitarian country in order to deal with a left-wing

The previously little-known Wisconsin senator Joseph McCarthy became the ugly face of midcentury anticommunism.

totalitarian threat. In short, we're not going to end democracy. We're going to keep the Bill of Rights on the books."

But throughout the 1950s, political debate essentially vanished in the United States as Eisenhower never publicly repudiated the extremist tactics of either the Red Scare or the "Lavender Scare" that targeted gays and lesbians.

Behind the scenes, the real power was being exercised by FBI Director J. Edgar Hoover, who had Eisenhower's full support. Tapping telephones, opening mail, installing bugs, breaking into offices and safes, Hoover often played up the phony threat of a surprise Soviet attack on the U.S. And in 1956, he briefed Eisenhower on the specter of a "dirty bomb" unleashed in Manhattan, killing hundreds of thousands of people and making New York uninhabitable for years.

Hoover was totally convinced communists were behind the black civil rights movement from World War I on and had spied on every single black leader since. His FBI was busy on a number of other fronts, leaking information to its high-level assets in the press and launching in 1956 a program of dirty tricks called COINTELPRO that was designed to disrupt ultimately some twenty-three hundred left-wing organizations. By 1960, the FBI had begun investigations of more than four hundred thousand individuals and groups—all with Eisenhower's support.

Patriotic pageants and loyalty oaths pockmarked the landscape. Paranoia was rampant.

A second, more damaging set of Hollywood hearings began. Artists and citizens were hauled before committees in order to name names.

To writer Mary McCarthy the purpose of the hearings was not to combat subversion but to convince Americans to accept "the principle of betrayal as a norm of good citizenship." It worked.

Renowned muckraking journalist I. F. Stone had earlier denounced the attempt to turn "a whole generation of Americans into stool pigeons."

The perception of our heroic World War II ally was now deeply tarnished in the U.S. by the Berlin airlift, the spies, the Korean War, and the further revelations of the brutalities of the Stalin purges. But the Red Scare itself was far more damaging to America. It certainly decimated the legal Communist Party U.S.A., whose membership had dropped from 80,000 in 1944 to below 10,000 by the mid-1950s, with probably 1,500 of them FBI informants.

More important, the Red Scare eviscerated the U.S. left, the labor unions, and political and cultural organizations that had spurred the reforms of the New Deal in the 1930s. With the exception of the civil rights and antinuclear movements, left-wing dissent and progressive reform would vanish in the 1950s and the labor movement would never recover.

To this day, the Eisenhower fifties are remembered as an era of the lonely, sad, capitalist corporation man and his gray flannel conformity. The public was cowed into silence and docile acquiescence.

Fearing defense spending would bankrupt the country, Eisenhower and Dulles called for a "New Look" defense policy that would cut the size of the army and rely on cheaper nuclear weapons, which would "be as available for use as other munitions," based on the assumption that any war with the Soviets would become a full-scale nuclear one.

Though he had once abhorred atomic weaponry, Eisenhower told the British ambassador, "I'd rather be atomized than communized," as he set out to convince a wary public that there was no difference between conventional and nuclear weapons. He told a reporter in 1955, "I see no reason why they shouldn't be used just exactly as you would use a bullet or anything else."

Churchill was shocked. So was Pulitzer Prize–winning *New York Times* columnist James Reston, who wondered why not a single congressman

Though Joseph McCarthy's name became synonymous with the Red Scare, it was FBI head J. Edgar Hoover who exercised the real power. By 1960, the FBI had begun investigations of more than 430,000 individuals and groups. Hoover also used his contacts in the media to fan the flames of anticommunist hysteria.

had questioned Eisenhower's commitment to "sudden atomic retaliation" without congressional approval.

In August of 1953, the Soviets exploded a four-hundred-kiloton prototype hydrogen bomb in Kazakhstan, shocking the world. They seemed to have closed the gap and now appeared to be only ten months behind the American H-bomb effort.

In December 1954, Eisenhower ordered 42 percent of atomic and 36 percent of hydrogen bombs deployed overseas, closer to the Soviet Union.

Meanwhile, he and Dulles intensified their efforts to vanquish the taboos surrounding the use of nuclear weapons.

In December 1953, Eisenhower had unveiled his "Atoms for Peace" program in a speech at the UN, mesmerizing the thirty-five hundred delegates. He promised "energy too cheap to meter," at home and abroad, ignoring scientists' warnings about the dangers of proliferation. Over the years, the administration would propose initiatives to use nuclear bombs for planetary excavation, creating harbors in Alaska, freeing inaccessible oil deposits, creating underground reservoirs, producing steam, and desalinizing water. There were schemes to blast a bigger and better Panama Canal and to alter weather patterns and even melt the polar icecaps.

But when a massive hydrogen bomb test in the Marshall Islands in March 1954 went awry and contaminated islanders and Japanese fishermen, international outrage ensued. The word "fallout" entered the lexicon, and opposition to nuclear testing grew globally. New organizations were spawned. People marched in the streets once more.

The respected nonaligned Indian prime minister Nehru publicly denounced U.S. leaders as "dangerous self-centered lunatics" who would "blow up any people or country who came in the way of their policy." Eisenhower told his National Security Council: "Everybody seems to think that we are skunks, saber-rattlers, and warmongers." Dulles worried: "Comparisons are now being made between ours and Hitler's military machine."

But in late 1953, Eisenhower could still speak eloquently and be believed. "I come here," he announced, "representing a nation that wants not an acre of another people's land; that seeks no control of another people's government; that pursues no program of expansion in commerce or politics or power of any sort at another people's expense."

There were other reasons, besides the nuclear buildup, for Nehru's denunciation of U.S. leadership in the world. Nehru knew more than the American public knew. He knew that Eisenhower was not telling the truth.

In Iran, the British turned for help to the CIA, with warnings about Middle Eastern oil coming under Soviet control. This oil-rich region, from the Caspian to the Persian Gulf, unlike Korea, was critical to Western interests.

Democratically elected, immensely popular prime minister Mohammad Mossadeq was the first Iranian to earn a doctor of laws degree from a European university. *Time* magazine named him 1951's Man of the Year. He inspired the Arab masses throughout the region, who pulsated with nationalist fever, ready to take over their own affairs.

John Foster Dulles and his brother Allen, who was now head of the CIA, knew Mossadeq was not a communist but feared a takeover by the small Communist Party. And with Eisenhower's full approval, they deployed the CIA to get rid of the "madman Mossadeq," buying up journalists, military officers, members of parliament, and, ominously, the services of the extremist Warriors of Islam—a terrorist gang.

Pro-Mohammad Mossadeq demonstration in Iran in February 1953. Enormously popular inside his country and well respected internationally, Mossadeq was overthrown by the CIA in 1953.

In August 1953, organized mobs caused chaos in Tehran—spreading rumors that Mossadeq was Jewish and communist. The CIA and British intelligence paid street thugs to destroy mosques. Among the rioters was Ayatollah Khomeini, Iran's future leader. Mossadeq and thousands of his supporters were arrested for treason, some executed.

Reinstating the shah on the throne in Iran, the U.S. turned on the financial spigots for the next twenty-five years, creating its strongest military ally in the Middle East.

Cutting down the British share, five U.S. oil companies now received 40 percent ownership of a new consortium. Though this was celebrated in the Western media as a great victory, the downside would be enormous. Instead of seeing a change of attitude at Stalin's death, the Soviets would perceive the U.S. imposing another puppet government on a nation with which they shared a two-thousand-kilometer border. Along with the NATO alliance, they now saw a Western strategy of encirclement.

"Blowback" is an espionage term for the violent unintended consequences of a covert operation on the civilian population of the aggressor nation. And, in this case, the United States, despite temporary success and a new supply of oil, had outraged the citizens of a proud nation.

It may have taken twenty-five more years for blowback to manifest, but, in 1979, it did. Fed up with fixed elections and the repressions of SAVAK—a despised intelligence agency given to torture—the people revolted, embracing the Islamic Revolution led by Ayatollah Khomeini, and forced out the shah.

The Iranian coup would poison U.S. relations with the Iranian people for another thirty years, into the presidencies of George W. Bush and Barack Obama.

The CIA had now come into its own, and the next year it organized the overthrow of Guatemala's popular leader Jacobo Árbenz Guzmán, who challenged the giant U.S. commercial interests in his impoverished Central American nation. He announced plans for a massive land reform program beginning with the nationalization of 234,000 acres of United Fruit Company land, more than 90 percent of which the company was not using. Foster Dulles believed Árbenz was secretly a communist and, if not stopped, would invite Soviet infiltration into the region. "The future of Guatemala lies," he warned, ". . . at the disposal of leaders loyal to Guatemala who have not treasonably become the agents of an alien despotism which sought to use Guatemala for its own evil ends." In reality, communist influence was minimal—a party of approximately four thousand members.

From bases in Honduras and Nicaragua, in June 1954, CIA-trained mercenaries attacked, and Árbenz surrendered to a military junta. Dulles crowed, "The events of recent months and days add a new and glorious chapter to the already great tradition of the American states."

Árbenz's replacement, anticommunist strongman Carlos Castillo Armas, set up a brutal military dictatorship, employing death squads, and was assassinated three years later.

The democratically elected Árbenz warned that "twenty years of fascist bloody tyranny" was coming. He was wrong. The tyranny that followed actually lasted forty years and took the lives of some two hundred thousand people.

The label "communist" was now being used not only to describe defenders of the Soviet system but anyone, anyplace, anytime who wanted to enact progressive changes in their country—be it a labor leader, a reformer, a peasant activist, a human rights worker, or even a priest reading the gospel and organizing self-help groups based on radical or pacifist messages.

Events of even greater significance were unfolding simultaneously in Vietnam. The British had yielded much of their empire, but the French, who had been humiliated by the German invasion of World War II, were still fighting for their vast colonies in Indochina and Africa.

As the British in Iran had done in order to receive American aid, the French demonized their enemy, Ho Chi Minh, as a communist fanatic, although they knew that he represented the same rebellion they had been fighting since the late 1800s. For the Vietnamese people it had always been a struggle for independence, well before the Russian Revolution and the concept of communism had taken root. But, in this time period, it was naturally assumed that Asian communism was directed from Moscow. The truth was that Stalin had almost always shown caution in Asia, denying significant aid to Mao, as he would to Ho Chi Minh, seeing little to gain by inflaming the French.

Ho, who'd received U.S. assistance when he led the resistance to the Japanese during World War II, had asked President Truman for help in setting up an independent Vietnamese state. He received no response. In 1950, he found out why. Truman was backing the other side.

In April 1954, Ho Chi Minh's peasant army hauled extremely heavy antiaircraft guns and howitzers through almost impassable jungle and mountain terrain to lay siege to an encircled French army at Dien Bien Phu.

Incredibly, the United States was paying 80 percent of the French war costs. Eisenhower justified this by describing the countries in the region falling like dominos, ultimately leading from Thailand, Indonesia, and Malaysia to Japan itself.

Though Eisenhower ruled out sending U.S. ground forces, the Joint Chiefs drew up plans for Operation Vulture, an air campaign against Viet Minh positions, which included the possibility of using two or three tactical A-bombs. Eisenhower would later dispute such accounts, but high-level French officials reported that Dulles had offered them two atomic bombs. Nonetheless, the French, alongside the British, rejected this option, and, on May 7, after fifty-six grueling days, the French garrison fell, and France's days of colonial conquest in Asia were over.

Despite the fact that his forces controlled most of the country, Ho gave in to pressure from the Soviets and Chinese, who feared U.S. intervention and accepted a proposal at Geneva that would temporarily divide Vietnam at the seventeenth parallel, with Ho's forces withdrawing to the north and French-backed forces retreating to the south.

A national election was scheduled for 1956 to unify the country. The U.S. promised not to interfere, but it did—installing a conservative, corrupt Catholic in a Buddhist country. Ngo Dinh Diem wasted no time in crushing rivals and jailing communists, thousands of whom were executed.

With U.S. backing, Diem then subverted the most important provision of the Geneva agreement, canceling the 1956 election. Eisenhower later explained that had the elections been held, "as of the time of the fighting, possibly 80 percent of the population would have voted for the Communist Ho Chi Minh." As a result, the insurgency was soon rekindled, and, within a few short years, the French war would become America's war.

Across the globe, in Africa, the Vietnamese struggle became an inspiration for the Algerian revolutionaries who would outlast the French in a brutal eight-year war from 1954 to 1962. This finally gutted the French Empire in Africa.

In 1953, Eisenhower offered a huge loan to feared fascist dictator Francisco Franco in return for the establishment of nuclear bases. Spain was then admitted to the United Nations in 1955, although communist China was still denied membership.

The U.S. also supported Portugal, which clung to an enormous ramshackle plantation and apartheid empire in southern Africa, as well as neighboring South Africa, where minority whites brutally suppressed the black majority.

By the mid-1950s, the reputation of the United States in the Third World reached rock bottom, as it allied itself with some of the world's most reactionary regimes.

Eisenhower and Dulles greet South Vietnamese president Ngo Dinh Diem at Washington National Airport. American leaders had maneuvered to replace the French puppet Bao Dai with Diem, who wasted no time in crushing his rivals and unleashing a wave of repression against former Viet Minh members in the south, thousands of whom were executed.

America's capacity for massive retaliation might keep the balance of power with the Soviets, but it would prove useless in preventing the revolutionary upsurge in the developing world, which wished to steer a nonaligned course between capitalist and socialist blocs and thought it obscene to spend billions of dollars on arms when money for development was in short supply.

From the nonaligned point of view, the American Cold War on Eisenhower's watch was not really a war against communism as much as it was a war against the poor peoples of the earth for the resources of the earth.

Twenty-nine Asian and African leaders met in 1955 at Bandung in Indonesia. The host was Indonesia's Sukarno, who had led the fight against Dutch colonialism. The stars were Yugoslavia's renegade leader Marshal Tito, who had, despite several assassination attempts, freed himself from

Stalin's grip, along with Nasser of Egypt, who had taken on the British Empire; Nehru, independent India's first leader; Ghana's Kwame Nkrumah; and Vietnam's Ho Chi Minh.

Israel, perceived as a U.S. ally, was not invited. Communist China was. They met on the beautiful island of Java in Indonesia, the world's fourth-largest nation, which combined the world's largest Muslim community and the third-largest Communist Party.

Dulles proclaimed neutrality an obsolete conception—immoral and shortsighted. And in one of the strangest and least-known episodes of this time period, the prime minister of China, Zhou Enlai, was targeted by Jiang Jieshi's nationalist government in Taiwan, secretly abetted by the CIA. A detonator and bomb were placed on his plane. But Zhou survived when he changed planes, although the sixteen people aboard were blown out of the sky under mysterious circumstances. Zhou maintained an enigmatic silence and the conference was considered a great success. But many of these independent leaders would, in time, be toppled by the U.S.

The Soviet Union was beginning to confront its own past. Premier Nikita Khrushchev, who like Eisenhower had come from humble origins and seen the worst of World War II up close as a political organizer at the Battle of Stalingrad, shocked the communist world in February 1956, emotionally giving voice to the darkest truths about his country's recent past. He detailed Stalin's murderous terror, which had killed millions and left his society frightened into a conformity far worse than that which had engulfed the U.S. He decried Stalin's cult of personality and initiated a much-needed policy of de-Stalinization.

The reaction across the communist world was incendiary—many were stunned. Mao in China was furious. Unrest swept much of Eastern Europe. Crowds gathered outside the parliament in Hungary and toppled the enormous statue of Stalin, lynching secret police officers in the streets.

Khrushchev allowed the revolt to take its course, but when the moderate Hungarian prime minister announced free elections and said that Hungary was withdrawing from the Warsaw Pact, which had been established in 1955 to counter the West's NATO, Khrushchev felt he had no other choice or he would be removed by his hardliners. Russian tanks

Dwight Eisenhower and Nikita Khrushchev had much in common. Each came from humble origins, and each believed deeply in the superiority of his own political system.

rolled into the old city and crushed the resistance. Some twenty-five hundred Hungarians lay dead. Although this number pales in comparison to the total casualties from America's interventions in Third World countries, Hungary became one of the biggest stories of the Cold War, symbolizing Soviet evil and domination.

Time magazine named the Hungarian Freedom Fighter "Man of the Year." At the same time, unknown to the American public, America's hard power continued to manifest globally.

Sukarno in Indonesia became a major target. CIA plans to unseat him were sometimes ludicrous, involving porno films and beautiful Russian blondes, and a military coup in 1957 in which CIA pilots bombed targets. Eisenhower denied U.S. involvement. But his deception was exposed when U.S. pilot Al Pope was shot down and paraded before a news conference. Infuriated by U.S. actions, Sukarno tacked closer toward the Soviets. It would take the U.S. another eight years to change the power structure in Indonesia in one of the bloodiest massacres of the century.

When Eisenhower was forced to send federal troops to Arkansas in the fall of 1957 to protect newly enrolled black high school students from violent, hateful mobs, the U.S. international image suffered another major blow.

The Soviet Union, on the other hand, won international acclaim for launching *Sputnik*, the first earth-circling satellite.

The U.S. had bombs. But, suddenly, the Soviets had space; they had rockets and missiles. Senate majority leader Lyndon Johnson said that the Soviets would soon "be dropping bombs on us from space like kids dropping rocks onto cars from freeway overpasses."

Eisenhower's response was lackadaisical. They "put one small ball into the air," he said. And to drive his point home, he reportedly played five rounds of golf that week.

The reason was, he knew the truth and could not reveal it—that U.S. technology had developed highly secret U-2 reconnaissance planes that had, for over a year, flown seventy thousand feet above Soviet airspace, photographing how far the Russians really lagged behind in the arms race. CIA director Allen Dulles later gloated, "I was able to get a look at every blade of grass in the Soviet Union."

A month later the Soviets launched the massive six-ton *Sputnik II*. Nonetheless, Khrushchev reached out to Eisenhower, calling for a peaceful space competition and an end to the Cold War. But Ike, feeling enormous political pressure, bragged publicly about America's vast and growing military superiority. "We are well ahead of the Soviets . . . both in quantity and in quality. We intend to stay ahead," he boasted, pointing to U.S. submarines and huge aircraft carriers now supplied with nuclear weapons.

Nonetheless, the Democrats seized the initiative. House Leader John McCormack declared that the U.S. faced "national extinction." Among those who jumped enthusiastically on this "missile gap" bandwagon was the junior senator from Massachusetts—John F. Kennedy. Eisenhower dismissed these critics as "sanctimonious hypocritical bastards," but gloom abounded.

He commissioned a secret security review that was authored essentially by Paul Nitze, the fiercely anticommunist Wall Street protégé of James Forrestal. His report, the Gaither Report, was devastating, and it was leaked, apparently by Nitze himself, to the *Washington Post,* which wrote that it "portrays a United States in the gravest danger in its history." In the best tradition of the yellow press, the newspaper pictured the nation moving to the status of a second-class power and urgently called for an enormous increase in military spending starting then and continuing through 1970.

The publication of Nevil Shute's novel *On the Beach* in 1957, followed two years later by an internationally acclaimed movie, chillingly showed a handful of survivors of nuclear war waiting in Melbourne, Australia, the world's southernmost city, for the fallout that had already wiped out the rest of humanity.

Winston Churchill, now in retirement, was attending a party when he was asked if he would send a copy of the novel to Eisenhower. The once ferocious Cold Warrior responded with despair: "It would be a waste of money. He is so muddle-headed now. . . . I think the earth will soon be destroyed. . . . And if I were the Almighty I would not recreate it in case they destroyed him too the next time."

After two heart attacks, Eisenhower still seemed a decent, well-meaning man, but he appeared lost, out of touch. Right under his nose, in America's backyard, in early 1959, Fidel Castro and his revolutionaries finally toppled Cuba's Batista dictatorship, under which American business interests controlled over 80 percent of Cuba's resources.

Castro set about redistributing land and reforming the education system. He seized large Cuban land holdings and over a million acres from United Fruit and two other companies—offering compensation, which United Fruit rejected. Like many nonaligned Third World leaders, Castro accepted offers of Soviet aid.

In April of 1959, he visited the U.S. and met briefly with Vice President Nixon, who dismissed Castro as naive about communism and later supported his elimination.

And when U.S. and British oil companies refused to process Russian crude at their Cuban refineries, Castro nationalized them and threatened to expropriate all American property on the island. Eisenhower announced a punishing trade embargo, denying the Cuban people, among other things, markets for their sugar, which the Soviets and Chinese offered to buy.

The embargo would take a terrible toll. Though it would be eased by the U.S. at the turn of the twenty-first century, it would last for more than fifty years and ten administrations. The embargo had been condemned repeatedly by a huge majority of the UN General Assembly. In 2011, 186 nations were against it; two nations supported it—the U.S. and Israel.

In March 1960, Eisenhower approved a CIA plan to organize a paramilitary force of Cuban exiles to overthrow Castro. This plan included the possibility of assassination. As a symbol to the rest of the world, Castro could not be allowed to succeed.

The Belgian Congo had been infamously portrayed in Joseph Conrad's "Heart of Darkness" in the early part of the century. Nothing much had changed. When the Belgians left in 1960, new socialist premier Patrice Lumumba, desperate for help, flew to Washington, but Eisenhower refused to see him. CIA chief Allen Dulles told Ike that Lumumba was an African Fidel Castro and persuaded Eisenhower to authorize a plan to assassinate him. It was bungled, but as the Congo descended into an anarchic civil war, Lumumba was removed in January 1961 by army mutineers in the presence of Belgian officers. He was tortured and murdered and quickly became a martyred nationalist hero to the Third World. Many blamed the U.S.

The CIA, abandoning the UN Peace Plan, backed Joseph Mobutu. Stealing billions of dollars in natural resources from the land, as well as from his U.S. supporters, and slaughtering multitudes to preserve his power, Mobutu ruled for three decades as a billionaire dictator and as the CIA's most trusted ally in Africa.

In his remarkable farewell address of January 1961, Eisenhower appeared to understand the monstrosity he had created and seemed almost to be asking for absolution. "We have been compelled to create a permanent arms industry of vast proportions. Three and a half million men and women are directly engaged in the defense establishment. . . . The total influence—economic, political, even spiritual—is felt in every city, every statehouse, every office of the federal government. . . . In the councils of government, we must guard against the acquisition of unwarranted influence, whether sought or unsought, by the military-industrial complex. . . . We must never let the weight of this combination endanger our liberties or democratic processes."

Privately, he told Allen Dulles, "I leave a legacy of ashes to my successor." He was close to the truth. Aside from overthrowing foreign governments and intervening freely around the globe, it was Eisenhower who did more than anyone else to create the very military-industrial complex he warned of.

Under Ike, the U.S. arsenal expanded from a little more than 1,000 to over 22,000 nuclear weapons. In total, he authorized more than 30,000 weapons, the remainder coming on line during Kennedy's presidency.

Nuclear bombs were now the foundation of America's empire and provided the new emperor, its president, with a mystical power that required more and more suffocating secrecy, and other powers that went far beyond the original limits of executive power defined in the Constitution.

And, although the bombs themselves were not expensive, the huge infrastructure was, requiring bases in the U.S. and abroad and enormous delivery systems by bomber, missile, aircraft carrier, and submarine.

Eisenhower additionally made it acceptable U.S. policy to threaten nuclear attack.

In a *Life* magazine interview in 1956, Dulles, defending his policy of brinksmanship, pointed to three different occasions on which the administration had walked to the brink of nuclear war and forced the communists to back down—in Korea, Vietnam, and the Formosa Straits. The U.S. would actually do so again against the Soviets, who also threatened to use their nuclear weapons during the Suez Crisis of 1956, and once more in the crisis with China over the small islands of Quemoy and Matsu in 1958.

Eisenhower's successors in the White House have all followed his example in threatening America's perceived enemies if they didn't accede to U.S. demands.

Additionally, what is little-known is that Eisenhower had delegated to theater commanders and other specified commanders the authority to launch a nuclear attack if they believed it were mandated by circumstances and they were out of communication with the president.

And with Eisenhower's approval, some of these commanders had in turn delegated the same authority to lower-level officers. Thus, there were now dozens of fingers on the trigger, at a time when there were no locking devices on nuclear weapons.

In August 1960, Eisenhower approved an operational plan to launch a nuclear attack simultaneously on the USSR and China within the first twenty-four hours of a war. The conservative estimate of the number of dead from U.S. bombs and fallout was 600 million people—more than one hundred Holocausts—and the possibility of a nuclear winter across the globe that would have ended all life.

In hindsight, Eisenhower, presiding over the world's most powerful nation during perhaps the tensest extended period in its history, could have, with bold action, put the world on a different path. Signs emanating from Moscow indicated that the Kremlin was ready to change course. But because of ideology, political calculations, the exigencies of a militarized state, and a limited imagination, Eisenhower repeatedly failed to seize the opportunities that emerged.

It's interesting to think that in 1953, when Eisenhower was becoming more of a Cold Warrior, his mentor, General George Marshall, became the only career military officer to be awarded the Nobel Peace Prize. Emphasizing the need for a better understanding of history and the causes of war, he said, "The cost of war is constantly spread before me, written neatly in many ledgers whose columns are gravestones."

Marshall, a conservative man who had lived through two world wars and a Depression, who, unlike many generals, rarely wore his medals in public and reportedly refused a large sum of money for his memoirs, stood, until he died in 1959, in a sort of respected but lonely grandeur, still ostracized by many on the right for moderation in a time of zealotry and a tolerance he was truly the embodiment of.

There is no question, the Eisenhower years are remembered as peaceful and prosperous, and at a time when war with the Soviet Union seemed quite possible, he certainly deserves credit for avoiding it. But the inescapable truth is that the esteemed Dwight Eisenhower put the world on a glide path toward annihilation with the most gargantuan expansion of military power in history and left the world a far more dangerous place than when he first took office.

CHAPTER EIGHT

*T*he 1960 presidential election was fought primarily on the issue of communism. Positioning himself, like Barack Obama in 2008, as the candidate of change, young challenger John F. Kennedy was able to take the strongly anticommunist Republican Richard Nixon to task for failing to prevent a missile gap and for permitting the establishment of a communist regime only ninety miles from the Florida coastline.

Kennedy, America's first Catholic president, won a narrow and perhaps a "stolen" election, but he did take Washington and the world by storm with his wit and graceful elegance. His administration was nicknamed Camelot after King Arthur's mythical Round Table of peace. His opportunistic but politically astute choice of Lyndon Johnson of Texas as vice president confirmed the liberal wing of the party's distrust of him.

Elected to the Senate in 1952, Kennedy had been a Cold War liberal who had avoided criticizing Joseph McCarthy, an old family friend. His younger brother Robert had even served on McCarthy's staff. Alluding to the title of his Pulitzer Prize–winning book *Profiles in Courage*, Eleanor Roosevelt said she wished that Kennedy had "had a little less profile and a little more courage."

His team, a combination of insiders from foundations, corporations, and Wall Street firms, as well as progressives and intellectuals, was labeled the best and the brightest for their intelligence, achievements, and

Kennedy's new administration recruited ambitious, highly intelligent establishment insiders, whom David Halberstam would later label, somewhat ironically, "the best and the brightest." They were typified by National Security Advisor McGeorge Bundy (with Kennedy, L), the dean of the Faculty of Arts and Sciences at Harvard, and Defense Secretary Robert McNamara (R), renowned for his computerlike mind and managerial brilliance.

can-do spirit, typified by National Security Advisor McGeorge Bundy—the first applicant to get perfect scores on all three Yale entrance exams.

At Defense, Kennedy brought in a civilian outsider—Robert Mc-Namara. Renowned for his computerlike mind and leading the Ford Motor Company, he earned the immediate distrust of his generals by putting the Pentagon under microscopic scrutiny. A devastating nuclear war plan had been handed down to them by Eisenhower. McNamara was appalled by what he found—a culture of paranoid worst-case scenarios. But when Kennedy asked the statistically minded McNamara to ascertain just how big the missile gap really was, it took three weeks to confirm that there was no gap and several months to find out that there was quite a huge difference. The U.S. had approximately 25,000 nuclear weapons, the Soviets 2,500. The U.S. 1,500 heavy bombers—1,000 of them in Europe within Soviet range—the Soviets 192. The U.S. 45 ICBMs, the Soviets 4.

In August 1957, the Soviet Union successfully tested the world's first intercontinental ballistic missile (ICBM). For the USSR, ICBMs could potentially offset the enormous military advantage the United States derived from bombers housed at NATO bases in Europe. When the Soviets used an ICBM to launch Sputnik *in October, some Americans panicked.*

Kennedy was briefed on Eisenhower's invasion plan for Cuba by Allen Dulles, who assured him that the Cuban people would rise in support. Several civilian advisors took sharp issue with the plan, but the inexperienced president feared blocking an operation backed by Eisenhower and the Joint Chiefs.

Three days before the operation, in April 1961, eight U.S. B-26 bombers flown by Cuban exiles incapacitated half of Castro's air force.

UN ambassador Adlai Stevenson, in an embarrassing prequel to Colin Powell's performance at the UN over Iraq in 2003, stated that the United States had committed no aggression against Cuba, and no strikes had been launched from Florida or from any other part of the United States. He showed a photograph of a plane, supposedly flown by a Cuban defector, but it was quickly exposed as belonging to the CIA.

Between fifteen hundred and sixteen hundred Cuban exiles arrived

Fidel Castro at a meeting of the UN General Assembly in September 1960. Castro led the revolution that overthrew Fulgencio Batista's U.S.-friendly dictatorship on New Year's Day 1959. When the United States tried to strangle the new regime economically, Castro turned to the Soviet Union for aid.

at the Bay of Pigs in seven ships, two of them owned by United Fruit. But Cuban troops were ready, and no popular uprising ever occurred.

The invaders begged for direct U.S. support, and, much to the shock of the CIA, Kennedy refused this support, as he had warned he would, fearing a Soviet countermove against West Berlin.

At a midnight meeting, military leaders and the CIA chief of clandestine services pressed Kennedy for three hours to send ground and air support. They expected it—Eisenhower would have done it. The chairman of the Joint Chiefs of Staff said it was "reprehensible, almost criminal" to pull the rug out. But Kennedy stood his ground. More than one hundred rebels were killed, roughly twelve hundred captured.

It was a chilling beginning to one of the most turbulent decades—and one that would ever change the world—the 1960s.

The entire sordid affair had a profound effect on the president, who told an influential journalist friend, "The first advice I'm going to give my successor is to watch the generals and to avoid feeling that just because they were military men their opinions on military matters were worth a damn." He seemed to begin to understand what Eisenhower was warning about, but his learning curve would need to be a sharp one to escape the steel trap of Cold War thinking.

Publicly, Kennedy took full responsibility for the fiasco. Privately he was furious at the Joint Chiefs "sons of bitches" and "those CIA bastards," threatening to "shatter the CIA into a thousand pieces, and scatter it to the winds." Incredibly, he fired Allen Dulles, albeit diplomatically, and two other top officials, and all CIA overseas personnel were placed under the local ambassador.

Kennedy's growing mistrust of his military and intelligence advisors made it easier to rebuff their pressure to send troops in 1961 into the tiny landlocked Asian nation of Laos—something that Eisenhower had warned him might be necessary to defeat the communists.

The Joint Chiefs wanted Kennedy to give prior commitment to a large-scale invading force.

Arthur Schlesinger, an aide and respected historian, later said, "After the Bay of Pigs, Kennedy had contempt for the Joint Chiefs. . . . He dismissed them as a bunch of old men. He thought [chairman of the Joint Chiefs Lyman] Lemnitzer was a dope." And as a result, Kennedy opted for a neutralist solution, which angered the Pentagon. This would come back to haunt him.

The mood was dark when Kennedy traveled to Vienna to meet Khrushchev at their first summit conference that June 1961. Khrushchev berated the young president for America's global imperialism. "We in the USSR," he later told a visiting senator, "feel that the revolutionary process should have a right to exist." The major issue for Khrushchev was Germany. What terrified him was the prospect of West Germany finally getting control over U.S. nuclear weapons deployed so close to the Soviet Union.

And also, by 1961, approximately 20 percent of the East German population—some 2.5 million people—had fled through the open border, seeking a better life in West Germany. It was an open-sore humiliation for the Soviets, who now wanted a treaty recognizing two separate Germanys and the withdrawal of Western forces from West Berlin.

Khrushchev explained to an American journalist: "We have a much longer history with Germany. We have seen how quickly governments in Germany can change and how easy it is for Germany to become an

During their June 1961 summit in Vienna, Khrushchev berated Kennedy about the United States' global imperialism. He declared that U.S.-Soviet relations hinged on resolution of the German question. Kennedy left frustrated, telling Khrushchev, "I see it's going to be a very cold winter."

instrument of mass murder. . . . We have a saying here: 'Give a German a gun; sooner or later he will point it at Russians.' . . . You like to think in the United States that we have no public opinion. Don't be too sure about this. On the matter of Germany, our people have very strong ideas. I don't think that any government here could survive if it tried to go against it. . . . We could crush Germany in a few minutes. But . . . we fear . . . the ability of . . . Germany to commit the United States . . . to start a world atomic war. How many times do you have to be burned before you respect fire?" Kennedy's parting comment to Khrushchev at Vienna was, "I see it's going to be a very cold winter."

Later that summer, Kennedy intensified the crisis with a saber-rattling speech: "The source of world trouble and tension is Moscow, not Berlin. And if war begins, it will have begun in Moscow and not Berlin."

Kennedy announced an additional $3.4 billion for defense, plans to increase draft calls to the army by three hundred thousand, and a national program to construct public and private fallout shelters. He reminded citizens, "In the thermonuclear age any misjudgments on either side

A model home fallout shelter designed by the U.S. Office of Civil and Defense Mobilization. The 1961 Berlin crisis infused the fallout shelter debate with a new sense of urgency.

about the intentions of the other could rain more devastation in several hours than has been wrought in all the wars of human history."

The Warsaw Pact nations responded in dramatic fashion. On August 13, East German troops began erecting barricades and roadblocks all across Germany to shut off the stream of escaping East Germans. The barbed wire was soon replaced with concrete. Kennedy, in defiance, sent fifteen hundred U.S. troops by road from West Germany into West Berlin, where they were met by Vice President Johnson.

That same month, Khrushchev resumed nuclear testing. When Kennedy learned of this, he erupted, "Fucked again!"

Despite the U.S.'s nuclear superiority, the air force wanted to increase the missile count to three thousand. McNamara fought them down to one thousand as the compromise number.

The Soviets, by October, were detonating a thirty-megaton bomb—the biggest yet exploded—and the next week, a fifty-plus-megaton bomb—over three thousand times as powerful as the one dropped on Hiroshima. Kennedy had inherited by now the full wrath of Dulles's brinksmanship.

To an outside observer, it might have seemed that Americans had taken leave of their senses in the summer and fall of 1961 as the nation conducted an extended conversation on building fallout shelters in people's homes, as well as the ethics of killing neighbors or friends to protect that shelter. It was known as the "gun-thy-neighbor" phenomenon.

Despite media pressure, surprisingly few people actually built shelters, either out of numbed resignation or because of the recognition of the difficulties of a meaningful survival.

In hindsight, the construction of the monstrous Berlin Wall actually defused the immediate threat of war, enabling Khrushchev to appease his hardliners. Kennedy confided, "It's not a very nice solution, but a wall is a hell of a lot better than a war."

In another part of the world, however, Kennedy had given his commitment to the politically important Cuban exile community in Florida to overthrow the Castro government. This would spark significant tensions with the Soviet Union.

In early November, he unleashed Operation Mongoose—a terror campaign overseen by his brother Robert and run by Edward Lansdale—designed to wreck Cuba's economy and, among other things, secretly continue the up-to-now-bungled assassination attempts on Castro.

Seeking a pretext for military action, the Joint Chiefs approved Operation Northwoods, which included a "Remember the *Maine*" incident modeled on the ship sinking that triggered the Spanish-American War in 1898. This plan included the U.S. staging a Cuban government hijacking, shooting down a civilian airliner, preferably with college students aboard, sinking boatloads of Cubans escaping to Florida, orchestrating a series of incidents around Guantánamo, and blaming the communist government.

Kennedy rejected the plan, but U.S. actions throughout 1962 convinced the Soviets that an invasion of Cuba was imminent. In January, the U.S. coerced Latin American countries to suspend Cuba's membership in the OAS. The U.S. conducted a series of large-scale military exercises in the Caribbean in the spring, summer, and fall of 1962—one involving 79 ships, 300 aircraft, and more than 40,000 troops. The last one, in October, with 7,500 marines set to participate, codenamed Ortsac, was a mock invasion of an island, replete with the overthrow of its government. The message was clear. "Ortsac" was "Castro" spelled backward.

Kennedy was equally intent on standing up to the communists in Vietnam. But, as a student of history, he must have harbored doubts about another land war in Asia. As a young congressman, he had visited Vietnam in 1951 during the debacle of the Korean War, and advised against aiding the French colonialists. He later spoke broadly of needing to win the support of Arabs, Africans, and Asians who "hated . . . the white man who bled them, beat them, exploited them, and ruled them." He had already pointed out the contradiction of supporting the French Empire in Africa and Asia while opposing Soviet moves in Hungary and Poland.

But he was now president and was soon defending a corrupt South Vietnamese government that was banning public assembly, some political parties, and even public dancing.

Embracing Eisenhower's domino theory, Kennedy was now insisting that Vietnam represented the cornerstone of the free world in Southeast Asia—"the finger in the dike."

Lyndon Johnson went to Vietnam in May 1961 and anointed Diem the "Winston Churchill of Southeast Asia," and, painting a bleak picture, pressed for a much larger U.S. involvement. The generals and McNamara agreed that only U.S. combat troops could forestall a communist victory. However, Kennedy, a decorated veteran of World War II, resisted sending in combat troops. He said to Arthur Schlesinger, "The troops will march in; the bands will play; the crowds will cheer; and in four days everyone will have forgotten. Then we will be told we have to send in more troops. It's like taking a drink. The effect wears off and you have to take another."

But he was an admirer of guerilla warfare in World War II, in which British and Americans had fought behind the lines in places like the Burma jungle, and he did approve his generals' other recommendations, expanding military involvement. U.S. personnel in Vietnam jumped from eight hundred when Kennedy took office, to over sixteen thousand advisors in 1963. He also allowed a growing army of CIA operatives and numerous American civilian contractors to flock to this new honeypot of enterprise. Under Kennedy's three-year watch, the CIA launched

A U.S. aircraft sprays herbicide over a South Vietnamese forest to defoliate a guerilla stronghold. The long-term environmental and health effects would prove disastrous for Vietnamese and Americans alike.

163 major covert operations worldwide—only seven fewer than had been conducted under Eisenhower in eight years.

Vietnam, in its early stages, was sometimes referred to as a "CIA war." At West Point, Kennedy reinforced this by saying it was "another type of war, new in its intensity, ancient in its origins . . . war by ambush . . . eroding and exhausting the enemy instead of engaging him." History knows the contrary proved to be true in Vietnam.

Under Kennedy, and mostly unknown to the American public, the U.S. began resettling villagers at gunpoint in barbed-wire-enclosed compounds guarded by unreliable South Vietnamese government troops and used herbicides to defoliate guerilla areas. The long-term environmental and health effects would turn out disastrously for Vietnamese and Americans alike.

But it would be the Cuban Missile Crisis in October 1962 that truly impressed upon Kennedy the potentially disastrous repercussions of his confrontational Cold War policies. On a Sunday, October 14, a U-2 surveillance plane brought back photographic evidence of Soviet medium-range ballistic missiles in position in Cuba. It was quite a shock.

Photo taken over Cuba by a U.S. U-2 surveillance plane on October 14, 1962. The photo revealed that the Soviets had placed medium-range ballistic missiles (MRBMs) on the island that were capable of delivering 1-megaton warheads to the continental U.S. This revelation sparked the Cuban Missile Crisis.

Khrushchev had lied to him, promising no offensive weapons in Cuba, but he was making a blunder of epic proportions. The last thing the Soviets wanted in 1962 was a direct military confrontation with the U.S. With little more than 10 ICBMs that could reliably reach U.S. soil and fewer than 300 nuclear warheads, they stood no chance against the U.S.'s 5,000 deliverable nuclear bombs and nearly 2,000 ICBMs and bombers.

Why did Khrushchev do this? The American public never understood. The media presented Soviet actions in Cuba as a case of outright Soviet aggression. But from the Soviet point of view, it was a reasonable response to repeated signs that the U.S. was preparing a first strike against the Soviet Union. The missiles might also deter the looming invasion of Cuba, which in a sense had now become a pawn in the game. The missiles would make the U.S. think twice before attacking—as Khrushchev said, giving the Americans "a little bit of their own medicine."

There was also no question that Khrushchev genuinely admired Castro, who had come to power on his own, without outside help, and had enormous symbolic value in the Third World. Finally, the missiles were an inexpensive way for Khrushchev to placate those who questioned his leadership in the communist world. But it was so dangerous, what he did—so dangerous.

Khrushchev had intended to announce the presence of the nuclear missiles on November 7 at the forty-fifth anniversary of the Bolshevik Revolution. But, as military analyst Daniel Ellsberg has pointed out, by keeping secret the fact that he had delivered tactical cruise and ballistic missiles, along with their nuclear warheads, Khrushchev had transformed a potentially effective means of deterring a U.S. invasion into a destabilizing provocation that backfired. The U.S. never understood the warheads had already arrived.

Even today, few realize the gravity of the Cuban Missile Crisis and even fewer seem to grasp its enduring lessons. Dulles's legacy of brinksmanship, of going to the edge, had finally spawned its Frankenstein monster.

Two days later, Kennedy met with his key advisors in a top secret meeting, hoping to stop the missiles before they were fully installed. Three days later, on October 19, he met with his Joint Chiefs. They pushed for a surgical air strike, without warning, to remove the missiles, followed by an all-out invasion of Cuba. LeMay assured Kennedy that the Soviets would not respond.

LeMay welcomed nuclear war as inevitable and a war that his country was currently in a position to win. There might not be a second opportunity. He fulminated against the Russian bear, "Let's take his leg off right up to his testicles. On second thought, let's take off his testicles, too."

After the meeting, Kennedy remarked to his aide Kenny O'Donnell, "If we listen to them, and do what they want us to do, none of us will be alive later to tell them that they were wrong."

With U.S. missiles in Turkey so close to the Soviet Union, McNamara contended that the strategic balance of power was not changed. Kennedy agreed, but, understanding the political symbolism, said that allowing the

*Kennedy meets with the Executive Committee (EXCOMM)
of the National Security Council during the crisis.*

missiles to stay would weaken the perception of the U.S. across the world and especially in Latin America.

He confided to his brother Robert that if he didn't take strong action now after what he'd done at the Bay of Pigs, he'd be impeached.

This moment became a crucial test of Kennedy's character. In the context of building that character, he'd fought bravely and saved men's lives as a naval lieutenant in the South Pacific, and was now no longer as intimidated by uniformed generals. In the coming days, he would reject the advice of such older men, as well as Paul Nitze, Dean Acheson, and even Dwight Eisenhower. He opted instead for a blockade, which he referred to as a "quarantine" to downplay the fact that this, too, was an act of war. On October 22, eight days after the pictures were taken, Kennedy solemnly informed the American people, "All ships of any kind bound for Cuba, from whatever nation or port will, if found to contain cargoes of offensive weapons, be turned back. . . . Should these offensive military preparations continue, thus increasing the threat to the hemisphere, further action will be justified."

He portrayed the U.S. as an innocent victim of unprovoked Soviet aggression, not revealing that the U.S. had been fighting a terrorist war against Cuba since late 1959.

The temperature of the world shot up. People were on edge, glued to their televisions and radios. Children watched the news, their parents full of fear. That same day, the Strategic Air Command went to DEFCON 3, and two days later, for the first time in history, to DEFCON 2, prepared to strike targets in the Soviet Union. The decision to go to the precipice of nuclear war was made, under the authority given by Eisenhower, by SAC commander General Thomas Power, without consulting the president. To make matters worse, instead of putting out this order in code as would be expected, it was sent out in the clear, to make sure that the Soviet radar operators would pick it up. Thereafter, the SAC fleet remained airborne, refueled by aerial tankers.

It was Power who told a defense analyst in 1960, "The whole idea is to kill the bastards! Look. At the end of the war, if there are two Americans and one Russian, we win!" The analyst responded wisely, "Well, you better make sure that they're a man and a woman."

A series of harrowing incidents occurred, any one of which could have triggered a holocaust. A SAC test missile was launched from the U.S. toward the Marshall Islands, and officials mistakenly reported that Tampa and Minnesota were under attack.

On October 25, Soviet leaders decided they would have to remove the missiles but still hoped to trade them in Cuba for U.S. Jupiters in Turkey. Before they could act on that decision, Khrushchev received faulty information that the invasion of Cuba was beginning.

By the twenty-sixth of October, American planes were flying over Cuba at treetop level, and 250,000 U.S. troops were assembled off the Florida coastline, ready to move. Two thousand bombing sorties were planned. Castro predicted a U.S. strike within seventy-two hours. The 42,000-plus-strong Soviet force, commanded by a Stalingrad veteran and backed by 100,000 Cubans, possessed, unknown to American intelligence, approximately 100 battlefield nuclear weapons.

Khrushchev was losing control of the situation. In an amazing moment, he asked his generals if they could guarantee that holding this course would not result in the death of 500 million people. "What good would it have done me in the last hour of my life to know that though our great nation and the United States were in complete ruin, the national honor of the Soviet Union was intact?"

In what McNamara described as "the most extraordinary diplomatic message I have ever seen," Khrushchev sent Kennedy an urgent letter asking simply for a promise not to invade Cuba. He warned that the two countries were heading inexorably toward war and "it would not be in our power to stop it . . . war ends when it has rolled through cities and villages, everywhere sowing death and destruction."

On October 27, an incident occurred that Schlesinger described as not only the most dangerous moment of the Cold War, but "the most dangerous moment in human history." The Russian ships were heading toward the quarantine line. One of four Soviet submarines sent to protect the ships was being hunted all day by the carrier USS *Randolph*. More than one hundred miles outside the blockade, the *Randolph* began dropping depth charges, unaware the sub was carrying nuclear weapons.

The explosion rocked the submarine, which went dark except for emergency lights. The temperature rose sharply; the carbon dioxide in the air reached near-lethal levels, and people could barely breathe. Men began to faint and fall down. The suffering went on for four hours. Then, the signals officer reported, "The Americans hit us with something stronger. . . . We thought—that's it—the end." Panic ensued. Commander Valentin Savitsky tried, without success, to reach the general staff. He assumed the war had already started and they were going to die in disgrace for having done nothing. He ordered the nuclear torpedo to be prepared for firing. He turned to the other two officers aboard. Fortunately for mankind, the political officer, Vasili Arkhipov, was able to calm him down and convince him not to launch—probably single-handedly preventing nuclear war.

In the midst of this harrowing confrontation, the breakpoint came when the National Security Council received word that a U-2 plane had been shot down over Cuba. Khrushchev had not authorized this. The Joint Chiefs wanted to act immediately and take out all the firing sites and missiles. Kennedy said, "No." The shooting down of the U-2 made both Kennedy and Khrushchev realize they were losing control of their enormous military machines. Americans, receiving continual television broadcasts, were paralyzed in the grip of something they had only dreamed about. Robert McNamara later described watching the sunset come over the Potomac, Saturday night the twenty-seventh of October, "It was a beautiful fall evening, the height of the crisis, and I went up into the open air to look and to smell it, because I thought it was the last Saturday I would ever see."

Soviet diplomats were burning their files in Washington and New York. Washington insiders had begun to quietly evacuate their families from the capital, telling wives and children to drive quickly as far south as possible.

In a last, desperate effort, Kennedy sent his brother to meet with Soviet ambassador Anatoly Dobrynin on that Saturday to tell him the United States was about to attack unless it received an immediate Soviet commitment to remove its bases from Cuba. He promised that the U.S. would not invade Cuba and that it would remove its Jupiter missiles from Turkey within four to five months.

Dobrynin conveyed the urgency to Khrushchev, who claimed in his memoirs that Robert Kennedy's message was even more desperate—that "the President is not sure that the military will not overthrow him and seize power."

The next morning—a Sunday, October 28—dawned with mercy. The Soviets announced they would withdraw the missiles. The world breathed as if there was only one collective breath for all. The crisis actually continued behind the scenes for three more weeks and finally ended on November 20, when the Soviets were able to regain control of their battlefield nuclear weapons and Il-28 bombers from the Cubans. The weapons would actually leave Cuba.

It's interesting to note in hindsight that during the entire crisis, Soviet missiles were never fueled; Red Army reservists were not called up, and no threats were made against Berlin.

Thirty years later, in 1992, McNamara was shocked when told that if American troops had invaded, not only were there four times as many armed Soviets in Cuba as believed and almost three times as many Cuban troops, but one hundred battlefield nuclear weapons would likely have been used. Realizing that one hundred thousand Americans would probably have died, McNamara said the U.S. would have responded by wiping out Cuba with the high risk of an all-out nuclear war between the U.S. and the Soviet Union. Hundreds of millions of people might have perished, possibly all mankind. Researchers have recently discovered that on the island of Okinawa, a large force of missiles with megaton nuclear warheads and F-100 fighter bombers armed with hydrogen bombs were preparing for action. Their likely target was not the Soviet Union, but China.

Military leaders were furious when the crisis ended without an attack on Cuba. McNamara recalled their bitterness: "The President invited the chiefs in to thank them for their support during the crisis, and there was one hell of a scene. Curtis LeMay came out saying, 'We lost. We ought to just go in there today and knock 'em off!'"

It was Khrushchev, even more than Kennedy, who deserves the lion's share of credit for having avoided war. And for this, he was vilified, as Mikhail Gorbachev would be three decades later when he democratically presided, against his will, over the dissolution of the Soviet Union. The Chinese charged Khrushchev with cowardice for caving in; Russian hardliners said he had "shitted his pants." Much of the Pentagon, however, believing that its willingness to go to war had forced the Soviets to back down, determined that superior force would also work elsewhere, especially in Vietnam, where once more U.S. officials believed it necessary to make a stand against communism.

The Soviets drew the opposite lesson, determined never again to be so humiliated and forced to capitulate from weakness. They began a massive buildup of nuclear weapons to achieve parity with the United States. Weakened by the crisis, Khrushchev would be forced out of power the following year.

But, first, he wrote Kennedy a long and remarkable letter: "Evil has brought some good . . . people have felt more tangibly the breathing of the burning flames of thermonuclear war." In light of this, he made a series of bold proposals for eliminating "everything in our relations capable of generating a new crisis." He suggested a nonaggression treaty between NATO and the Warsaw Pact nations. Why not, he asked, "disband all military blocs," cease testing all nuclear weapons—in the atmosphere, in outer space, underwater, and also underground. He proposed solutions to conflicts over Germany and China.

It's interesting to note that there was a tremendous revival of Christianity at the same time, with the short-lived papacy of Pope John XXIII, one of the most popular popes ever. He called together the Second Vatican Council, which issued a new encyclical that shook up the Catholic world. It was called *Pacem in Terris*—Peace on Earth—and ushered in a change in thinking—particularly in Latin America, where priests, nuns, and laypersons took the message of the Gospels to the poor and the persecuted, encouraging them to take their fate into their own hands to overcome the misery of their existence. What became known as "liberation theology" led to many ensuing problems with Kennedy's successors in the backyard of the United States.

Although more tepid to Khrushchev in his response, Kennedy's thinking was evolving, and, in the year following the missile crisis, underwent a remarkable transformation. He began to see Vietnam as one place to step back from the East-West confrontation, but he knew it would not be easy.

The debate over Kennedy's true intentions in Vietnam has at times been quite acrimonious, and his own contradictory statements and mixed signals have added to the confusion. Clearly he was under enormous pressure to stay the course. And as late as July 1963, Kennedy told a news conference that "for us to withdraw . . . would mean a collapse not only of South Vietnam but Southeast Asia."

In private, however, he was voicing doubts. In late 1962 he asked respected Senate majority leader Mike Mansfield to go there and evaluate the situation. Mansfield returned with a highly pessimistic assessment, recommending the U.S. withdraw its forces. Aide Kenny O'Donnell described Kennedy's reaction: "The president was too disturbed by the senator's unexpected argument to reply to it. He said to me later when we talked about [it], 'I got angry with Mike for disagreeing with our policy so completely, and I got angry with myself because I found myself agreeing with him.'"

On the eleventh of June 1963, in an image that shocked the world, Vietnamese Buddhist monk Thich Quang Duc burned himself to death at a busy Saigon intersection to protest the corrupt South Vietnamese government.

McNamara began pressing the Joint Chiefs for a plan of phased withdrawal. Kennedy approved the plan in May 1963 but could not formalize it. The first thousand men were set to depart at the end of that year. In September, he sent McNamara and his trusted new Joint Chiefs chairman, General Maxwell Taylor, on a ten-day fact-finding expedition to Vietnam. They gave the president their report on October 2. It called for withdrawing troops before the end of 1963 and completing the withdrawal by the end of 1965.

Kennedy now formalized his commitment in his National Security Action Memorandum 263, which he signed on October 11 and released to the press. Kennedy, no doubt, was torn. He'd explained to O'Donnell: "In 1965, I'll become one of the most unpopular presidents in history. I'll be damned everywhere as a communist appeaser, but I don't care. If I tried to pull out completely now from Vietnam, we would have another Joe McCarthy Red Scare on our hands, but I can do it after I'm re-elected. So we better make damn sure I am re-elected."

The Republicans were after his scalp. New York governor Nelson Rockefeller charged that he was soft on communism, naively believing the Soviet leaders were "reasonable . . . and desirous of reaching a fundamental settlement with the west." Rockefeller, who was a moderate Republican, said, "The foundations of our safety are being sapped." Kennedy hadn't stopped communist aggression in Laos. He had failed to provide air support during the Bay of Pigs and stood "idly by while the wall was being built in Berlin." Coming up behind Rockefeller was the extremist Republican senator Barry Goldwater, who would actually win the nomination in 1964.

As late as October 1963, in the hope that the situation in South Vietnam could improve, Kennedy supported the overthrow of the oppressive Diem regime but not the assassination of Diem. When the Vietnamese president and his brother were killed by the South Vietnamese military, Kennedy was visibly and extremely upset. Nonetheless, his mind-set did not change.

Among those who later came forward with confirmation of Kennedy's intention to withdraw were Robert McNamara, Arthur Schlesinger, Mike Mansfield, Assistant Secretary of State Roger Hilsman, Ted Sorensen,

Senator Wayne Morse, Kenny O'Donnell, and Speaker of the House Tip O'Neill.

Daniel Ellsberg, later in 1967, interviewed Robert Kennedy, before the 1968 shift in public opinion on the war. Kennedy said that his brother "was absolutely determined not to send ground units." Ellsberg asked him if his brother would have accepted defeat at the hands of the communists and Robert Kennedy replied, "We would have fuzzed it up. We would have gotten a government in that asked us out or that would have negotiated with the other side. We would have handled it like Laos." Ellsberg asked him why his brother was so clearheaded, when most of his senior advisors were still committed to prevailing. Robert responded emotionally, "Because we were there! We were there, in 1951. We saw what was happening to the French. We saw it. My brother determined, determined, never to let that happen to us."

During the remarkable last few months of his life, Kennedy even contemplated a course reversal on Castro's Cuba—a relationship in which his policies were consistently wrongheaded. But just as he clung to the hope of victory in Vietnam while taking steps toward withdrawal, he endorsed a new round of CIA sabotage in Cuba, while exploring several avenues of discreet contact with Castro himself. He told Jean Daniel, an influential French journalist who was about to meet Castro, "I believe that there is no country in the world . . . where economic colonization, humiliation and exploitation were worse than in Cuba, in part owing to my country's policies during the Batista regime." Daniel finally met with Castro two days before Kennedy's assassination. Castro, expressing criticism of U.S. behavior, but admiring Kennedy's potential, also held out hope for a new departure. Kennedy, Castro averred, "still has the possibility of becoming, in the eyes of history, the greatest president of the United States, the leader who may at last understand that there can be coexistence between capitalists and socialists."

Kennedy, in the heart of the Cold War, was facing the abiding truth of American politics: One must be strong. And if one is perceived as soft or weak, one does not endure. And that is the confusing thing about power. Kennedy himself was quite ill from Addison's disease and the effects of spinal operations from World War II injuries. Addicted to painkillers and his own ravenous appetites, finding himself in a cocoon of deceits, not only to himself, but to his wife, to his Cuba and Vietnam policies, and to the country, John Kennedy yet seemed aloof from fear. Like Roosevelt, he embodied a grace that forgave much in the new era of television reality.

In June 1963, in a commencement address at American University, without input from the Joint Chiefs, the CIA, or the State Department, Kennedy gave one of the most extraordinary presidential speeches of the twentieth century. The address was actually based on a draft submitted by *Saturday Review* editor and anti-nuclear activist Norman Cousins, who had been serving as a liaison between Kennedy and Khrushchev. In it, Kennedy encouraged his listeners to think about the Soviet people in human terms—and called for an end to the Cold War:

"What kind of peace do I mean? What kind of peace do we seek? Not a Pax Americana enforced on the world by American weapons of war. . . . Let us re-examine our attitude toward the Soviet Union . . . it is sad to . . . realize the extent of the gulf between us. And if we cannot end now our differences, at least we can help make the world safe for diversity. For, in the final analysis, our most basic common link is that we all inhabit this small planet. We all breathe the same air. We all cherish our children's futures. And we are all mortal."

In September of that year, the Senate passed the Partial Nuclear Test Ban Treaty by a vote of eighty to nineteen. Presidential speechwriter Ted Sorensen believed that "no other accomplishment in the White House ever gave Kennedy greater satisfaction."

And in another stunning reversal, Kennedy called for replacing the space race, perhaps his signature initiative, with joint U.S.-Soviet exploration of space and an expedition to the moon. He said, "International law and the United Nations Charter will apply. Why should man's first flight to the moon be a national competition?"

By the time John Kennedy drove into downtown Dallas to begin his re-election campaign for 1964, he had made powerful enemies in the upper echelons of the intelligence, military, and business communities, not to mention the Mafia, southern segregationists, and both pro- and anti-Castro Cubans. In their minds he was guilty of not following through

Kennedy's most emphatic response to Khrushchev's overtures for peace during the previous year came in his 1963 commencement address at American University. Aided by Ted Sorensen and Norman Cousins, he had drafted the speech without input from the Joint Chiefs, the CIA, or the State Department.

on the Bay of Pigs, disempowering the CIA, firing its leaders, resisting involvement in Laos, concluding the test ban treaty, planning to disengage from Vietnam, abandoning the space race, encouraging Third World nationalism, flirting with ending the Cold War, and, perhaps most damningly, accepting a negotiated settlement in the Cuban Missile Crisis. The rage toward him was visceral.

Kennedy had read the bestselling 1962 novel *Seven Days in May*, which portrays a coup d'état by a Joint Chiefs of Staff furious over a liberal president's new nuclear treaty with the Soviets.

He told a friend: "It's possible. It could happen in this country." If there were a third Bay of Pigs, it could happen.

The Warren Commission, strongly influenced by ex–CIA director Allen Dulles, later concluded that Lee Harvey Oswald was the lone assassin, although, unlike most single assassins with a cause, he firmly denied his guilt. The case against him was made effectively by the national media, but

John F. Kennedy delivered a ringing inaugural address that both reached out to the Soviet Union in hopes of building friendship and reaffirmed his generation's willingness "to defend freedom in its hour of maximum danger" and "pay any price, bear any burden, meet any hardship" in order to do so.

four of the seven Warren Commission members expressed doubts. Lyndon Johnson, Robert Kennedy, and Governor John Connally, who had been wounded in the attack, also questioned the findings. The public found the report unconvincing. We may never know who was responsible or what their motive was, but we do know that Kennedy's enemies included some of the same forces who had cut down Henry Wallace in 1944 when he was trying to lead the United States down a similar path of peace.

Khrushchev would suffer an equally ignominious though less bloody fate as he was ousted by Kremlin foes the following year. He became a critic of the Soviet government and smuggled his memoirs out of the country to be published in the West under the title *Khrushchev Remembers*—it became a bestseller. When he died in 1971, he was buried in a corner of a Moscow cemetery; no monument was erected for years.

Future generations owe an enormous debt, and possibly their very existence, to these two brave men who stared into the abyss and recoiled from what they saw. And they owe a special debt to an obscure Soviet submarine officer who single-handedly blocked the start of a nuclear war.

With the ascension of Vice President Lyndon Johnson, there would be important changes in many of Kennedy's policies—-particularly toward the Soviet Union and in Vietnam.

In his inaugural address, in the morning of that decade, in January 1961, Kennedy had delivered his message of hope: "Let the word go forth, from this time and place, to friend and foe alike, that the torch has been passed to a new generation of Americans."

But with his murder, the torch was passed back to an old generation—the generation of Johnson, Nixon, Ford, and Reagan—leaders who would systematically destroy the promise of Kennedy's last year, as they returned the country to war and repression. Though the vision Khrushchev and Kennedy had expressed would fall with them, it would not die. The seeds they had planted would germinate and sprout again long after their deaths.

For those of us who lived through the 1960s, the Cuban Missile Crisis, coming on the heels of the war scare over Berlin, was a terrifying event. It was one of many nightmares, call it punches to the stomach of a new generation of Americans who had never seen history unfold so quickly, so dramatically, and in such a violent fashion. It would soon be followed by the war in Vietnam—a bloodbath, a nightmare of America's own making, that would eat Vietnamese and Americans alive for almost a decade. More horrifying things were to come by the end of that decade, but, in hindsight, on that afternoon in Dallas when John Kennedy's head was blown off in broad daylight, it was as if a giant horrific Greek Medusa had unearthed its hideous face to the American people, freezing us with an oracle of things yet to come.

CHAPTER NINE

*I*n April 1967, Nobel Peace Prize winner Dr. Martin Luther King, Jr., broke his silence about the U.S. invasion of Vietnam: "As I have walked among the desperate, rejected, and angry young men, I have told them that Molotov cocktails and rifles would not solve their problems. . . . But they asked, and rightly so, 'What about Vietnam?' . . . If America's soul becomes totally poisoned, part of the autopsy must read Vietnam. . . . A nation that continues year after year to spend more money on military defense than on programs of social uplift is approaching spiritual death. . . . This need to maintain social stability for our investments, accounts for the counter-revolutionary action of American forces in Guatemala. It tells why American helicopters are being used against guerillas in Colombia and why American napalm and Green Beret forces have already been active against rebels in Peru. . . . They ask if our own nation wasn't using massive doses of violence to solve its problems, to bring about the changes it wanted. Their questions hit home and I knew that I could never again raise my voice against the violence of the oppressed in the ghettos without having first spoken clearly to the greatest purveyor of violence in the world today—my own government."

Two days into office, on Sunday—the day before John Kennedy was buried—Lyndon Johnson met with his military advisors and said he was not going to lose Vietnam. He'd never agreed with Kennedy's memorandum to withdraw and two days later he issued a new memo, signaling

Lyndon Johnson taking the oath of office following Kennedy's assassination on November 22, 1963. The new president was worlds apart from his fallen predecessor in every imaginable way.

the U.S. would be taking a more hands-on approach. His foreign policy thinking was profound in a primitive way. "There are 3 billion people in the world," he reasoned, "and we have only 200 million of them. We are outnumbered fifteen to one. If might did make right, they would sweep over the United States and take what we have. We have what they want."

Who were "they"? His analogies may have been coarse, but stated in other words the struggle was not really about communism, but was between the First World and the Third World.

Abandoning Kennedy's attempts at reform, Johnson made it clear in the new "Mann doctrine" that all Latin American countries would be judged on how they protected the $9 billion in U.S. investments, not on how they defended the interests of their own people. The U.S. would no longer discriminate against right-wing dictatorships and would regard military aid as a wiser investment than Kennedy's economic aid.

The fifth largest country in the world, resource-rich Brazil, would be the first to suffer. In 1964, new democratically elected president João Goulart implemented land reform and sought controls on foreign capital. Recognizing Cuba was the last nail in his coffin. Castro's example could

Brazilian president João Goulart in New York in April 1962. After refusing to impose austerity measures on his people and instead instituting a program of land reform and control of foreign capital and recognizing Cuba, Goulart was overthrown in a coup backed by the United States.

not be emulated. Johnson sharply reduced U.S. aid. Inflation skyrocketed. The CIA financed large antigovernment rallies, and the U.S. embassy prodded right-wing officers to overthrow the government.

Within days, the new regime declared a state of siege. Fifty thousand were arrested the first month alone. Torture was instituted. U.S. aid and investment flowed into Brazil, and a repressive military regime ruled for the next twenty years, producing the largest gap between rich and poor on the earth. The dominos—in this case the democracies—began falling once again across South America.

In 1965, Johnson sent twenty-three thousand troops into the Dominican Republic to crush a popular uprising seeking to restore constitutional order after a military coup. Johnson told his lawyer, "There ain't no doubt about this being Castro now. . . . They are moving other places in the hemisphere. It may be part of a whole communistic pattern tied in with Vietnam."

In Greece, the birthplace of democracy, where the Cold War had gotten jump-started and the U.S. had supported a right-wing government for many years, a new yearning for democracy appeared certain

Honduran troops en route to the Dominican Republic to support the U.S. invasion of the country in 1965. The United States crushed a popular uprising intended to restore constitutional order and return to power the democratically elected president Juan Bosch, who had recently been ousted by the military.

to bring the veteran liberal George Papandreou back as prime minister. Johnson called in the Greek ambassador and actually said: "Listen to me, Mr. Ambassador—fuck your Parliament and your Constitution! America is an elephant, Cyprus is a flea. Greece is a flea. If these two fleas continue itching the elephant, they may just get whacked by the elephant's trunk—whacked good! . . . We pay a lot of good, American dollars to the Greeks, Mr. Ambassador. . . . If your prime minister gives me talk about democracy, parliaments, and constitutions, he, his parliament, and his constitution may not last very long."

In fact, it didn't. The military junta seized power in 1967, banning miniskirts, long hair, and foreign newspapers, making church attendance compulsory while engaging in numerous incidents of sexually oriented torture and cruelty. Its new prime minister, who had been a captain in a Nazi security battalion tracking down Greek resistance fighters, became the first CIA agent to become the premier of a European country.

But it was Asia that posed the greatest resistance to U.S. goals, aside from Japan, which was becoming a prosperous client state that was paying the U.S. to maintain bases. China exploded its first atomic bomb in October of 1964, catching Washington totally off-guard. In Indonesia, sitting astride Southeast Asia's principal sea lanes, where 3.5 million members made its Communist Party the third largest in the world behind the Soviets and Chinese, Sukarno, having survived repeated U.S. attempts to remove him, further irritated the U.S. by declaring he would test an atomic bomb. But he was denied help from China. And, when he recognized North Vietnam, expropriated U.S. rubber plantations, and threatened to nationalize American oil companies, Lyndon Johnson struck hard. Almost half the officer corps had received some U.S. training, and, in October 1965, with CIA support, General Suharto led the army in crushing Sukarno's supporters.

In the following months, Suharto's militias and civilian mobs went from house to house, killing a half million to a million suspected communists and their families. U.S., British, and Australian intelligence provided thousands of names of communists, educators, and reformers to the army.

Sukarno was forced out finally in 1967 and replaced by Suharto, who enriched himself, his family, and U.S. corporations for decades, until he was overthrown by the people, led by student activists, in 1998.

Largely unknown to the public, the coup in Indonesia was hailed inside Washington as the CIA's greatest single operation in its history. In 1968, the CIA acknowledged that the Indonesia massacre ranked as one of the worst mass murders in the twentieth century.

President Kennedy's national security advisor McGeorge Bundy, later criticizing the U.S. Vietnam War policy, wrote that Indonesia was the true breaking point in Asia—far more important to U.S. goals than Vietnam, which was, he said, "unnecessary." Yet, now in history, even Indonesia's bloodbath pales in comparison to what the United States inflicted on Vietnam.

Johnson and his advisors understood very little about Vietnam's history and its strong resistance to Chinese and French invasions over the centuries. They totally underestimated the nationalist aspect of Ho Chi Minh's movement and assumed if they wreaked enough havoc and killed enough people, the Vietnamese would submit. Within two months of JFK's death, in January 1964, Johnson and McNamara escalated covert military activities against North Vietnam, dropping intelligence and commando teams to destroy bridges, railways, and coastal installations, kidnapping North Vietnamese, and bombing border villages.

Johnson was pathological in his ability to lie. As with the search for weapons of mass destruction in Iraq in 2003, the American people would eventually discover the false origins of the Vietnam War.

In August 1964, Johnson and McNamara used a fabricated incident in North Vietnam's Gulf of Tonkin as an excuse to further escalate the war. The media echoed the line that a U.S. ship had been attacked.

Johnson rushed to Congress to authorize direct U.S. military action. And the House, after forty minutes of debate, passed the resolution 416 to 0. In the Senate, it passed by 88 to 2.

A few days later, Johnson told his undersecretary of state, "Hell, those dumb, stupid sailors were just shooting at flying fish." Senator Wayne Morse presciently commented, "I doubt that the American people understand what this resolution really is. It is a resolution that seeks to give the president of the United States the power to make war without a declaration of war."

In the election of 1964, Johnson crushed Arizona senator Barry Goldwater, who threatened to use nuclear weapons in Vietnam. It was billed as a landslide for peace. But following the election, Johnson began a steady process of escalation, sharply expanding the "free-fire zones," in which anything that moved was considered a legitimate target. The U.S. arsenal of acceptable weapons grew to include napalm, cluster bombs, and white phosphorus, which burned from the skin straight through to the bone, causing horrific deaths. All of these would have been considered illegal chemical weapons at the Nuremberg trials.

Johnson's lies about his plans snowballed, and, by April 1965, he'd sent seventy-five thousand combat troops to Vietnam—and more than half a million by the end of 1967. The monthly draft reached thirty-five thousand men, as the U.S. set out to find Vietnam's breaking point.

Yet, when his Joint Chiefs of Staff at a meeting asked for more firepower or an all-out war, Major Charles Cooper recalled Johnson started

ABOVE: *President Sukarno during a 1956 visit to the U.S.*

BELOW: *President Nixon greets President Suharto, who seized power in Indonesia after the U.S.-aided massacre of between a half million and a million communists and other leftists in what the CIA later called "one of the worst mass murders of the 20th century."*

Napalm (ABOVE) and white phosphorous (BELOW) bombs being dropped over Vietnam. Under Johnson, the U.S. arsenal of acceptable weapons in Vietnam grew to include napalm, cluster bombs, and white phosphorus, which burned straight to the bone, causing horrific and painful deaths.

General Nguyen Van Thieu with Johnson (background) and Air Marshal Nguyen Cao Ky with McNamara (foreground). Ky and Thieu headed the South Vietnamese government that seized power in May 1965. William Bundy later commented that the new regime "seemed to all of us the bottom of the barrel, absolutely the bottom of the barrel."

screaming obscenities: "Imagine that you're me—that you're the president of the United States—and five incompetents come into your office and try to talk you into starting World War III. . . . The risk is just too high. How can you fucking assholes ignore what China might do? You have just contaminated my office, you filthy shitheads. Get the hell out of here right now."

The generals got out. And, after a pause, Johnson continued to escalate the bombing of North Vietnam.

In his inimitable way, he explained to George McGovern his strategy of intensifying the bombing without provoking a strong response from China and North Vietnam: "I'm going up her leg an inch at a time. . . . I'll get to the snatch before they know what's happening."

The U.S. dropped three times as many bombs on tiny Vietnam as it did in all of World War II. On the ground, in a policy sanctioned by Kennedy, more than 5 million peasants were forced out of villages and resettled in barbed-wire camps. Tens of thousands of supposed communists, many of them reformers or critics of the government, were assassinated as part of a "Phoenix Program," but it did little to slow the resistance movement. The murder of civilians became commonplace, as the U.S. military leadership exaggerated body counts to tell the public that the communists were on their last legs, while still asking for more and more troops.

Five South Vietnamese governments came and went, the last clinging to power through massive corruption and violence against its own people.

America's college campuses began to buzz with activism. In October 1967, one of the first violent confrontations took place at the University of Wisconsin. Johnson, convinced that communists were behind the antiwar movement, ordered the CIA to uncover proof, with massive surveillance and other information-gathering efforts. Codenamed "Chaos," the CIA's illegal domestic operations lasted almost seven years, compiling a computer index of three hundred thousand citizens and organizations and extensive files on more than seven thousand individuals, but failed to prove communist involvement.

Among the FBI's principal targets was Nobel Peace Prize winner Dr. Martin Luther King, Jr. Black America was in a state of near rebellion. Riots had rocked U.S. cities for several years, but now twenty-five major riots, lasting two days or more, and thirty minor ones shattered the summer of 1967. Police and National Guard troops killed twenty-six blacks in Newark and forty-three in Detroit.

A *Ramparts* magazine March 1967 exposé revealed that the CIA had been funding the National Student Association. Other liberal groups were exposed as Agency fronts, with CIA money going to anticommunist professors, journalists, aid workers, missionaries, labor leaders, and civil rights activists, who did the Agency's dirty work. Among the discredited were the Ford Foundation, Radio Free Europe, Radio Liberty, and the Congress for Cultural Freedom.

Even McNamara, with his characteristic rationality, was having doubts. In October 1967, one hundred thousand people marched on the Pentagon. Armed infantry prevented them from reaching it, but McNamara ordered them not to load their weapons. He watched alone from a command post on the roof.

Now isolated within the establishment, McNamara despaired. Rumors

LEFT: Peter Kuznick speaking at an antiwar rally on the campus of Rutgers University in New Brunswick, New Jersey. As stories of atrocities in Vietnam reached the United States, the antiwar movement continued to grow.

BELOW: In 1967, Oliver Stone enlisted in the U.S. Army and volunteered for combat duty in Vietnam, where he served for fifteen months and was wounded twice. He was awarded a Bronze Star for combat gallantry and a Purple Heart with an Oak Leaf Cluster.

Antiwar protestors at the October 1967 march on the Pentagon. As popular opposition to the war exploded, the FBI tried to disrupt the antiwar movement.

of a possible mental collapse reached Johnson. "We just can't afford to have another Forrestal," he said. When McNamara argued that more bombing would not work, Johnson was livid. He demanded loyalty, saying of another aide: "I don't want loyalty. I want LOYALTY. I want him to kiss my ass in Macy's window at high noon and tell me it smells like roses. I want his pecker in my pocket."

Johnson ousted McNamara and announced that he would become president of the World Bank. At his last cabinet meeting, an aide reported that McNamara finally broke down: "The goddamned bombing campaign, it's been worth nothing; it's done nothing. They've dropped more bombs than in all of Europe in all of World War II and it hasn't done a fucking thing!"

The year 1968 was one of extraordinary change. In January, on the same day, the North Vietnamese and Vietcong forces unleashed shock attacks on most of Vietnam's major cities and provincial capitals. The attacks were ultimately repelled, with great losses to the Vietnamese, but the mood in Washington was despair.

A bipartisan group of elder statesmen reassessed the situation. It was time to get out.

Lyndon Johnson, his enormous ego deeply wounded by the doubts of his leadership, besieged by enemies internal and external, his popularity plummeting, announced shockingly in March 1968 that he would

A visibly upset Johnson with McNamara during a Cabinet Room meeting in February 1968. After McNamara drew the president's ire by expressing doubts about the war, Johnson surprised McNamara by appointing him to head the World Bank.

not run for a second term. The country was stunned. The leader of the war effort was giving up.

To those against the war, this was a great victory. But to many Americans, as well as neutral countries and allies alike, the U.S. now appeared as a rudderless, immoral country—an emperor without clothes. The Chinese said "a paper tiger."

Racked by inner demons, Johnson allowed his heartfelt dream of being a great social reformer to be buried in the killing fields of Vietnam. "Losing the Great Society," he lamented later in the decade to a historian, "was a terrible thought, but not so terrible as the thought of being responsible for America's losing a war to the communists. Nothing could possibly be worse than that." Here was a man, a potential giant, who, in denying his compassion, suffered from a truly American obsession—the fear of weakness.

Hoover's FBI was doing everything it could to disrupt the antiwar movement, as it had done for years to the civil rights movement. Hundreds of agents infiltrated New Left organizations. FBI and CIA news flacks went to great lengths to marginalize the war's critics and impugn their patriotism.

Hoover was especially worried that the antiwar protests would merge with the black liberation struggle, as a disproportionate number of black soldiers died on the front lines.

Forever convinced that communists were behind the civil rights movement, Hoover pursued Martin Luther King with a vengeance, doing nothing to protect him, until the moment King himself was shot and killed by another supposedly lone-nut assassin in April 1968. Hoover had even encouraged him to commit suicide in one threatening, notorious, anonymous hate-filled letter.

Race riots once more erupted across America. The Berrigan brothers, who were priests, went to jail for burning draft files. Benjamin Spock, the world's most prominent pediatrician; William Sloane Coffin, a Yale University chaplain; Jane Fonda, a young movie star; and heavyweight boxing idol Muhammad Ali were all speaking out.

Across America, in 1968, a newly charismatic Robert Kennedy captured the imagination of young and old tired of the war. Fulfilling his brother's legacy, he was calling for a new America. White, black, brown— it didn't matter. His eyes had Camelot in them. Once more the fire of change and reform was afoot.

Johnson, secretly hoping to be a last-minute choice for president, if called, feared him as much as any man. But the fates were cruel beyond imagining to the Kennedy brothers, as on the hot June night of his victory in the California primary Robert was brutally gunned down in another strange, hard-to-believe set of circumstances by a supposedly deranged young Palestinian. This was a serious and devastating blow to the heart of the reform movement.

Postwar baby boomers had begun flooding college campuses in 1964. Imbued with idealism, dismissive of Cold War ideology, upset with their parents' conformist values and fears, their protests spread worldwide. Students and workers convulsed industrial nations; confrontations shook Prague, Tokyo, West Berlin, Turin, Madrid, Rome, and Mexico City, where soldiers massacred hundreds of protesting students.

In the summer of 1968, at the Democratic convention, ten thousand

ABOVE: *A Cabinet Room meeting during a summit of the "Wise Men." In March 1967, following two days of meetings by these elder statesmen, Dean Acheson summed up the consensus view that they could "no longer do the job we set out to do in the time we have left and we must begin to disengage."*

BELOW: *Johnson's March 31, 1968, press conference announcing that he would not run for re-election. Johnson's presidency would be far from Vietnam's last casualty.*

A distraught Johnson listens to a tape sent from Vietnam in July 1968. To the detriment of both his presidency and the nation, Johnson chose Vietnam over the Great Society.

protesters were manhandled, along with the media, by Chicago police. Television was now presenting a reality the public had never seen before: American authority figures acting as aggressors both at home and abroad. It seemed that the country was coming apart. People spoke of the gulf between the antiwar left and prowar right as a civil war, like the one that had ripped the country apart over a hundred years earlier.

It was in the midst of this terrifying turmoil that the staunchly anticommunist Richard Nixon, so bitterly denied the presidency by John Kennedy in 1960, found his life's destiny. But he almost lost. Stunningly, in this climate, the right-wing segregationist Alabama governor George Wallace, running with the retired General Curtis LeMay, was polling 21 percent and threatening Nixon's chances for victory barely a month before the election. Riding the resentment of what he later called the "silent majority," Nixon's law and order message resonated with white voters, scared of ghetto rebellions, campus disruptions, and rising crime, and he eked out the narrowest of victories.

Nixon was also claiming a "secret plan" to end the war in Vietnam, refusing to divulge its details. What Richard Nixon actually delivered to the country was not peace, law, or order, but war, chaos, and disorder—as the only president to resign his office in disgrace.

Nixon and his national security advisor and later secretary of state, Henry Kissinger, actually expanded the war, which lasted seven more years. Half the total of U.S. casualties from the war occurred under Nixon. Kissinger later said: "I refuse to believe that a little fourth-rate power like North Vietnam does not have a breaking point."

And he and Nixon set out to find it. Nixon's secret plan to end the war turned out to be withdrawing U.S. forces, starting in April 1969, and replacing them with U.S.-trained and -equipped Vietnamese, while systematically and ruthlessly bombing the North Vietnamese and the Viet Cong into submission.

Drawing parallels with Eisenhower's nuclear threats in Korea, which he said ended that war, Nixon boasted to an aide: "I call it the madman theory. . . . I want the North Vietnamese to believe I've reached the point where I might do anything to stop the war. We'll just slip the word to them that . . . 'Nixon is obsessed about communists. We can't restrain him when he's angry—and he has his hand on the nuclear button'—and Ho Chi Minh himself will be in Paris in two days begging for peace."

Two months into office, Nixon began a secret bombing campaign inside neighboring Cambodia to destroy North Vietnamese military sanctuaries. He took extraordinary measures to hide it from Congress. Even the crew members involved believed they were hitting targets in South Vietnam.

Though most Americans remained in the dark about the country they were invading, the truth occasionally seeped out, as when freelance journalist Sy Hersh, in November 1969, broke the news that a year and a half earlier U.S. forces had massacred up to five hundred civilians in the village of My Lai, nicknamed "Pinkville" for its strong enemy sympathies.

Babies, pregnant women, and old people had been raped, scalped, and mutilated, as command of the situation broke down. Not a single shot had been clearly fired at U.S. forces. Indicative of the growing dehumanization of this time and resembling U.S. attitudes toward the Japanese in World War II, 65 percent of Americans told pollsters they were not bothered by the news of the massacre.

Nixon during the 1968 campaign. Riding the resentment of antiwar protesters by what he called the "silent majority" and claiming that he had a secret plan to end the war in Vietnam, Nixon narrowly defeated Hubert Humphrey.

The only officer found guilty was given a partial pardon by Nixon. Public opinion strongly favored it.

There were few limits to Nixon's thinking. He and Kissinger planned for a savage attack, possibly using nuclear weapons, in the fall of 1969, but were thwarted when millions participated nationwide in an October moratorium, and three quarters of a million protesters flocked to Washington in November. Still, Nixon recklessly put the military on secret alert, flying eighteen nuclear-armed B-52s over the polar ice cap toward the Soviet Union, trying to force Soviet leaders—once again unsuccessfully—to pressure the North Vietnamese to accept U.S. peace terms.

Le Duan, who took over the leadership when Ho Chi Minh died in 1969, later told a visiting journalist that the U.S. had threatened to use nuclear weapons on thirteen different occasions. But that had not changed their policies.

Although they would pay a terrible price for their independence, the

South Vietnamese soldiers undergo U.S. training in 1970. In April 1969, Nixon approved plans to withdraw U.S. forces and replace them with U.S.-trained and -equipped Vietnamese. If this approach didn't work, Nixon felt he could always play his "madman" card: threaten North Vietnam with nuclear attack.

Vietnamese understood a basic truth that America's leaders never grasped. The Vietnamese foreign minister later said: "We knew that they could not stay in Vietnam forever, but Vietnam must stay in Vietnam forever."

The Vietnam War was about independence and time, not territory or body counts. America's sixth president, John Quincy Adams, a century before, had warned that a nation should not go "abroad, in search of monsters to destroy." It was here, in Vietnam, that the U.S. ran into its ultimate monster—a people who could not be defeated because they were fighting to protect their homeland against foreign invaders. The U.S. would win every major battle, but it never won the war.

According to his lawyer John Dean and other insiders, Nixon was actually obsessed with war protesters and often adjusted his bellicosity to diminish their outrage.

But now, steeling himself by drinking heavily and watching the movie *Patton* over and over again, Nixon, in April 1970, announced a joint

U.S.–South Vietnamese ground invasion of Cambodia to destroy bases along the border.

Six students were shot and killed at Jackson State in Mississippi and Kent State in Ohio. Four million students and 350,000 faculty members took part in protests. Over a third of the country's colleges and universities suspended classes. Thirty ROTC buildings were burned or bombed in one week. Protests and violent confrontations spread to over seven hundred campuses.

Kissinger described Washington as "a besieged city" with "the very fabric of government . . . falling apart."

The air war intensified. "I want everything that can fly to go in there and crack the hell out of them," Nixon said in 1970. Sounding more like a gangster than a statesman, Kissinger conveyed the order to bomb "anything that flies or anything that moves"—words that could have been spoken by a defendant in the dock at Nuremberg.

When Nixon, after he resigned, was confronted with his lawbreaking, he replied: "Well when the president does it, that means that it is not illegal." By this time Cambodia had been subjected for five years to a brutal air bombardment and an escalating civil war that left hundreds of thousands of Cambodians, many of them civilians, dead.

The bombing campaign in Cambodia continued until August 1973 when Congress cut funding for the war. The U.S. hit more than one hundred thousand sites. The economy devastated, refugees flooded into the capital of Phnom Penh.

The communist rebels, the Khmer Rouge, used these atrocities to recruit angry peasants from the countryside and grew exponentially during the bombing. They finally seized power in 1975 from a corrupt U.S.-backed military dictatorship and then unleashed new horrors on their own people. On top of the half million Cambodians killed in the U.S. phase of the war, one and a half million more perished during Pol Pot's monstrous regime. Perhaps 25 percent of Cambodia's population died during this period.

Meanwhile, in Vietnam, many troops were making individual choices about whether to go into combat. In a remarkable admission in 1971, the *Armed Forces Journal* revealed that the demoralization of the troops in

The bodies of dead Vietnamese in the aftermath of the U.S. massacre at My Lai. In November 1969, Americans learned from the journalist Seymour Hersh that U.S. forces had, the previous November, slaughtered some five hundred civilians in a village of mostly women, children, and old men.

Vietnam was exceeded only by the mutiny of the French army and the collapse of the Russian army in 1917.

Still Nixon persisted. While bombing Cambodia and continuing the secret, crippling bombing of tiny Laos, which had started in 1964, Nixon bombed North Vietnamese cities for the first time since 1968. Civilian casualties soared.

And after a landslide electoral victory against antiwar candidate George McGovern in 1972, Nixon unleashed a twelve-day "Christmas bombing" on the North—the heaviest yet of the war. The outcry in the world was deafening. A peace agreement was concluded the next month in Paris. It was essentially the same deal that had been offered to Lyndon Johnson in 1968, and which Richard Nixon had secretly undermined in order to win the election.

The U.S. agreed to pay the North $3.25 billion in reparations but

Nixon during his April 30, 1970, press conference, announcing the invasion of Cambodia. The president's decision prompted outrage on campuses across the country and ignited a dramatic wave of protests.

later reneged. Elections were promised promptly, but South Vietnam dithered and delayed for the next year and a half.

Nixon brought home the last American combat troops in March 1973. As it would decades later in Iraq and Afghanistan, the U.S. invested huge amounts of money in training and equipping a corrupt South Vietnamese ally to fight for itself.

It did not work, nor did Nixon's madman thesis. In April 1973, trying to buy time for the South Vietnamese army, he ordered the most intense bombing of the entire war of both North and South. But overwhelmed by Watergate revelations, he was forced to rescind the order.

The war dragged on for two more years, until the South Vietnamese army simply collapsed and fled. North Vietnamese forces overran Saigon in April 1975. Disturbing images of fleeing civilians, deserting South Vietnamese soldiers, their officers a step ahead of them, and U.S. embassy marines beating down desperate U.S.-connected Vietnamese trying to escape on the last helicopters off the embassy roof would remain indelibly imprinted in the American psyche. They also added fuel to complaints of already angry war supporters who, like Nixon, contended that the media had sold out Vietnam.

Nixon, meanwhile, caught in a web of crimes known as the Watergate scandal, paranoid over his domestic enemies and further revelations that would expose his illegalities on several fronts, grew increasingly erratic. His defense secretary instructed military leaders not to respond to Nixon's orders. The system was truly beginning to crack. His support having eroded, Nixon announced his resignation.

Nixon thus avoided impeachment, but more than forty of his people were convicted of crimes, several of them going to jail. Nixon was pardoned by his newly appointed vice president, Gerald Ford, who had replaced him. As the war, Lyndon Johnson, and Richard Nixon faded from American television screens, the trust between the presidency and the American people had been betrayed.

Kissinger, now serving also as secretary of state, came through unscathed. He and North Vietnam's Le Duc Tho were awarded the 1973 Nobel Peace Prize. Kissinger won international acclaim as the guiding sane force in the sinking Nixon administration. Knowing peace had not yet been achieved, Le Duc Tho had the grace to turn the prize down.

The U.S. licked its wounds, but few in power reflected on the deeper meaning of what had occurred. The Eisenhower domino theory proved to be a myth. The feared virus had not spread. Thailand, Malaysia, Singapore, Indonesia, Taiwan, the Philippines, and, most important, Japan all prospered and remained firmly in the Western camp.

Worried about U.S. loss of prestige in Asia, and clearly not having understood the repercussions of supporting dictatorships, Nixon and Kissinger turned with fresh eyes to Latin America to reassert U.S. power.

Chile had survived as a model democracy since 1932. It would not survive Nixon and Kissinger.

When socialist Salvador Allende won the election of 1970, promising to nationalize U.S. companies like IT&T that essentially controlled the Chilean economy, Nixon told his CIA chief, "Make the economy scream." All of the international institutions, including the World Bank, with Robert McNamara at its helm, conspired to bring down the regime. The CIA funded opposition parties, pushed propaganda and disinformation, offered bribes, and organized demonstrations and violent strikes against the government. And finally it condoned the murder of the most powerful Chilean general who vowed to defend democracy.

When Salvador Allende took his case against the U.S. to a packed General Assembly at the UN in December 1972, he was cheered wildly but may well have signed his death warrant: "We find ourselves opposed by forces that operate in the shadows, without a flag, with powerful weapons, from positions of great influence. . . . We are potentially rich countries, yet we live in poverty. We go here and there, begging for credits and aid, yet we are great exporters of capital. It is a classic paradox of the capitalist economic system."

The CIA urged its Chilean agents to act. Military leaders, directed by General Augusto Pinochet, executed their coup d'etat on September 11, 1973. As the military closed in, Allende made a final radio address from the presidential palace: "I will not resign. . . . Foreign capital—imperialism united with reaction—created the climate for the army to break with their tradition. . . . Long live Chile! Long live the people! These are my last words. I am sure that my sacrifice will not be in vain. I am sure it will be at least a moral lesson, and a rebuke to crime, cowardice, and treason."

Allende took his own life with a rifle given him by Fidel Castro. Pinochet seized power. His junta killed or disappeared more than thirty-two hundred opponents and jailed and tortured tens of thousands more in a reign of terror led by the Caravan of Death. For the Chilean people, 9/11 has a far more tragic meaning than our 9/11. It marked the end of their government at the hands of the United States. Argentina would follow with a terrifying "Dirty War" against leftists that would last from 1976 to 1983 and kill or disappear somewhere between nine thousand and thirty thousand people.

The new Pinochet regime in Chile was quickly recognized and given aid and lasted in power until 1998. Chile's American-trained intelligence service was masterminded by Colonel Manuel Contreras, who became a paid CIA agent. He organized death squads that hunted down political opponents in Latin America, Europe, and the U.S. His secret police even sent agents to Washington, D.C., to blow up a former Chilean diplomat critical of the regime. Called Operation Condor, the assassination ring

North Vietnam began its final offensive in March 1975. Without the aid of U.S. forces, the South Vietnamese army simply collapsed. Images of South Vietnamese soldiers shooting their way onto planes and U.S. marines beating down desperate Vietnamese trying to escape on the last U.S. helicopters lifting off the U.S. embassy roof would remain indelibly imprinted in the American psyche for decades to come.

included the right-wing governments of Chile, Argentina, Uruguay, Bolivia, Paraguay, and Brazil. Assassination squads tracked down and killed more than thirteen thousand dissidents outside their home countries. Hundreds of thousands more were thrown into concentration camps. At a minimum, the U.S. facilitated communications among these intelligence chiefs.

An internal CIA history that was declassified in 2007 revealed that under the leadership of counterintelligence chief James Jesus Angleton, who was obsessed with the idea of the Soviet Union infiltrating his organization and taking over ultimately most of the world, the CIA had been actively involved in creating and using foreign police forces and counterterrorism units and training close to eight hundred thousand military and police officers in twenty-five countries, including secret police and death squad leaders.

Salvador Allende outside his home on October 24, 1970, after learning he'd been elected president of Chile. The new president took office on November 3. Two days later, Nixon called for his ouster.

After a dismal decade marked by Vietnam, Watergate, and initial congressional investigations into the activities of the CIA, Americans felt confused. What kind of country were we? The answer was a perturbing one. Despite the deep rift between left and right and young and old, Americans were enjoying rising standards of living and a loosening of strict sexual, gender, and moral codes. There was even halting progress in race relations.

No war taxes were levied and the draft was finally mothballed. Those who could afford a college education by and large did not go to Vietnam. The working class did.

Most Americans happily enjoyed the fruits of the 1960s economic boom, a boom driven in part by the military-industrial complex with its huge arms sales. For example, the U.S. lost and needed to replace more than five thousand of its close to helicopters twelve thousand, in Vietnam. Between 1951 and 1965, the state of California alone received $67

Augusto Pinochet greeting Kissinger, June 1976. After overthrowing Allende in a CIA-aided coup ordered by Nixon himself, Pinochet seized power and proceeded to murder more than 3,200 opponents and jail and torture tens of thousands more. Kissinger saw to it that the United States quickly recognized and provided aid to the murderous regime.

billion in defense contracts, which helped revitalize the empty American West, employing huge numbers in new cities and towns. This, in turn, redistributed the power in Congress, with many representatives throughout the gun belt becoming dependent on the arms industry for their positions in government.

And, as it would later in Iraq and Afghanistan, the government paid for the war by printing more dollars, straining its ability to convert dollars into gold, inflating the currency, and helping to create a deficit that grew from $3 billion in the early 1960s to a staggering $25 billion by 1968. Speculation flourished; tax havens were sought out; productive reinvestment lagged.

Corruption also abounded in Vietnam, where the U.S. shipped huge warehouses of goods to the war zone. Enormous base camps with giant merchandizing centers called PXs flowered in a primitive landscape like mini–Las Vegases, fueling dreams of consumption. Black markets thrived, as cars, refrigerators, TV sets, food, and drink distorted a Third World economy. Deadly weapons disappeared, stolen by racketeering insiders—both U.S. soldiers and civilians—who greedily sold to both South and North Vietnamese. Financial scandals, as in most wars, were buried in the debris and chaos.

Ominous signs began to emerge. Factories fled either to developing countries or to the nonunion South, as older, northern industrial cities began to decay from unemployment, poor housing and schools, and drugs. Real wages not only stagnated, they would actually decline for the next thirty years, as the middle and working classes' standard of living steadily eroded.

In 1971, Nixon removed the United States from the thirty-five-dollar-an-ounce gold standard and abrogated the Bretton Woods Treaty that had governed the postwar economic alliance.

OPEC, an organization of oil-producing countries, mostly in the Middle East, now felt powerful enough to punish the United States for supporting Israel in the 1973 war. Oil prices quadrupled in the next year. The U.S., which before the 1950s produced all the oil it needed, was now importing one-third of its supply.

The country would suffer deep cycles of inflation and recession, with Wall Street profiting from the increasing volatility and insecurity of a speculative bubble economy that reached its nadir in the great recession of 2008.

The Vietnam War would indeed spell the end of the last significant period of social and political reform the United States had seen.

Was the country now a "paper tiger," living on borrowed money and time? This question would haunt the national imagination through the 1970s and even the 1980s into the 1990s, when, with the fall of the Soviet Union, the sense of American domination re-emerged.

The accepted mythology of the time was that the United States lost the war in Vietnam. But as linguist, historian, and philosopher Noam Chomsky has pointed out, "It's called a loss, a defeat, because they didn't achieve the maximal aims, the maximal aims being turning it into something like the Philippines. They didn't do that . . . they did achieve the major aims. It was possible to destroy Vietnam and leave." Elsewhere he wrote, "South Vietnam . . . had been virtually destroyed, and the chances that Vietnam would ever be a model for anything had essentially disappeared."

When an aging and wiser Robert McNamara returned to Vietnam in 1995, he conceded, somewhat in shock, that despite official U.S. estimates of 2 million Vietnamese dead, 3.8 million Vietnamese had perished—the equivalent of 27 million Americans at that time. In comparison, 58,000 Americans died in the fighting and 200,000 were wounded. The U.S. had destroyed 9,000 of South Vietnam's 15,000 hamlets. In the North, it devastated all 6 industrial cities, 28 of 30 provincial towns, and 96 of 116 district towns. Unexploded ordnance still blankets the countryside. Nineteen million gallons of herbicide had poisoned the environment and wiped out almost all of Vietnam's ancient triple-canopy forests.

The effects of chemical warfare alone lasted for generations and can be seen today in the hospitals in the South where Agent Orange was used—dead fetuses kept in jars, surviving children born with horrid birth defects and deformities, and cancer rates much higher than in the North.

And yet, incredibly, the chief issue in the United States was for many years the hunt for thirteen hundred soldiers missing in action—a few hundred of them alleged to have been taken as captives by the North Vietnamese. High-grossing action movies were made out of it.

No official apology from the United States has ever been issued and there has been absolutely no appreciation of the suffering of the Vietnamese. President Bill Clinton finally recognized Vietnam in 1995—twenty years later.

Ever since the war, American conservatives have struggled to vanquish the "Vietnam Syndrome," which became a catchphrase for Americans' unwillingness to send troops abroad to fight.

For a war that so mesmerized and defined an entire generation, surprisingly little is known about Vietnam today among American youth. This is not accidental. There has been a conscious and systematic effort to erase Vietnam from historical consciousness, such as when Ronald Reagan said, "It's time that we recognized that ours was, in truth, a noble cause. . . . We dishonor the memory of fifty thousand young Americans who died in that cause when we give way to feelings of guilt, as if we were doing something shameful."

It was not only conservatives who whitewashed history. Bill Clinton joined the chorus of falsifiers when he said, "Whatever we may think about the political decisions of the Vietnam era, the brave Americans who fought and died there had noble motives. They fought for the freedom and the independence of the Vietnamese people." No wonder an astounding 51 percent of 18- to 29-year-olds told Gallup pollsters in 2014 that the Vietnam War had been worth fighting.

The outcome has been shrouded in sanitized lies. The Vietnam Veterans Memorial in Washington, dedicated in November 1982, contains the names of 58,280 dead or missing Americans. The message is clear—the tragedy is the death of those Americans. But imagine if the names of 3.8 million Vietnamese, and millions of Cambodians and Laotians, were also included. The wall, whose length is 493 feet, would be over eight miles long.

The supposed shame of Vietnam would be finally avenged by Ronald Reagan, the two Bushes, and even, to an extent, Barack Obama, in the decades to come. The irony is that the Vietnam War represented a sad climax of the World War II generation, from which Johnson, Nixon, Reagan, George H. W. Bush, and all the generals and high command came—those proclaimed by the mainstream media in the late 1990s as the "greatest generation." Yet that same media ignored the arrogance of a generation that, overconfident after World War II, dismissed Vietnam as a fourth-rate power that could be easily defeated. From what the ancient Greeks called hubris, or arrogance, comes the fall.

And from this initially obscure war came a great distortion of economic, social, and moral life in America—a civil war that polarizes the country to this day—with much denied, little remembered, nothing regretted, and, perhaps, nothing learned. History must be remembered, or it will be repeated until the meanings are clear.

The second president of the United States, John Adams, once said, "Power always thinks it has a great soul . . . and that it is doing God's service when it is violating all his laws," which makes the details of the oncoming history a sad, inevitable bloodbath that repeats itself, again and again, as the U.S.A., much too often, has stood on the side of the oppressors.

Propping up allies with financial and military aid, war on drugs programs, police and security training, joint military exercises, overseas bases, and occasional direct military interventions, the U.S. empowered a network of tyrants who were friendly to foreign investors who could exploit cheap labor and native resources on terms favorable to the empire.

Such was the British and French way, and such would be the American way. Not raping, looting Mongols but rather, benign, briefcase-toting, Ivy League–educated bankers and corporate executives who would loot local economies in the name of modernity, democracy, and civilization to the benefit of the United States and its allies.

During the Cold War, politicians and the media sidestepped debate over the basic morality of U.S. foreign policy by mouthing platitudes about U.S. benevolence and insisting that harsh or even dirty tactics were needed to fight fire with fire. The Kissingers of the world called it "realpolitik."

But even when the Soviet Union collapsed in the early 1990s, our nation's policies did not change. The U.S., time and again, has taken the side of the entrenched classes or the military against those from below seeking change. This was the American war against the poor of the earth—the most easily killed—the collateral damage.

But was this all really about fighting communism, or was that a way to disguise policymakers' real motivation?

It was George Kennan, America's leading early Cold War strategist, who went to the heart of the matter in a memorandum written in 1948—writing that with "50 percent of the world's wealth, but only 6.3 percent of its population . . . we cannot fail to be the object of envy and resentment. Our real task . . . is to devise a pattern of relationships which will permit us to maintain this position of disparity. . . . To do so, we will have to dispense with all sentimentality and daydreamings. . . . We should cease to talk about vague and . . . unreal objectives such as human rights, the raising of the living standards, and democratization . . . we are going to have to deal in straight power concepts. The less we are then hampered by idealistic slogans, the better."

But George Kennan, who lived to be 101 years old in 2005, was an intellectual who never sought political office. Never in his wildest dreams could he have imagined the barbaric proportions of the upcoming presidency of Ronald Reagan.

CHAPTER
TEN

*I*n 1970, Attorney General John Mitchell gloated, "This country is going so far right you are not even going to recognize it." But how much further to the right could the U.S. go? In 1970, there was Vietnam, Cambodia, Laos, nuclear threats, surveillance, sabotage, dirty tricks, official lies, racial polarization, and crime, and still to come were the war on drugs, Chile, and Watergate. But compared to the world that Ronald Reagan and George W. Bush would usher in, one could almost look back nostalgically on the Nixon era.

Right-wing forces have always operated freely and openly in the dark chasms of American life, where racism, militarism, imperialism, and blind devotion to private enterprise festered. The raw underbelly of fanaticism has spawned groups as disparate as the Ku Klux Klan, the Nazi Party, the Liberty League, the America Firsters, the John Birchers, the Mc-Carthyites, and the Tea Party, spewing either hatred, bigotry, or simply ignorance of history.

Beginning with Nixon's courting of a new Republican South and the success of George Wallace as a third-party candidate, these forces migrated from the fringes of American politics and the nether reaches of rationality to a new home in the Republican Party, which gradually banished its once-thriving moderate and liberal wings.

Nixon had once said that domestic politics interested him about as much as "building outhouses in Peoria." But on his watch, whether he liked it or not, eighteen-year-olds won the vote, censorship declined, and gays and lesbians emerged from the shadows. He established the EPA, the Environmental Protection Agency, supported the Equal Rights Amendment and new regulations protecting the health of workers, and even strengthened the Voting Rights Act. He even endorsed a guaranteed annual income for all Americans.

His former right-wing allies were belatedly recognizing that this was not the 1950s anticommunist hatchet man Richard Nixon they had known. Though he was pulverizing Southeast Asia, he horrified the right when he turned around and, seeking to ease the stresses of the U.S. land war in Asia, recognized Red China in 1972. And on top of that, he went to the Soviet Union and signed the historic SALT I Treaty, placing limits on missile and antimissile systems.

When Nixon took the country off the gold standard and imposed wage and price controls in 1971, and then pulled all remaining U.S. troops out of Vietnam in 1973, it seemed he had lost his mind and totally betrayed his base.

By the time of Watergate, Nixon had made far too many enemies on both left and right—more than he could afford. Facing probable impeachment, he resigned on August 9, 1974. The presidency was now in the hands of the amiable Gerald Ford, a man who Lyndon Johnson said could not fart and chew gum at the same time. Ford announced that "our long national nightmare is over," but, sending all the wrong signals, pardoned Nixon. Even more troubling for the future was that Nixon's fall brought out the deepest impulses of rage and revenge from the core of Nixon's new Republican Party. His legendary anger became theirs, but now directed against the government itself. Reinvigorated by anger at a so-called liberal media, which had played such a toxic role in their mind in distorting Vietnam and driving Nixon from the presidency, a network of conservative think tanks as well as rich foundations invested large sums of money to push for their agendas. Among these was a radical return to the concept of privatization, which had been in their minds destroyed by Roosevelt's loathed New Deal. Roosevelt's old enemies—the money class—were back.

This burgeoning right-wing network had little use for a relative moderate like Gerald Ford and itched to put a real right-winger like former

*Gerald Ford being sworn in as president upon
Nixon's resignation in August 1974.*

California governor Ronald Reagan into the White House. Bowing to the
pressure, Ford and Donald Rumsfeld, a young congressman who'd made a
name attacking the Soviets in the 1960s, engineered a major cabinet shake-
up, known as the "Halloween Day Massacre," in October 1975. Rumsfeld, whom Nixon had called a "ruthless little bastard," took over Defense.
Kissinger, staying on at State, lost his national security post to General
Brent Scowcroft. George H. W. Bush took over the CIA and Dick Cheney,
a protégé of Rumsfeld's, replaced him as chief of staff. Vice President Nelson Rockefeller, a relative moderate, was forced off the ticket in 1976.
Rumsfeld helped block a new SALT Treaty, and Ford banished the term
"détente," associated now with Henry Kissinger, from the White House.

But the people wanted change, and they entrusted the presidency in
1976 to Governor Jimmy Carter, a former peanut farmer and longtime
Sunday School teacher from Plains, Georgia, who narrowly defeated Ford.

Carter was anything but a typical candidate. He sought to end the
arms race, revive détente, restore America's moral standing, and learn
from Vietnam, saying, "Never again should our country become militarily involved in the internal affairs of another nation unless there is a direct

Trying to placate their critics on the right, Ford and his chief of staff, Donald Rumsfeld, engineered a major cabinet shake-up in October 1975, known as the "Halloween Day Massacre." Among other changes, Rumsfeld took over for James Schlesinger as secretary of defense. Many saw Rumsfeld, whom Nixon had described as a "ruthless little bastard," behind the shake-up. From his new post at the Pentagon, Rumsfeld began warning that the Soviets threatened to overtake the United States in military strength and that détente was not in the United States' interest.

and obvious threat to the security of the United States or its people." He vowed never to repeat the "false statements and sometimes outright lies" that his predecessors had used to justify the U.S. invasion of Vietnam. He said at the United Nations that the U.S. would cut its nuclear arsenal by 50 percent if the Soviets did the same.

Following his gut, Carter scored some significant early successes. He helped secure the Camp David Accords in 1978, leading to Israeli withdrawal from Egyptian territory captured in the 1967 war, and established diplomatic relations between the two countries. He negotiated a SALT II Treaty with the Soviets, mandating a reduction in nuclear missiles and bombers.

But Carter knew little about foreign policy and had been deeply influenced by the ideas of Zbigniew Brzezinski, his national security advisor.

LEFT: Ford with Henry Kissinger. From the start, Ford sent all the wrong signals. Among them was announcing that Kissinger would stay on as both secretary of state and national security advisor.

BELOW: Henry Kissinger speaking on the phone in Deputy National Security Advisor Brent Scowcroft's office during the fall of South Vietnam. By the beginning of Ford's administration, Kissinger was feeling despondent over the future of the American Empire. He told the New York Times' James Reston, "As a historian, you have to be conscious of the fact that every civilization that has ever existed has ultimately collapsed. History is a tale of efforts that failed, of aspirations that weren't realized, of wishes that were fulfilled and then turned out to be different from what one expected. So as a historian, one has to live with a sense of the inevitability of tragedy."

(LEFT) Jimmy Carter leaves a church while campaigning in Jacksonville, Florida. (RIGHT) A Carter supporter holds up a campaign sign at the 1976 Democratic National Convention in New York City. A millionaire peanut farmer and longtime Sunday School teacher from Plains, Georgia, Carter narrowly defeated Ford. Running as a populist and an outsider, appealing to blacks, farmers, and disaffected youth, he promised to restore trust in government and heal the wounds resulting from divisions over Watergate, the Vietnam War, and years of generational, gender, and racial discord.

An author, professor, and fierce anticommunist, Brzezinski tapped the rising, though still little-known Carter for membership in the Trilateral Commission, a group founded by Chase Manhattan Bank chairman David Rockefeller in 1973 to bolster the world capitalist order.

Its 180 elite members in offices on three continents generally rejected the rigidity of right-wing anticommunism. But Brzezinski, like Kissinger before him, marginalized the more liberal secretary of state and engineered a return to Cold War orthodoxy. He bragged about being the first Pole in three hundred years in a position to really stick it to the Russians.

Massive U.S. arms sales to Iran, half of all U.S. sales worldwide, had kept the unpopular shah in power, and, despite the shah's dismal human rights

Carter and Soviet leader Leonid Brezhnev sign SALT II. For all the treaty's fanfare, it was only a measured success. Both sides were actually allowed to continue their nuclear buildups at a reduced rate.

record, the Carters shared a lavish 1978 New Year's Eve in Tehran. Jimmy Carter gushed, "There is no leader with whom I have a deeper sense of personal gratitude and personal friendship." Within a year, the shah had imposed martial law, and his troops shot down hundreds in the street.

Fearing that the Soviets would occupy Iran's oil fields in this chaos, Brzezinski warned Carter that the United States now faced "the most massive American defeat since the beginning of the Cold War, overshadowing in its real consequences the setback in Vietnam."

Two months later, the shah fled for his life. Ayatollah Khomeini returned from exile, demanding the shah's return to face trial. Carter, under pressure from Brzezinski, Kissinger, and David Rockefeller, allowed the shah into the United States for medical treatment for cancer, infuriating the Iranian public. In November, students burst into the American embassy in Tehran and seized fifty-two American hostages, whom they held for 444 days—effectively destroying Carter's presidency.

Carter with Zbigniew Brzezinski, whose selection as national security advisor would help doom Carter's progressive agenda. The hawkish son of a Polish diplomat and an obsessed anticommunist, Brzezinski set out to deliberately and systematically shape Carter's thinking on foreign policy. Overwhelming the president with Cold War orthodoxy, Brzezinski eventually wore him down and won him to a hard-line view.

Crises seemed to be flaring all over. Central America, after suffering decades of poverty, brutality, and corruption under U.S.-backed right-wing dictators, was ready to explode by the late 1970s.

In Nicaragua, the Sandinistas seized power in July 1979—Latin America's first successful revolution since Cuba's twenty years earlier—and began an ambitious program of land, education, and health reform. Brzezinski argued for military intervention, fearing the revolutionary ferment would embolden forces in neighboring Guatemala, Honduras, and El Salvador—where forty families had ruled for over a century. Right-wing death-squad murders and torture increased, and the progressive Salvadorian archbishop Oscar Romero was assassinated in 1980. Later that year, the FMLN insurgents were on the brink of another successful revolution when Carter, pressured by Brzezinski, restored military aid to the government.

Another storm was brewing in Afghanistan, an impoverished remnant from the British Empire, where life expectancy was forty years. Only one

Despite the Iranian ruler's dismal human rights record, President Carter never ceased to support the beleaguered shah, outraging most Iranians. At a lavish 1978 New Year's Eve celebration with the shah in Tehran, as protesters demonstrated in both nations' capitals, Carter offered his host this adulatory toast: "Our talks have been priceless, our friendship is irreplaceable, and my own gratitude is to the Shah, who in his wisdom and with his experience has been so helpful to me, a new leader. There is no leader with whom I have a deeper sense of personal gratitude and personal friendship." Riots broke out soon after the Carters left. In January 1979, the shah fled Iran.

Protest against the Shah during the Iranian Revolution.

in ten could read, and most lived as nomads or farmers in muddy villages, scarcely different from when Alexander the Great had passed through two thousand years before. It was in July 1979 that Brzezinski had Carter sign a little-known directive for secret aid to the Islamic fundamentalist opponents of the pro-Soviet regime in Kabul. And that day, Brzezinski proudly noted that "this aid was going to induce a Soviet military intervention." His intention was to drag them into their own Vietnam.

Brzezinski understood the Soviets' fear that the Afghan insurgency might spark an uprising by the 40 million Muslims in Soviet Central Asia. He even compared it, in its effect on the U.S., to a communist insurgency in Mexico. The Soviets concluded correctly that the Americans were instigating the insurgency, possibly with help from China. But they still hesitated to intervene. Veteran foreign minister Gromyko knew that "we would be largely throwing away everything we achieved with such difficulty, particularly détente, the SALT II negotiations . . ."

With their top-heavy, bureaucratically ossified economy stagnating, the Soviets saw arms control as their chance to finally escape the wartime treadmill.

But the provocation worked. President Brezhnev, a stolid, unimaginative Soviet leader, insisting the war would be over in three to four weeks, launched a full-scale invasion by eighty thousand Soviet troops into Afghanistan on Christmas Day 1979.

The inexperienced Carter hyperbolically called the invasion the greatest threat to world peace since World War II. A *New York Times* columnist felt compelled to remind him of the Berlin blockade, the Korean War, the Suez crisis, the Cuban Missile Crisis, and the U.S. invasion of Vietnam.

Carter withdrew the U.S. ambassador and took SALT II off the table. He cut trade between the two countries, banned U.S. athletes from the upcoming Moscow Olympics, and sent his defense secretary to sound out Chinese leaders about military ties.

He effectively extended the Truman Doctrine to the adjacent Persian Gulf region, including Iran, which would now be regarded as a U.S. vital interest.

Muslim nations condemned the Soviet aggression. Saudi Arabia sent money, and thousands of young Muslims from all over the Middle East

An Afghan fighter demonstrates the positioning of a handheld surface-to-air missile. To keep Gorbachev from being able to withdraw Soviet troops from Afghanistan, Reagan and Casey transformed Carter's tentative support for the mujahideen into the CIA's largest covert operation to date, totaling more than $3 billion.

began the journey to Afghanistan for jihad—holy war against the Soviet infidels.

Brzezinski traveled to meet with the dictators of Pakistan and Saudi Arabia to work out financial and military aid for the holy warriors, who were particularly upset over the Soviet-supported government's reforms to emancipate and educate their women. Brzezinski has repeatedly denied having any regrets about fueling Islamic fundamentalism, which would blow back against the United States on 9/11 and plague it for years to come. He later asked, "What is more important in world history? The Taliban or the collapse of the Soviet Empire? Some agitated Muslims or the liberation of Central Europe and the end of the Cold War?"

At what price? In seeking to destroy the Soviet Empire, Brzezinski instead destroyed Jimmy Carter's presidency. Carter never fulfilled his promise to reduce defense spending, increasing it from $115 billion to $180 billion. Carter more than doubled the number of warheads aimed at the Soviet Union. Carter even repudiated his earlier criticism of the

Vietnam War. Vietnam veterans became freedom fighters who "went to Vietnam without any desire to capture territory or to impose American will on other people."

Carter's policy, in the end, ironically, laid the groundwork for the even more extreme views that Ronald Reagan would bring to the White House.

There's never been a president quite like Ronald Reagan, with his charm, humor, elegant good looks, and driving compulsion to transform America into a conservative fortress.

A folksy, homespun actor turned General Electric pitchman, Reagan served eight years as California's governor. He was underrated by many as a B actor in Hollywood and titled his first autobiography *Where's the Rest of Me?* based on his 1942 movie *King's Row*, a gothic classic about small-town America. In the film, his legs were amputated by his girlfriend's sadistic, perhaps castrating, surgeon father. The film marked his transition from New Deal liberal to Cold War conservative. He later discovered his missing half in his fight against communism—a fight that as president of the Screen Actors Guild turned him into a highly public crusader against the Red Menace as well as a secret FBI informant who denounced colleagues as communists.

Political consultant Roger Ailes, who would later create Fox News, drawing on tactics he developed with Richard Nixon, reminded the seventy-three-year-old Reagan that he got elected on themes—not details—happy thoughts like "Morning in America" or the Puritan belief that America was the shining city on a hill. Reagan's critics were defeatists who would "blame America first."

Or there were dark fictional themes such as "We're in greater danger today than we were the day after Pearl Harbor. Our military is absolutely incapable of defending this country."

The facts never quite mattered if there was a good punch line. He loved to tell the story about the Chicago welfare queen with eighty names, thirty addresses, and twelve Social Security cards who had a tax-free income of $150,000, although the numbers changed to match the credulity of his listeners.

He preferred films to reading and his staff prepared visual aids on issues such as the Soviet threat or the problem in the Middle East.

For meetings, even with a few people in the room, Reagan would read his lines like an actor from three-by-five index cards. At one meeting, with top U.S. automobile manufacturers, he read at length from the wrong cards until, noting their embarrassment, he finally caught on. He liked to go home to his beloved wife, Nancy, punctually, late in the afternoon, exercise, eat dinner in his pajamas, watch TV, and be in bed early.

In June 1987, Reagan went to Berlin and exhorted Soviet leader Mikhail Gorbachev, "General Secretary Gorbachev, if you seek peace, if you seek prosperity for the Soviet Union and Eastern Europe, if you seek liberalization: Come here to this gate! Mr. Gorbachev, open this gate! Mr. Gorbachev, tear down this wall!"

Less than two and a half years later, the wall did indeed come crashing down, and, in 1991, the Soviet Empire collapsed. The Cold War was over. Many credit Reagan with winning it. Admirers lionize him as the greatest president since World War II—one of the greatest ever. But the real story is far more complex. Reagan left behind a bloody trail of death and destruction but also came excruciatingly close to achieving enduring greatness.

Reagan's disengaged style and lack of foreign policy experience left a void that the administration's anticommunist hawks scrambled to fill.

Leading the pack was William Casey. The movies could not have invented a man like Casey—a Catholic Knight of Malta, he attended mass daily and proclaimed Christianity to anyone who asked his advice. Statues of the Virgin Mary filled his Long Island mansion. He'd been head of the Securities and Exchange Commission and before that he'd worked with the OSS. According to Casey's CIA deputy Robert Gates, "The Reaganites saw their arrival as a hostile takeover." Casey had read Claire Sterling's apocryphal *The Terror Network* and was convinced that the Soviet Union was behind international terrorism, including the recent assassination attempt on the Polish-born pope, a fellow Catholic.

The head of the CIA's Office for Soviet Analysis, Melvin Goodman, said that much of Sterling's evidence was based on "black propaganda," anticommunist allegations that the CIA itself had planted in the European press. Yet Casey told analysts that he had learned more from Sterling than from all of them. Al Haig, the hard-core secretary of state,

Ronald Reagan was one of the least intellectually curious men to ever occupy the White House. Counterterrorism coordinator Anthony Quainton recalled being summoned to the White House early in the new administration: "I gave that briefing to the President, who was joined by the Vice President, the head of CIA, the head of the FBI, and a number of National Security Council members. After a couple of jelly beans, the President dozed off. That . . . was quite unnerving."

agreed and alleged that the Soviets had tried to assassinate him when he was the head of NATO. Experts knew that Sterling had exaggerated Soviet support for the nihilist terrorist groups of Western Europe. But Casey and Gates purged analysts who refused to knuckle under, crippling the Agency in such a way that when the Soviet Union fell apart later in the decade, the Agency was unable to anticipate it.

At his first press conference, using the language of John Foster Dulles and James Forrestal, Reagan quickly reversed almost two decades of progress in easing Cold War tensions when he declared, "The only morality they recognize is what will further their cause, meaning they reserve unto themselves the right to commit any crime, to lie, to cheat, in order to attain that, and that is moral, not immoral, and we operate on a different set of standards." America's morality, he insisted, was superior:

Reagan with CIA Director William Casey, a multimillionaire Wall Street lawyer and devout Irish Catholic, who had come to the CIA, according to his deputy Robert Gates, "to wage war against the Soviet Union." Under Casey, the CIA painted a picture of a hostile, expansionist USSR, an image that didn't accord with the facts.

"I'd always felt that from our deeds it must be clear to anyone that Americans were a moral people who . . . had always used our power only as a force for good in the world."

In reality, Reagan's election encouraged right-wing impulses throughout the Third World, prodding extremists to recoup perceived losses of land or power or government, resulting from indecisive American leadership since Vietnam. The methods would be cruel. In Latin America especially, death squads, massacres, disappearances, rapes, and torture followed the 1980 shift in American ideology.

The colonel who headed the U.S. advisory team in El Salvador said, "Real counterinsurgency techniques are a step toward the primitive," an apt description of U.S. leaders' efforts to test their new post-Vietnam counterinsurgency doctrines and defeat uprisings without a large commitment of U.S. forces. Many top Salvadoran, Honduran, and Guatemalan army officers were trained at the U.S. Army School of the Americas in Panama, and then, after 1984, Fort Benning in Georgia. The emphasis on counterinsurgency techniques honed in Vietnam was expanded.

Visiting neighboring Honduras in 1982, Reagan met with Guatemalan president General Efraín Ríos Montt, a born-again evangelical Christian who had recently seized power in a coup. Reagan complained that Montt had received "a bum rap" and called him "a man of great personal integrity." Under his rule, the Guatemalan army would kill roughly one hundred thousand Mayan peasants living in the region of the leftist insurgency between 1981 and 1983.

Across the Nicaraguan border in Honduras, former members of Somoza's thuggish national guard gathered, and, with Casey's assistance, plotted a return to power. They called themselves the counter-revolutionaries, or "contras."

The war began in March 1982. Congress then banned the use of government funds to overthrow the Sandinista government. But Casey and National Security Council official Oliver North concocted a plot right out of the World War II OSS days. In an elaborate, illegal operation, aided by Israeli arms dealers, the United States sold missiles to its enemies in Iran at exorbitant prices and used the profits to fund the contras, with Latin American drug dealers often serving as intermediaries and receiving easier access to American markets in return. The fifteen-thousand-man contra army, employing kidnapping, torture, rape, and murder, targeted health clinics, schools, agricultural cooperatives, bridges, and power stations.

Reagan and Casey lied to Congress about what the CIA was up to. According to his deputy, Gates, "Casey was guilty of contempt of Congress from the day he was sworn in."

Reagan defended the covert war by saying in 1984, "The Nicaraguan people are trapped in a totalitarian dungeon, trapped by a military dictatorship . . . made . . . all the more dangerous by the unwanted presence of thousands of Cuban, Soviet, and radical Arab helpers." He went so far as to call the contras "the moral equivalent of the Founding Fathers and the brave men and women of the French resistance." These "moral

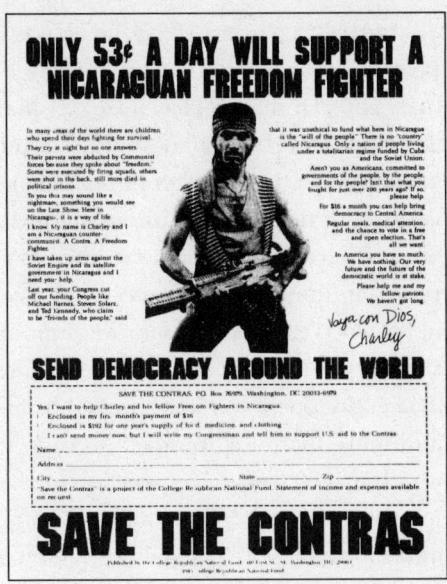

Echoing Reagan, who anointed the contras "the moral equivalent of the Founding Fathers," the College Republicans distributed this flyer calling for support for "Nicaraguan Freedom Fighters." Those "Freedom Fighters" were notorious for torturing, mutilating, and slaughtering civilians.

equivalents" were responsible for most of the deaths of twenty thousand to thirty thousand Nicaraguan civilians during the war.

Similar atrocities occurred in neighboring El Salvador, where U.S.-trained troops stabbed, decapitated, raped, and machine-gunned 767 civilians in the village of El Mozote in late 1981, including 358 children under age thirteen.

Congress ended up funneling almost $6 billion to this tiny country, making it the largest recipient of U.S. foreign aid per capita in the world. Wealthy landlords were running the right-wing death squads that murdered thousands of suspected leftists. The death toll from the war reached seventy thousand. The Salvadoran population of the U.S. expanded five times to half a million by 1990, many of these illegal entries. Yet more Nicaraguans, supposedly fleeing communist oppression, if not the contra war, were allowed into the U.S. Many Salvadorans were turned back.

Bogged down in protracted proxy wars in Nicaragua and El Salvador and haunted by the memory of defeat in Vietnam, which he called a "noble cause," Reagan hungered for an easy military victory to restore Americans' self-confidence.

In 1983, a powerful truck bomb was set off by Hezbollah, an anti-Israeli political organization that often resorted to terrorist tactics. The Al-Qaeda of its time, Hezbollah blew up a U.S. Marine barracks in Lebanon, leaving 241 dead and dealing another devastating blow to U.S. pride. Two days later, U.S. troops invaded not Lebanon, but Grenada—a tiny Caribbean island with one hundred thousand inhabitants. Reagan claimed it was "a Soviet-Cuban colony, being readied as a major military bastion to export terror and undermine democracy." We got there just in time. As in one of his old Westerns, he sent American soldiers into battle. Banning media supposedly for their own safety, he offered government footage instead. The entire operation was bungled from the start. Nineteen soldiers died, and more than one hundred were wounded, as a small force of mostly poorly armed Cuban construction workers resisted. Nine helicopters were lost. The invasion, from a military point of view, was a farce, with the army awarding almost 275 medals for valor to seven thousand troops—of whom only about twenty-five hundred saw a limited form of combat.

Reagan proudly announced, "Our days of weakness are over. Our military forces are back on their feet and standing tall."

Halfway across the world, Reagan and Casey transformed Carter's limited support for the Afghan insurgents into the CIA's largest covert operation to date, totaling over $3 billion. They channeled aid through Pakistan's General Zia, a corrupt dictator who funneled the arms and dollars to the most extreme Afghan Islamist faction under Gulbuddin Hekmatyar, a man of legendary cruelty, whose forces were rumored to patrol the bazaars of Kabul throwing vials of acid in the faces of women not wearing full burkas and specialized in skinning prisoners alive. The CIA provided the insurgents between two thousand and twenty-five hundred U.S.-made Stinger missiles.

The U.S. helped both sides in the bloody Iran-Iraq War. Reagan, in 1983, sent special envoy Donald Rumsfeld to Baghdad to reassure Saddam Hussein of U.S. support. Under a license from the Commerce Committee, U.S. companies shipped several strains of anthrax, later used in Iraq's biological weapons program, and insecticides for chemical warfare.

As president, Reagan persisted in the scare talk, labeling the Soviets "the evil empire" and calling them "the focus of evil in the modern world."

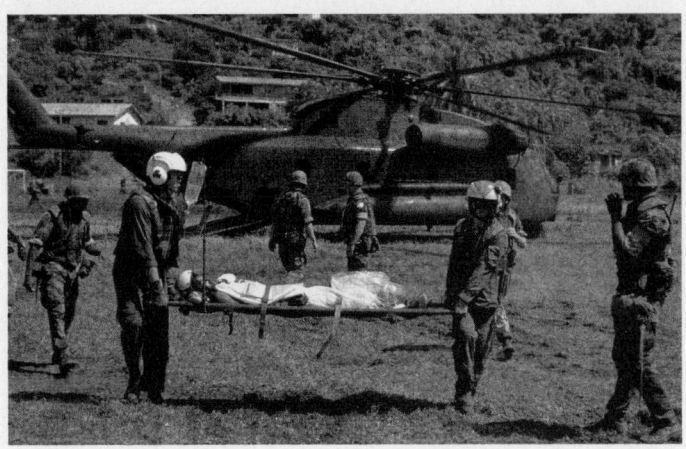

ABOVE: *In late 1983, the United States used instability in Grenada as a pretext to invade the tiny island nation and topple Maurice Bishop's revolutionary government. In a logistically bungled operation, nineteen U.S. soldiers died and more than a hundred were wounded. Nine helicopters were lost. Most of the troops were quickly withdrawn.*

BELOW: *Medical students wait to be evacuated during the U.S. invasion of Grenada. Reagan claimed that the invasion was necessary to rescue the endangered students, but the students were actually in little danger. When polled by the dean of the medical school, 90 percent said they wanted to stay.*

In late 1982, although the U.S. was ahead in every meaningful category, he said, "Today, in virtually every measure of military power the Soviet Union enjoys a decided advantage." And he amped up defense spending, which by 1985 had increased 35 percent over 1980 expenditures.

The U.S. arsenal now contained 11,200 strategic warheads to the Soviets' 9,900. New and upgraded weapons systems rolled off assembly lines, including the long-delayed and very costly MX program, which moved missiles around loops that hid their precise location, making them invulnerable to a Soviet first strike. Despite massive protests throughout Europe, the U.S. deployed ground-launch cruise missiles to Britain and Pershing II missiles to West Germany in November 1983. Some Soviet officials were convinced that a U.S. attack was imminent, as relations reached their lowest point in more than two decades.

To finance this, Reagan slashed federal support for discretionary programs, effectively transferring $70 billion from domestic programs to the military. He waged war on labor and the poor, busting the air traffic controllers union, meanwhile giving elegant parties in the White House for his millionaire friends. A sense of the 1890s Gilded Age—"the 400" of American society—returned to Washington.

In June 1982, almost a million people rallied against nuclear weapons in New York's Central Park. Among them was a young Columbia undergraduate named Barack Obama. The movement unnerved Reagan, who saw it as a serious threat to his re-election.

Despite all his bluster, Reagan, too, feared the possibility of nuclear war, which he associated with the biblical Armageddon. After watching the enormously popular 1983 ABC TV movie *The Day After*, Reagan wrote in his diary that it "left me very depressed."

And whether influenced by his wife or by her astrologer, we don't know, but, concerned about the bad blood he had engendered, Reagan began to rethink his approach to the Soviet Union. He later wrote in his memoirs, "Three years had taught me something surprising about the Russians. Many people at the top of the Soviet hierarchy were genuinely afraid of America and Americans." Incredibly, if this diary is to be believed, it had never dawned on President Reagan that the Soviets might indeed fear a U.S. first strike.

Hoping possibly to appease the growing antinuclear sentiment, in March 1983 Reagan proposed the Strategic Defense Initiative (SDI)—a space-based defense shield around the nation itself. Or as his critics called it: "Star Wars."

The fantasy of Star Wars became an enormously expensive antiballistic missile system. The Pentagon had begun research, in the 1970s, to counter a supposed Soviet breakthrough in energy beam weaponry, despite the fact that no such Soviet project existed.

In March 1985, an extraordinary development changed the course of history. Fifty-four-year-old Mikhail Gorbachev came to power in the Soviet Union. Like Henry Wallace years before, he was an agricultural expert. Like Khrushchev, he exhibited a rare degree of honesty while using diplomacy and luck to navigate a minefield of inefficiency and lies. He had traveled widely in the West and, like Khrushchev, sought above all to improve the lives of his people.

He saw the problem with clarity—to achieve parity with the U.S., the Soviets were spending nearly a quarter of their gross domestic product on defense. Some estimated even higher. Defense production consumed an enormous proportion of the Soviet budget. Their planned economy, which had stagnated since the late 1970s, was run by a military-industrial-academic establishment immune from reality. To revitalize society, he knew he would have to slash military spending.

Gorbachev set out to end the arms race and redeploy resources. He also took steps to end the war in Afghanistan, a conflict he thought from the beginning was a "fatal error" and a "bleeding wound."

As a very young man, he had witnessed the horrors of war, and in a series of extraordinary letters to Reagan proposed, like Henry Wallace forty years earlier, friendship and peaceful competition.

Reagan responded encouragingly. The two leaders met for the first time in Geneva in November 1985, connecting on a human level, if not a political one. Gorbachev continued writing letters through 1986, calling for the elimination of all nuclear weapons by 2000.

It didn't change Reagan's mind-set. The U.S. announced plans for a new series of nuclear tests and increased support for the mujahideen in Afghanistan.

In October 1986, Reagan and Gorbachev met in Reykjavik, Iceland. The two leaders would come within a few words of changing history forever.

Gorbachev offered a stunningly bold set of disarmament proposals. Even Paul Nitze, who had done so much to harm relations between the two countries, observed that the Soviet proposal was "the best we have received in twenty-five years." Nitze and Secretary of State George Shultz urged Reagan to accept a sweeping arms control deal. Reagan turned to ideologue Richard Perle, who feared such a deal would strengthen the Soviet economy. Perle warned that the agreement would effectively kill Reagan's Star Wars plan. Perle and the other advisors knew Reagan's vision of SDI was a pipe dream, a fantasy, and a costly one. Only Reagan believed it would work.

When negotiations stalled, Gorbachev urged Reagan to act boldly.

Reagan's response shocked observers. "It would be fine," he said, ". . . if we eliminated all nuclear weapons." Shultz agreed—"Let's do it." Gorbachev said he was ready to eliminate nuclear weapons if Reagan restricted SDI testing to the laboratory for ten years. Gorbachev and Soviet scientists knew that SDI would do nothing to protect the United States from a full-scale Soviet attack, but they feared U.S. moves to weaponize space and recoiled at the thought of abandoning the Anti-Ballistic Missile Treaty, one of the few tangible constraints on the nuclear arms race.

Shultz and even Paul Nitze tried to change Reagan's mind—tragically, they failed. Reagan explained that confining these tests to the laboratory would damage him politically at home, especially with his right-wing base. They had reached an impasse. The meeting ended.

As they were leaving the building, Gorbachev tried one last time. "Mr. President, I am prepared to go back inside right now and sign the documents . . . agreed upon if you will refrain from plans to militarize space." Reagan answered: "I'm extremely sorry." The two superpowers had come within a hairsbreadth of beginning the process of eliminating nuclear weapons, thwarted by a Star Wars fantasy that had hardly entered the laboratory in 1986. Gorbachev was furious and blamed the failure on Reagan's plan to exhaust the Soviet Union economically through an arms race. He explained to the Politburo that he was dealing not only with the "class enemy"—the capitalist United States—but with President Reagan, "who exhibited extreme primitivism, a caveman outlook, and

ABOVE: Reagan delivers a national television address explaining his Strategic Defense Initiative (SDI). Nicknamed "Star Wars," the cockamamie scheme for a missile defense shield would prove a deal breaker in Reagan's negotiations with Soviet leader Mikhail Gorbachev.

BELOW: Reagan and Gorbachev shake hands at a plenary session during the 1985 Geneva summit.

Gorbachev and Reagan meet during the summit in Reykjavík. Catching Reagan completely off guard, Gorbachev arrived with a strikingly bold set of disarmament proposals.

intellectual impotence." The U.S. has subsequently spent well more than $100 billion on SDI, with final costs projected to exceed a trillion dollars. With the problem of multiple decoys overwhelming the system, along with other issues, creation of an effective Strategic Defense Initiative, to this day, remains highly uncertain.

Both sides hoped to revive the talks. But, before that could happen, a scandal that same month rocked Reagan's administration. In October 1986, a cargo plane was shot down over Nicaragua. The only survivor admitted it was a CIA operation. Congressional hearings revealed an administration up to its eyeballs in illegality, corruption, blundering, and subterfuge involving American hostages in Lebanon, arms sales to both Iraq and Iran, ill-fated attempts to cultivate nonexistent "moderates" in Tehran, and collaboration with a whole set of unsavory characters, including Manuel Noriega in Panama.

In a flagrant violation of Congress's ban on U.S. support for overthrowing the Nicaraguan government, Americans also learned that the

Disappointed, Reagan and Gorbachev depart from Reykjavík. The two leaders had come remarkably close to completely eliminating nuclear weapons, but Reagan's refusal to abandon SDI shattered the prospect of total nuclear disarmament.

CIA mined Nicaraguan harbors, which provoked the conservative icon Senator Barry Goldwater to scold Bill Casey. "I am pissed off," he wrote. "This is an act violating international law. It is an act of war."

Details of the murky, convoluted operation consumed much of Reagan's last two years. Pathetically, he told a news conference that he was not fully informed of the Iran policy, one aspect of which was seriously flawed, and walked off. It was apparent that he had little grasp of, and less control over, what his underlings were up to. Reagan addressed the nation, stating, "A few months ago, I told the American people I did not trade arms for hostages. My heart and my best intentions still tell me that's true. But the facts and the evidence tell me it is not." As an apology, it wouldn't have worked for Nixon. But perhaps Ronald Reagan had too kindly an aura to have to defend himself, much less go to prison. And the Washington establishment apparently concluded that the country could not withstand another impeachment or forced resignation and thus allowed Reagan to serve out his term. He left office a befuddled old man.

His subordinates were not so lucky. Among those convicted of crimes were two national security advisors, one of whom attempted suicide, as well as Oliver North and Assistant Secretary of State Elliott Abrams, who would re-emerge in the second Bush administration. Defense Secretary Caspar Weinberger, Abrams, and several others were convicted or indicted but pardoned by the next president. The CIA director cheated his fate, dying of a brain tumor the day after the hearings began. Vice President George H. W. Bush managed to avoid prosecution. He insisted he was "out of the loop—no operational role." But in his private diary, which he never thought he'd be forced to release, he admitted, before the scandal began to break, "I am one of the few people that know fully the details." As a result, the independent counsel's final report noted that the criminal investigation of Bush was regrettably incomplete.

In the midst of this sordid affair, Gorbachev, wanting to salvage something, came to Washington in December 1987 and signed the Intermediate-Range Nuclear Forces Treaty, a major milestone. It was the first agreement ever to destroy an entire class of nuclear weapons, one in which the Soviet Union had superiority.

In Afghanistan, the Soviet withdrawal began in May 1988. When the Soviets sounded out the U.S. on collaborating to curb Islamic extremism, the U.S., having achieved its goals, washed its hands of the problems it had helped to create. Up to twenty thousand Arabs had flooded into Pakistan to join the jihad against the Soviet infidels, among them a very young Saudi construction heir able to support an army of volunteers—Osama bin Laden. Thousands more flocked to Pakistan's madrassas, where they were indoctrinated in radical Islam and recruited for jihad, often with books developed at the University of Nebraska at Omaha's Center for Afghanistan Studies with USAID funding and distributed by the CIA. The Saudis in the 1980s spent $75 billion to spread their brand of Wahhabi extremism.

A million Afghans died in the war. Five million—one-third of the population—had fled to Pakistan and Iran. In the late 1980s, Islamists linked to Pakistani intelligence seized control of Afghanistan. RAND expert Cheryl Benard, whose husband, Zalmay Khalilzad, served as U.S. ambassador to Afghanistan, said, "We made a deliberate choice . . . to throw the worst crazies against [the Soviets]. . . . We knew exactly who these people

Reagan with Lieutenant Colonel Oliver North and Nicaraguan contra leader Adolfo Calero in National Security Advisor Robert McFarlane's office. McFarlane and North, a gung-ho but unstable marine with delusions of grandeur and a knack for embellishment, were the principal plotters in the administration's illegal scheme to sell weapons to the Iranian government in order to fund the contras.

were, and what their organizations were like, and we didn't care. The reason we don't have moderate leaders in Afghanistan today is because we let the nuts kill them all." Among the victims of these American-armed and -trained fanatics were Afghan women, who were driven back into the dark ages. Warned repeatedly that the fanaticism he was unleashing would threaten U.S. interests, Bill Casey insisted the partnership between Christianity and Islam would endure, and in the spring of 1985 even backed mujahideen cross-border raids into the Soviet Union in the hopes of inciting Soviet Muslims to revolt.

Although Reagan left office in near disgrace, conservatives have anointed him one of the nation's great presidents, crediting him with restoring America's faith in itself after the failed presidencies of Johnson, Nixon, Ford, and Carter.

But what is Reagan's real legacy? Once a Roosevelt Democrat, he developed a contempt for government that was legendary. Yet, he spent enormous sums on the military while cutting social programs for the poor. He reduced taxes on the wealthy, doubled both the military budget and the national debt, and, in a revolutionary change, transformed the United States from the world's leading creditor nation in 1981 into the biggest debtor nation by 1985.

He deregulated industries, eroded environmental standards, defiantly ripping down the solar panels that Jimmy Carter had put on the White House roof, weakened the middle class, busted unions, heightened racial divides, widened the gap between rich and poor, and abetted companies in shipping manufacturing jobs abroad. He deregulated savings and loans institutions, which led to the first giant "too big to fail" government bailouts of troubled banks and failed savings and loans. By 1995, this would cost the taxpayers $87 billion.

Under the guise of privatization, and backed by Reagan's extolling of market forces, Wall Street went on an enormous "Greed Is Good" looting binge that resulted in October 1987 in the worst stock market collapse since the Great Depression.

In a parting gift to future conservatives, in 1987 the FCC, with Reagan's help, repealed the Fairness Doctrine, which had required broadcasters since the 1940s to give adequate and fair coverage to opposing views on issues of public importance. As a result Rush Limbaugh and talk radio exploded on the scene, finding a massive audience.

This and the gradual loosening of limitations on the number of stations a company could own had, by 1996, enabled the growth of a right-wing media empire. With it came a number of interlocked, well-funded conservative think tanks that helped shape a new Washington groupthink.

Playing up fears, resentments, and hatred of government, by the end of the 1990s, Clear Channel, Rupert Murdoch's Fox News, Talk Radio Network, Salem Radio, the U.S.A. Radio Network, and Radio America, as well as the proliferation of cable television networks, had created a movement that would dramatically lower the standards of American political discourse and doom the prospects for progressive change.

The Hoover Institution at Stanford, a respected conservative mecca, described Reagan as a man whose "spirit seems to stride over the country, watching us like a warm and friendly ghost." Even Democratic presidents like Clinton and Obama, whether pandering to conservative forces or suffering from historical amnesia, would bow to pressure to flaunt their religiosity, extol the virtues of a free capitalist marketplace, perpetuate the myth of the universal middle class, and trumpet the notion of American exceptionalism. They would feed the insatiable appetite of the military-industrial complex, expand the search for threatening enemies at home and abroad, and move heaven and earth to maintain the resulting empire.

Even in Nicaragua, though scolded, Reagan won the long contra war, wrecking its economy and exhausting the local population, who would soon lose faith in the Sandinistas' ability to bring progress to the country. By 1990, the religious, pro-Washington candidate, helped by U.S. funding as well as its embargo, triumphed in a democratic election, allowed by the supposedly communist Sandinistas, who stepped aside peacefully.

As far as Reagan's much-vaunted role in winning the Cold War, the lion's share of credit goes to Mikhail Gorbachev—a true visionary and, it turns out, the real democrat. If Reagan had entered into the sincere partnership offered by Gorbachev, as Roosevelt had done with Stalin in World War II, the world would have been transformed.

But Ronald Reagan, at the least, let the chance to rid the world of nuclear weapons slip through his fingers because he wouldn't let go of a space fantasy.

Appreciating Gorbachev's extraordinary effort, a leading Soviet expert on the U.S. warned his American counterparts, "We will do the most horrible thing to you; we will leave you without an enemy."

Unfortunately, he was wrong.

CHAPTER ELEVEN

or a glorious moment in the late 1980s, the world was a hopeful, even joyous, place. Protracted and bloody wars were ending in Afghanistan, Angola, Cambodia, and Nicaragua, and between Iran and Iraq. PLO leader Yasser Arafat, under pressure from Moscow, renounced terrorism and implicitly recognized Israel's right to exist.

Addressing the United Nations in December 1988, Mikhail Gorbachev made another dramatic bid to change the course of history. Gorbachev unilaterally declared that the Cold War was over: "the use or threat of force no longer can . . . be an instrument of foreign policy. This applies above all to nuclear arms. . . . Let me turn to the main issue—disarmament, without which none of the problems of the coming century can be solved. . . . The Soviet Union has taken a decision to reduce its armed forces . . . by 500,000 men. . . . We have decided to withdraw by 1991 six tank divisions from East Germany, Czechoslovakia, and Hungary, and to disband them. . . . Soviet forces stationed in those countries will be reduced by 50,000 men and their armaments, by 5,000 tanks. All Soviet divisions remaining . . . will become clearly defensive."

He promised to reveal Soviet plans for the "transition from the economy of armaments to an economy of disarmament" and called upon other military powers to do likewise through the United Nations. He proposed a 50 percent reduction in offensive strategic arms, asked for joint action to eliminate "the threat to the world's environment," urged banning weapons in outer space, and demanded an end to exploitation of the third world, including a "moratorium of up to 100 years on debt servicing by the least developed countries."

Still, he was not finished. He called for a UN-brokered cease-fire in Afghanistan as of January 1. In nine years of war, the Soviets had failed to defeat the Afghan insurgents despite deploying 100,000 troops, working closely with local Afghans, and building up the Afghan army and police. He proposed an international conference on Afghan neutrality and demilitarization and held out an olive branch to the incoming administration of George H. W. Bush, offering a "joint effort to put an end to an era of wars, confrontation and regional conflicts, to aggressions against nature, to the terror of hunger and poverty as well as to political terrorism. This is our common goal and we can only reach it together."

The *New York Times* proclaimed that not since Roosevelt and Churchill's Atlantic Charter had a world leader demonstrated a vision like Gorbachev's: "Breathtaking. Risky. Bold. Naive. . . . Heroic . . . his ideas merit—indeed, compel—the most serious response from President-elect Bush and other leaders." The *Washington Post* called it "a speech as remarkable as any ever delivered at the United Nations."

George H. W. Bush had not yet moved into the White House after trouncing Massachusetts governor Michael Dukakis in the 1988 election. Trailing by seventeen points that summer, Bush had struggled to overcome the so-called wimp factor.

It's odd that the recipient of the Distinguished Flying Cross, who had flown fifty-eight combat missions as a navy pilot during World War II and been shot down in the Pacific, would be derided as a "wimp. WASP. Weenie." "Every woman's first husband." "Bland conformist."

But, because of his nasal voice, sheltered upbringing, Yale education, and oil money background, he appeared to be the ultimate insider establishment candidate.

Most of his political offices had been appointments—ambassador to the United Nations and China and CIA chief. But none of Ronald Reagan's charisma had rubbed off on him. Reagan hadn't wanted him on the ticket.

Seeking to improve his chances, Bush followed the advice of, among

Reagan and Bush meeting with Gorbachev on Governors Island during Gorbachev's visit to New York for the UN address. Gorbachev sought their help on arms control and troop withdrawal, but Bush's advisors remained skeptical and the CIA, ravaged by right-wing "reformers," completely misread the changes occurring in the Soviet Union.

others, his oldest son, George W., adopting a more aggressive strategy against the reserved, stoic Dukakis, who came from Greek immigrant roots and was reluctant to counterattack.

He questioned Dukakis's patriotism and openly played the race card with a campaign ad about the furloughed murderer Willie Horton. Like Nixon, Bush appealed to voters' racism and fears of crime.

The strategy turned the tide, and Bush took office in January 1989, placing the destiny of much of mankind in the hands of two men who had witnessed firsthand the ravages of war—Bush as a victor, Gorbachev as a young eyewitness to Germany's brutal destruction of the USSR.

In the 1990s, with America searching for a new role in a rapidly changing world, the mass media began elevating the World War II generation to especially heroic dimensions. At the fiftieth anniversary of D-Day in 1994, the "Greatest Generation" was anointed. This became a nostalgic concept and sales of books, movies, and TV programs boomed. D-Day became the climactic battle of World War II. Even Pearl Harbor, in glorious Technicolor, was turned into a victory.

Conveniently, the media ignored or overlooked the fact that influential Americans, opposed to Roosevelt's New Deal, had aided and abetted the Third Reich—after the true nature of Hitler's anti-Semitic, murderous regime was known. The motive, whether hatred of communism, fascist sympathies, or simply greed, was rarely openly discussed.

Among these men was President Bush's own father, Prescott Bush. German coal and steel magnate Fritz Thyssen had been one of Hitler's early backers and much of his wealth was protected overseas by the Brown Brothers Harriman investment firm, through the holding company Union Banking Corporation, in an account managed by Prescott Bush.

In 1942, the U.S. government seized Union Banking Corporation, along with four other Thyssen-linked accounts managed by Bush. And after the war, the shares were returned to the American shareholders, including Bush. Bush wasn't alone in his dealings with the Nazis. Ford, GM, Standard Oil, Alcoa, ITT, General Electric, the munitions maker Du Pont, Eastman Kodak, Westinghouse, Pratt & Whitney, Douglass Aircraft, United Fruit, Singer, and International Harvester all continued to trade with Germany up to 1941, and many of their subsidiaries carried on operations throughout the war, from which the firms would later reap the profits.

Thus, almost fifty years after the start of World War II, in January 1989, the past once more echoed the present. Could Prescott Bush's son George, like John Kennedy, repudiate his father's murky past and partner with the communist Gorbachev in changing the world?

Bush perhaps pondered his options, but he was neither a deep nor a bold thinker. Several times he had scorned what he called the "vision thing," distrusting individualistic thinking. Like Harry Truman after World War II, he surrounded himself with communist-hating conservatives.

Among them were the strongly anticommunist Dick Cheney as his defense secretary, and as his deputy national security advisor, Robert Gates, the man who'd made his stripes as deputy to the fanatic William Casey. They all agreed that reaching out to Gorbachev would weaken Western resolve.

Whereas Gorbachev was calling for eliminating tactical nuclear weapons in Europe, an offer most Europeans applauded, the United States countered that the Soviet Union should remove 325,000 troops in exchange for a U.S. cut of 30,000.

Bush neglected to pursue real progress with the Soviet Union, but when hundreds of prodemocracy demonstrators were slaughtered in Beijing at Tiananmen Square by the Peoples Liberation Army—he placated Chinese leaders by condemning the crackdown publicly and banning military ties, but, behind the scenes, making it clear this would not jeopardize relations between China and the U.S.

Gorbachev pursued the reform of the Soviet system, rejecting the long-held view that controlling Eastern Europe was necessary to Soviet security. In a few extraordinary months in 1989 and 1990, all the Eastern and Central European communist governments fell, one by one, as the world watched in disbelief. It was possibly the most peaceful people's revolution ever carried out in recorded history—Poland, Estonia, Lithuania, Latvia, Hungary, Czechoslovakia, East Germany, and Romania changed their governments without fear.

On November 9, 1989, East and West Berliners jointly tore down the Berlin Wall, desecrating the Cold War's most reviled symbol. It was a grand moment, evidence of a new beginning. Yet many Americans hailed these actions as the ultimate vindication of the capitalist West after decades of Cold War. State Department policy planner Francis Fukuyama made a name for himself, declaring, "It was the end of history"—proclaim Western liberal democracy the final form of human government.

At Yalta, in early 1945, on the eve of Germany's surrender, Roosevelt, Stalin, and Churchill had gone a long way toward dividing Europe and Asia into Western and Soviet spheres of influence. This structure essentially lasted through proxy wars, near nuclear conflagrations, intense propaganda, and espionage activity for forty-five years.

Now, this was all changing—and quickly. Gorbachev hoped that a new trust might lead to the dissolution of NATO and the Warsaw Pact. And, astonishingly, he was even willing to allow East and West Germany to reunite, on the understanding that NATO would not expand eastward. Bush led him to believe so, but would be out of power by 1993.

Celebrants atop the falling Berlin Wall on November 9, 1989. Gorbachev saw Soviet communism's collapse as a new beginning, but many U.S. policy makers hailed it as the ultimate vindication.

And Gorbachev would pay the price for trusting America, as the Clinton and second Bush administrations expanded NATO right up to Russia's doorstep.

The Russians felt thoroughly betrayed, and although U.S. officials over the years have insisted that no such promises were ever given, recently released statements from the U.S. ambassador to the Soviet Union at the time and previously classified British and West German documents substantiate the Russian claims that there was a clear commitment.

It was becoming equally clear to some that the United States was not changing its colors to celebrate this new mood of peace. Barely a month after the Berlin Wall fell, in December 1989, with words of praise for Gorbachev's restraint in Eastern Europe barely out of his mouth, Bush launched an invasion of Panama.

Panamanian strongman Manuel Noriega had long been one of the

U.S. Drug Enforcement Administration (DEA) agents escort General Manuel Noriega onto a U.S. aircraft. Despite the fact that the Panamanian strongman had long enjoyed CIA funding and U.S. protection for assisting the contras in Nicaragua and fingering his drug cartel's rivals to the DEA, in December 1989, Bush sent some 15,000 troops to assist the 12,000 already in the country to overthrow Noriega and take down his Panamanian Defense Forces. Latin Americans angrily condemned the return to gunboat diplomacy.

U.S.'s errand boys in Central America. On the CIA payroll since the 1960s, corrupt and unscrupulous, he profited by assisting Colombia's Medellín drug cartel. His assistance to the contras in Nicaragua won him protection from top Reagan officials including Casey and Oliver North.

But a 1988 U.S. drug indictment and his overturning of Panama's 1989 presidential election convinced Bush that Noriega was more liability than asset. He acted. "Operation Just Cause," he called it, sending in fifteen thousand troops to assist the twelve thousand already in-country and leveling the impoverished Panama City neighborhood of El Chorillo, which abutted the headquarters of the Panamanian Defense Forces, killing hundreds of civilians.

This was justified as part of the "war on drugs" declared by Nixon in 1971, which was now being shifted to fight production at the source, which meant, among other things, targeting foreign countries, if need be, for military action. Noriega would be sent to jail in the U.S. for drug trafficking.

To much of the world, the invasion was shocking and illegal, but to most Americans, indoctrinated with the idea of a war on drugs, it was business as usual in America's backyard.

Congress further failed to challenge Bush's flagrant violation of the 1973 War Powers Act. The new message was clear.

Joint Chiefs chairman Colin Powell declared, "We have to put a shingle outside our door saying 'Superpower Lives Here,' no matter what the Soviets do." Soviet hardliners, concerned about Gorbachev's reforms, understood that their concessions would not curb U.S. bellicosity or predatory behavior. They might in fact embolden the U.S. to act more recklessly. It did—within fourteen months, Bush once again showed how tough he could be. This time in the Middle East.

The Reagan administration had cozied up during the Iran war to Iraq's Saddam Hussein, turning a blind eye to his repeated use of chemical weapons, sometimes against his own people, made in part from U.S.-supplied chemicals. When tensions flared between Iraq and oil-rich Kuwait, the U.S. ambassador April Glaspie personally assured Saddam that Bush "wanted better and deeper relations" and had "no opinion" on Iraq's border dispute.

Hussein took this as a green light from Bush and, the following week, with an estimated 250,000 troops and fifteen hundred tanks, took over Kuwait with little resistance. Glaspie effectively confirmed that she had led Hussein on, telling the *New York Times*, "I didn't think—and nobody else did—that the Iraqis were going to take all of Kuwait."

Long desiring a stronger footprint in the Middle East, the U.S. sent Secretary of Defense Cheney, General Powell, and General Norman Schwarzkopf to meet with Saudi King Fahd, to convince him to accept a large American military force as a buffer.

When they showed the king photos of Iraqi troops and tanks at the Saudi border, and even across it, the king, upset, reacted and asked for help. But the U.S. photos had been doctored to show that Iraqi forces were digging in with fortifications and trenches close to the border. There is no evidence that Hussein ever intended to invade Saudi Arabia.

Secretary of Defense Dick Cheney meets with Crown Prince Sultan, the Saudi minister of defense and aviation. After U.S. ambassador April Glaspie met with Saddam Hussein in Baghdad on July 25, 1990, assuring him that Bush "wanted better and deeper relations" and had "no opinion" on Iraq's border dispute with Kuwait, Cheney, along with Generals Colin Powell and Norman Schwarzkopf, rushed to meet with the Saudis, showing them doctored photos of an alleged Iraqi troop buildup on their border with Kuwait. Convincing King Fahd to allow a large U.S. military force onto Saudi soil, the U.S. gained its long-sought toehold in the region.

The deception was exposed when a Japanese newspaper obtained photos taken by a Soviet commercial satellite company showing no military activity near the border. *Newsweek* followed up, calling it "the case of the 'missing' military presence."

Pressure nonetheless mounted quickly. If Hussein took Saudi Arabia, he'd have control of at least one-fifth, if not more, of the world's oil supply. The Israeli press led the charge, decrying, in the words of one newspaper editorial, "U.S. impotence and the weakness of . . . Bush [who] resembles Chamberlain in his knowing capitulation to Hitler."

The ever-adaptable Bush turned the tired analogy on its head, repeatedly comparing Saddam to Hitler. Concerned that Saudi Arabia might come up with an alternative solution to the crisis, he quickly announced U.S. troops were headed to the Persian Gulf. Meanwhile, Kuwaiti officials hired the world's largest public relations firm, Hill & Knowlton, to orchestrate the largest foreign-funded effort ever undertaken to manipulate U.S. public opinion.

In October 1990, in a congressional caucus organized by Hill & Knowlton, a fifteen-year-old Kuwaiti girl testified that she'd been a volunteer in a Kuwaiti hospital when Iraqi troops burst in. She claimed tearfully, "They took the babies out of the incubators. They took the incubators and left the children to die on the cold floor."

It was a masterful performance. Bush cited the story repeatedly in making the case for war. "It turns your stomach," he said, "to listen to the tales of those that have escaped the brutality of Saddam the invader. Mass hangings, babies pulled from incubators and scattered like firewood across the floor."

It was later discovered that the young witness had never been at the hospital but was the daughter of the Kuwaiti ambassador to the U.S. and a member of the ruling family. By the time the fraud was exposed, U.S. bombing of Baghdad had begun.

The U.S. public was nonetheless divided. The leaders of Saudi Arabia and especially the loathsome anti-Semitic regime of Kuwait were cruel despots—hardly enamored of democracy for their own people. Nor were crucial U.S. interests at stake, when Iraq's and Kuwait's oil combined constituted less than 10 percent of U.S. imports.

In late November, Cheney warned that Iraq could have a nuclear device within a year and would likely use it. It was a card Cheney would play again in coming years. NSC Advisor Brent Scowcroft added a terrorist threat for good measure.

Stung by the criticisms of his illegal Panama invasion, Bush took the measure to Congress, and, though antiwar protesters filled the streets, Congress narrowly passed the resolution in January 1991. By that time, more than 560,000 U.S. troops were in the region. The total would reach 700,000.

Schwarzkopf claimed the U.S. was facing a million-man Iraqi land force, with high-quality Soviet tanks, that was willing to use chemical weapons.

Operation Desert Storm, which began on January 17, 1991, by openly sending combat troops in huge numbers into a Middle Eastern country, marked the beginning of a new era in American geopolitics. It would take the country deeper into a rabbit hole it had never been in before.

For five weeks with new, awe-inspiring, television-friendly, high-tech weapons, including cruise and Tomahawk missiles and laser-guided bombs, U.S. airstrikes pulverized Iraq's communications, military, and industrial infrastructure. On television, the American population had never seen firepower like this. It was the beginning of the video game era, and it was dazzling as Iraq was reduced, according to the UN, to a near-apocalyptic preindustrial age. The ground invasion lasted one hundred hours, with U.S. and Saudi forces routing demoralized, poorly trained Iraqi troops from Kuwait. U.S. forces slaughtered escaping Iraqis along what became known as the "highway of death." A new category of weapons made out of depleted uranium was born. Their radioactivity and chemical toxicity would produce cancers and birth defects. Victims would include U.S. soldiers who suffered mysteriously for years from what became known as Gulf War Syndrome.

Enough of the Republican Guard escaped to ensure that Saddam would retain his hold on power. Bush and his advisors decided not to push to Baghdad to overthrow the regime, as such a move would bolster Iraq's enemy, Iran, and might antagonize America's Arab allies.

But American officials urged the Iraqis to rise up and topple Hussein themselves. When Iraqi Kurds and Shiites responded in large numbers, the U.S. stood idly by while the government crushed the uprisings using poison gas and helicopter gunships. Despite this bloodletting, Bush crowed, "The ghosts of Vietnam have been laid to rest beneath the sands of the Arabian desert." He called it a New World Order.

But among those who saw through what he called a "burst of triumphalism" was the notoriously peevish conservative *Washington Post* columnist George Will, who wrote: "If that war, in which the United States and a largely rented and Potemkin coalition of allies smashed a nation with the GNP of Kentucky, could . . . make America feel 'good about itself,' then America should not feel good about itself."

More than two hundred thousand Iraqis died in the war and its immediate aftermath—approximately half of them civilians. The U.S. death toll stood at less than two hundred.

RIGHT: Antiwar protesters filled the streets in January 1991.

BELOW (LEFT TO RIGHT): General Colin Powell, General Norman Schwarzkopf, and Paul Wolfowitz listen to Dick Cheney (not pictured) at a press conference during Operation Desert Storm. The United States' use of a gargantuan force of 700,000 troops during the war was justified by the massive estimates of Iraqi troops by Powell, Cheney, and Schwarzkopf, who predicted a half million, a million, and a million, respectively.

Operation Desert Storm began on January 17, 1991. The United States pummeled Iraqi facilities for five weeks with its new high-tech weapons. After crippling Iraq's communications and military infrastructure, U.S. and Saudi forces attacked battered, demoralized, and outnumbered Iraqi troops in Kuwait, who put up little if any resistance. U.S. forces slaughtered escaping Iraqis along what became known as the "highway of death."

"By God, we've kicked the Vietnam syndrome once and for all!" Bush rejoiced. But privately, in his diary, he was more circumspect, admitting he was experiencing "no feeling of euphoria . . . no battleship *Missouri* surrender . . . to make this akin to World War II, to separate Kuwait from Korea and Vietnam." Something was clearly missing. The laurels of victory and a true peace would be squandered, not in the sands of Kuwait, but in Bush's lack of foresight and vision in failing to acquire a true ally in the Soviet Union. Just a few weeks after signing the START I Treaty, as he prepared to move toward greater autonomy for the Soviet republics, Gorbachev was placed under house arrest by communist hardliners in August 1991.

Boris Yeltsin, president of the Russian Republic, led a popular uprising that returned Gorbachev to power, but time was running out. For the people, there had been too many changes too fast and not enough order.

Condemned and rejected, on Christmas Day 1991, Gorbachev, one of the most visionary and transformative leaders of the twentieth century, resigned, having been rejected by the Russian people, who had no idea what was in store for them.

But neither did George Bush. His 91 percent approval rating at the end of the Persian Gulf War blinded leading Democrats to his electoral vulnerability, leaving the door open for little-known Arkansas governor Bill Clinton to run as a "new kind of Democrat."

A charming, compassionate man who wanted to be all things to all people, Clinton defied the odds and upset George Bush. His victory was abetted by third-party candidate Ross Perot, a conservative businessman, who siphoned off 19 percent of the popular vote.

It seemed like a golden moment. The United States had been blaming social and political upheaval on the Soviet Union for the previous forty-six years. Now, with a Democrat in the White House, how could the U.S. justify the bloated military budget that for decades had diverted resources, as in the Soviet Union, from needed development? Would there at last be the celebrated peace dividend?

The euphoria over Clinton proved short-lived. Republicans wounded Clinton out of the gate by blocking his plan for the open admission of gays into the military, also questioning his avoidance of service during Vietnam. Even more damagingly, the Republicans and their business allies waged a propaganda war to frighten and confuse the public and defeat Clinton's ambitious health care plan that would have covered tens of millions of uninsured citizens. Future Tea Party leader Richard Armey, the chair of the House Republican Conference, called it "the Battle of the Bulge of big-government liberalism."

Among advanced industrial countries, only the United States and apartheid South Africa lacked a national health care system. With the conservative media trumpeting this Republican victory and exaggerating its significance, a Republican "renaissance" gained momentum. In the 1994 midterm elections, Republicans achieved control of both branches of Congress for the first time in forty years. Amazingly, at a time when there were no international crises, both parties lurched further to the right.

Clinton, without much of a mandate and vulnerable, ended Aid to Families with Dependent Children, which had helped poor families since the Great Depression. He supported the war on drugs and

Bush and Gorbachev sign the START I treaty at the Kremlin in Moscow. The treaty would limit both sides to 6,000 strategic nuclear warheads and 1,600 delivery systems. Gorbachev also pushed for the elimination of tactical nuclear weapons, a move endorsed in a study commissioned by Joint Chiefs Chairman Colin Powell. But that was rejected by the Pentagon. Despite the setbacks, both sides made significant unilateral cuts in their nuclear arsenals that would reduce, though not eliminate, the danger of nuclear holocaust.

tough-on-crime legislation. The U.S. prison population exploded from a half million in 1980 to 2 million by 2000, many of whom were convicted of victimless drug crimes.

Meanwhile, post-Soviet Russia was moving drastically to the right. Yeltsin turned to Harvard economist Jeffrey Sachs and other experts such as Undersecretary of the Treasury Lawrence Summers for help in privatizing the economy. With them came the G7, the International Monetary Fund, and the World Bank, advocating a form of economic "shock therapy" yet unknown to the Russian people.

The flirtation with unfettered, brass-knuckles capitalism proved surreal and disastrous. Yeltsin quickly deregulated the economy, privatized state enterprises and resources, eliminated desperately needed subsidies and price controls, and established privately owned monopolies.

The people called it the "great grab," as the nation's factories and resources were sold for a pittance to opportunistic private investors, including former communist officials who became multimillionaires overnight.

While a younger, moneyed generation was celebrating its new freedoms, most Russians' life savings were wiped out by hyperinflation, and tens of millions lost their jobs. Life expectancy plummeted from 67 to 57 years for men, 76 to 70 for women. Russia's economy shrank to the size of that of the Netherlands, as it was rapidly becoming a Second World power.

The Western aid and debt relief that Sachs had promised never materialized. Sachs later blamed Cheney and Paul Wolfowitz for pursuing "long-term U.S. military dominance over . . . Russia." Gorbachev, in his recent memoir *Alone with Myself*, reflected that Yeltsin was preferred by Bush's inner circle and eventually Bush himself as "his goals—to dismember and liquidate the USSR—matched the goals of the American leadership." The idea was that a "weakened Russia under Yeltsin was more in line with U.S. interests than the prospect of a renewed USSR that Gorbachev was struggling for."

Anti-Americanism came back into vogue. Russians bristled as Clinton pushed U.S. involvement in the energy-rich Caspian Basin and expanded NATO to include Hungary, Poland, and the Czech Republic. Ninety-two-year-old Cold War architect George Kennan called this "an enormous and historic strategic error."

Many Russians were coming to believe that the U.S. was imposing "a reverse Iron Curtain" on Russia's borders. Though Clinton professed himself a friend of Yeltsin, polls showed 77 percent of the Russian population preferring order over the 9 percent choosing this form of "democracy," with many pining for the "good old days" of Stalin.

Perceiving the increasingly unpopular Yeltsin as a drunkard, they deplored his illegal shutdown of and armed assault on the elected parliament. He suspended the constitution and ruled primarily by decree for the rest of the decade.

Polling single-digit approval ratings, Yeltsin resigned on the eve of the new century, to be replaced by former KGB officer Vladimir Putin, who brought Russia back from the brink by restoring a strong, tyrannical, centralized power—in the Old Russian style.

Throughout the 1990s, Clinton's administration, eager to take

President Clinton and Russian leader Boris Yeltsin share a laugh during a press conference at FDR's home in Hyde Park, New York, in October 1995. Though Clinton extolled Yeltsin as the architect of democracy, the Russian people deplored his illegal shutdown of and armed assault on the elected parliament, his launching of bloody wars against the breakaway republic of Chechnya in 1994 and again in 1999, and his stewardship of the collapsing economy. Gorbachev denounced Yeltsin as a "liar" who had more privileges than the Russian tsars.

economic advantage wherever possible, pushed for building pipelines to ship the rich oil and gas reserves, valued in the $3 trillion to $6 trillion range, from former Soviet republics in Central Asia along routes that bypassed Iran and Russia.

Meanwhile, the fundamentalist Taliban took over Afghanistan and welcomed back the wealthy Saudi jihadist Osama bin Laden to establish Al-Qaeda—"The Base"—in their country. Although he'd been a part of the CIA netherworld of the 1980s, bin Laden was now totally focused on driving the U.S. and its allies out of the Muslim world—decrying especially the presence of U.S. troops in Saudi Arabia, Islam's holiest land. Pointing as well to blind U.S. support for Israel, in 1992 he issued his first religious fatwa. Two mysterious bombings followed in Saudi Arabia, killing more than twenty U.S. military personnel.

Bin Laden denied Al-Qaeda's involvement, and the Saudi government, with its close ties to the very rich bin Laden family, steered the FBI investigation toward Iran, a perceived U.S. enemy.

In 1998, U.S. embassies in Kenya and Tanzania were bombed, killing more than two hundred. In 2000, bin Laden claimed responsibility for Al-Qaeda striking the U.S. Navy ship *Cole*, killing seventeen.

Since the Gulf War, UN weapons inspectors had been overseeing destruction of Iraq's weapons of mass destruction (WMD) as U.S.- and British-enforced no-fly zones and harsh UN sanctions had caused immense suffering. The Clinton administration falsely blamed the deaths of some estimated half million children from disease and malnutrition on dictator Saddam Hussein.

In a *60 Minutes* interview, correspondent Lesley Stahl confronted Secretary of State Madeleine Albright. "We have heard," Stahl said, "that a half million children have died . . . that's more children than died in Hiroshima," and asked, "Is the price worth it?" Albright replied, "I think this is a very hard choice, but . . . we think the price is worth it."

The tough-talking Albright insisted that Hussein's use of WMD was a great threat to U.S. security. And on another occasion, she said quite openly, "If we have to use force, it is because we are America; we are the indispensable nation. We stand tall and we see further than other countries into the future."

Although the United States faced no clear threat from hostile nations, the Clinton administration proved even more tough-minded on defense than its Republican adversaries and squandered the promised peace dividend in a new wave of spending.

In January 2000, his administration added $115 billion to the Pentagon's projected five-year defense plan.

It continued spending profusely on missile defense. Clinton also refused to sign the Ottawa Landmines Treaty and oversaw a significant increase in U.S. arms sales to almost 60 percent of the world's market by 1997—the lion's share going to countries with deplorable human rights records.

Political scientist Chalmers Johnson summed up these years in 2004: "In the first post–Cold War decade, we mounted many actions to perpetuate and extend our global power, including wars and 'humanitarian' interventions in Panama, the Persian Gulf, Somalia, Haiti, Bosnia, Colombia and Serbia, while maintaining unchanged our Cold War deployments in East Asia and in the Pacific."

This emerging bipartisan foreign policy seemed set in stone. There would be no debate. Clinton saw U.S. actions abroad not as those of an aggressive, resource-hungry empire but as a necessary force for stability in a new world order based on America's concepts of democracy and free markets. He did nothing in the end to challenge the basic structures of this empire.

Although his last two years were severely damaged by a sex scandal with an intern and an embarrassing trial for impeachment that once more blinded a sensationalist media to far more significant events, "Slick Willie," as some called him, in his inimitable way, avoided major disasters. Benefiting from a resurgent global economy favoring U.S. markets and finance, Clinton left behind a temporarily prosperous country with a huge surplus. Expecting to capitalize on parts of this legacy, his party nominated Vice President Al Gore in 2000. An increasingly forward-looking, experienced man who repeatedly warned of a looming world ecological disaster caused by a changing climate that needed controlling, he would back away from this issue considerably during the final campaign, the here and now being of more importance to the average voter.

The Republicans countered with a self-proclaimed "compassionate conservative," Texas governor George W. Bush, son of George H. W. and grandson of Prescott.

The debates between the candidates thoroughly misled voters about the policies Bush would actually pursue once in office.

Moderator: "Welcome to the second election 2000 debate between the Republican candidate for president, Governor George W. Bush of Texas, and the Democratic candidate, Vice President Al Gore."

Moderator: "People watching here tonight they want to base their vote on differences between the two of you as president, is there any difference?"

Gore: "I just think, Jim, that this is an absolutely unique period in world history and have a fundamental choice to make, are we going to step up to the plate as a nation the way we did after World War II, the way that generation of heroes said, okay, the United States is going to be the leader. And the world benefited tremendously from the courage that they showed in those postwar years. I think that in the aftermath of the Cold War it's time for us to do something very similar, to step up to the plate, to provide the leadership, leadership on the environment, leadership to make sure the world economy keeps moving in the right direction. Again, that means not running big deficits here and not squandering our surplus, it means having intelligent decisions that keep our prosperity going and shepherds that economic strength so that we can provide that leadership role."

Bush: "Yeah, I'm not sure that the role of the United States is going around the world and say, this is the way it's got to be. We can help, and maybe it's just our difference in government, the way we view government. You know I want to empower people, I want to help people help themselves, not have government tell people what to do. I, I just don't think it's the role of the United States to walk into a country and say, 'We do it this way, so should you.' So I'm not exactly sure where the vice president is coming from, but I think what we need to do is convince people who live in the lands they live in to build the nations. Maybe I'm missing something here. I mean are we going to have kind of a nation-building corps from America. Absolutely not. Our military is meant to fight and win war. That's what it's meant to do, and when it gets overextended morale drops. But I want to be judicious as to how to use the military. It needs to be in our vital interest, the mission needs to be clear and the exit strategy obvious."

As he embarked on one of the country's most ambitious periods of nation-building, George Bush actually did more in his eight years in office than any other president to bury the World War II myth of an American power moderated by fairness. In hindsight, it was his capacity to conceal his reactionary intentions that years later still confounded and shocked many Americans.

It started with the 2000 election itself—the most scandalous in U.S. history—wounding perhaps fatally the legitimacy of the political process in this country. Coming as it did at the beginning of a new century, it felt to many like an ominous oracle.

Al Gore won the popular mandate by more than 540,000 votes but lost Florida when more than 10 percent of African Americans were disqualified by an antiquated state voting system, overseen by Florida governor Jeb Bush, George's younger brother, and Florida secretary of state Katherine Harris, Bush's state campaign manager.

Mimicking the shenanigans of a banana republic, the U.S. Supreme Court, without precedent, surprisingly intervened in the Florida election process and voted five to four to stop a recount, thus handing Bush the election. The majority of these justices had been appointed in administrations in which Bush's father was either president or vice president.

If it had happened in another country, it would have been denounced by the United States as a coup.

The dissenting judges wrote, "Although we may never know with complete certainty the identity of the winner of this year's presidential election, the identity of the loser is perfectly clear. It is the nation's confidence in the judge as an impartial guardian of the rule of law."

On a drizzly January day in 2001, George W. Bush, the forty-third president, was given the oath of office. His inauguration betokened the lack of accountability that would characterize his administration. Thousands of protesters were isolated in zones far from the cameras. In a manner befitting a Roman emperor, surrounded by an entourage of true believers, Bush would hold fewer press conferences than any other president in history.

Compassion would be in limited supply, as most of his top appointees hailed from a little-known group called the Project for the New American Century (PNAC), spearheaded by William Kristol and Robert Kagan, which had been organized in 1997 to rekindle the neoconservative vision of unchallenged U.S. hegemony.

It included Defense Secretary Donald Rumsfeld, his deputy Paul Wolfowitz, and Vice President Dick Cheney. They deplored the fact that the U.S. had lost its way under Clinton and called for a return to moral clarity and Reaganesque military strength. They demanded increased defense spending, complete domination of space, deployment of a sweeping missile defense system, and the ability to "fight and decisively win multiple, simultaneous major theater wars" and to police "critical regions," especially the oil-rich Middle East. Their first order of business was toppling Iraq's Saddam Hussein, circumventing the UN Security Council if necessary.

Gloomy and pathologically secretive Dick Cheney would dominate the administration to an extent no vice president had ever done before and made it clear that, with Republicans controlling both houses of Congress, the U.S. was playing by a much tougher set of rules.

The first President Bush and Bill Clinton had made efforts at diplomacy and coalition-building, but Bush the younger, in his sense of defiance toward his father, came to resemble more a degenerate heir to an admired Roman emperor.

In Bush's mind, both his father and the sexually undisciplined Bill Clinton were weak. Ronald Reagan was his idea of "strength" and a higher father. After all, Bush and the neocons believed that Reagan beat the Russians.

Ironically, in early 2001, *Gladiator* was named the best film of 2000—a worldwide success celebrating Rome's harsh militarism and depicting a perverted leadership that spelled the fall of the Roman Empire.

Neoconservatives' contempt for the United Nations had always been a given, but now it seemed they were isolating themselves almost entirely from the world community. The U.S. failed to ratify the International Criminal Court treaty that Clinton and virtually every other Western democratic leader had negotiated.

The administration rejected the comprehensive Test Ban Treaty, which 150 nations had signed. Bush repudiated the Kyoto Protocol on Global Warming and, to the shock of the Russians, abrogated the crucial 1972 anti–ballistic missile treaty in order to expand the unproven Missile Defense Program. The media asked few questions about these abrupt reversals in policy.

Bush suspended talks with North Korea on its long-range missile program and disavowed the Middle East peace process. But that did not reflect disinterest in the Middle East. To the contrary, as Ralph Nader put it, the Bush administration was "marinated in oil." Cheney put together a highly secretive energy task force that laid out plans to control the world's oil supply.

Cheney had made his intentions clear in 1999 to oil industry executives when he said, "The Middle East, with two-thirds of the world's oil and the lowest cost, is still where the prize ultimately lies."

Signs of an impending attack on the U.S. abounded in the summer of 2001. Intercepted Al-Qaeda messages said that "something spectacular" was about to happen. Counterterrorism chief Richard Clarke testified that CIA director George Tenet was running around Washington with his "hair on fire," trying to get the attention of National Security Advisor Condoleezza Rice and President Bush.

But Defense Secretary Rumsfeld and Rice, a former Chevron board member, with a double-hulled oil tanker named after her, were preoccupied with ballistic missile defense and reforming the Pentagon. Intelligence agencies issued threat reports with headlines like "Bin Laden Threats Are Real" or "Bin Laden Determined to Strike in U.S." But Bush could not focus his attention, as he spent more time away from Washington than any recent president, often at his Crawford, Texas, ranch chopping wood. He did not enjoy riding horses, unlike his hero Reagan.

At his presidential daily briefing on August 6, at which the threat of Al-Qaeda operatives' hijacking planes was discussed, Bush disdainfully told his CIA briefer, "All right. You've covered your ass, now." Yet with a straight face, Bush told a news conference in April 2004, "Had I any inkling whatsoever that the people were going to fly airplanes into buildings, we would have moved heaven and earth to save the country."

Rice was equally disingenuous: "I don't think anybody could have predicted . . . that they would try to use an airplane as a missile, a hijacked airplane as a missile," though the FBI was issuing reports of individuals taking flying lessons who had no interest in learning how to land.

As dissatisfaction was mounting over Bush's incompetent governance, the terrorists struck the U.S.A. in a highly ingenious and dramatic fashion—9/11, it was thereafter to be called. The hijackers flew planes into the premier symbols of U.S. imperial power—Wall Street and the Pentagon. More than 3,000 people lost their lives. In New York, more than 2,700 people were killed, including some 500 who hailed from ninety-one different countries.

The nation watched in horror as flames engulfed the Twin Towers of the World Trade Center before their stunning collapse. How could this happen to the U.S.? Who would dare attack us in the heart of our empire, in a manner so naked, so low-tech? Where was this New World Order? Had we, as a nation, not gotten it right? Were we not good enough? Had we not contained the evil for sixty years since World War II? Had we not restrained ourselves from dropping the bomb since Hiroshima and Nagasaki?

And now, to some very powerful American leaders, it was as if they, the outliers of empire, these terrorists, had dropped Hiroshima on us, or at the very least another Pearl Harbor. The neocons called for all-out war.

On that day, a prodigious anger was unleashed on the world. An enormous Pandora's box of dark energy and pent-up fear of chaos reminiscent of the late-eighteenth-century French Revolution all came together in a self-righteousness that would spawn a crusade against not only bin Laden and his followers but against all "evil" in the world.

For Bush, not only was it his destiny to be a war president, but this was a Great Awakening—on a global scale. From atop the rubble at the World Trade Center, Bush proclaimed: "Our responsibility to history is already clear, to answer to these attacks and rid the world of evil."

The world, for the most part, responded with great empathy for America. Vladimir Putin of Russia was one of the first to offer help. Major Islamic figures denounced the attacks as a crime against humanity and Osama bin Laden as a fraud, a person who had no right to issue religious edicts and no religious training.

Chris Hedges, a veteran Middle East journalist, wrote several years later: "The tragedy was that if we had the courage to be vulnerable, if we had built on that empathy, we would be far safer and more secure today than we are. We responded exactly as these terrorist organizations wanted us to respond. They wanted us to speak the language of violence."

In the recent past, American leaders, especially Harry Truman at the end of World War II, Lyndon Johnson, Richard Nixon, and Ronald Reagan, had dangerously overreacted to the appearance of vulnerability—Johnson most dramatically, sacrificing the Great Society to his fear of failure in Vietnam. Perhaps this is the Achilles' heel of the American political process. Compassion or empathy is in short supply and easily dismissed

The smoldering rubble of the fallen World Trade Center buildings in New York City two days after the Al-Qaeda attacks of September 11, 2001.

as naiveté or softness. Yet it is compassion for the other that, in the end, has distinguished our greatest leaders, be they Washington, Jefferson, Lincoln, Roosevelt, or, on other fronts, people such as Martin Luther King, Jr.

Had Al Gore been in office instead of being derided by the media as an annoying know-it-all, might he not have emotionally connected to a world that had hardened in its hatred of U.S. policies? Might he not have acted in humbler fashion and pursed the terrorists with the traditional structures of diplomacy, intelligence services, and firm police action? Would not the same results have been achieved without making new enemies, who could be perceived as martyrs to a young generation of emerging radicals? Would he have kicked off a truly virtual World War III?

George Bush instead put the world on notice: "Every nation, in every region, now has a decision to make. Either you are with us or you are with the terrorists." He proclaimed it a monumental struggle between good and evil. Bush told the world's citizenry, "You're either with us or against us," and many reacted with disgust and anger.

Chalmers Johnson wrote that "Americans like to say the world changed as the result of September 11," but that it was more accurate to say that America was becoming "a new Rome, the greatest colossus in history no longer bound by international law, the concerns of allies, or any constraints on its use of military force. . . . The American people were still largely in the dark about why they had been attacked or why their State Department began warning them against tourism in an ever-growing list of foreign countries. . . . But a growing number finally began to grasp what most non-Americans already knew and had experienced over the previous half century—namely, that the United States was something other than what it professed to be, that it was, in fact, a military juggernaut intent on world domination."

Instead of explaining the real reasons for the attacks—Al-Qaeda's fierce opposition to U.S. troops in Saudi Arabia and to U.S. support for Israel in its struggle with the Palestinians—Bush mouthed platitudes, asking, "Why do they hate us?" He answered, "They hate our freedoms—our freedom of religion, our freedom of speech, our freedom to vote and assemble and disagree with each other."

How ironic that Bush 41 had actually squandered world peace by unleashing in Panama and the first Iraq attack the furies of war, and that his son, striking out blindly and virtually bankrupting his nation precisely as bin Laden hoped he would, had now found his destiny in his father's ancestral genes as "America's War President"—in a war that by Dick Cheney's reckoning could "last forever."

CHAPTER
TWELVE

For most Americans, 9/11 was a terrible tragedy. For George Bush and Dick Cheney it was that plus more—a chance to implement the agenda that their neoconservative allies had been working up for decades. The Project for the New American Century's recent report titled "Rebuilding America's Defenses" had stated that "the process of transformation . . . is likely to be a long one, absent some catastrophic and catalyzing event—like a new Pearl Harbor." Al-Qaeda, in their minds, had given them their Pearl Harbor. And within minutes of the attack, the Bush team leaped into action.

With Bush in Florida, Vice President Cheney and his legal counsel, David Addington, took charge, arguing that the president, as a wartime commander-in-chief, could act virtually unfettered by legal constraints.

On September 12, already looking past Al-Qaeda's Osama bin Laden group in Afghanistan, Bush, back in Washington, instructed counterterrorism chief Richard Clarke, "See if Saddam did this. See if he's linked in any way."

Clarke recalled, "It was Iraq, Saddam, find out; get back to me." An interviewer asked, "And the reaction you got that day from the defense secretary, Donald Rumsfeld, from his assistant, Paul Wolfowitz?" Clarke replied, "Well, Donald Rumsfeld said, when we talked about bombing the Al-Qaeda infrastructure in Afghanistan, he said there were no good targets in Afghanistan. Let's bomb Iraq. And we said but Iraq had nothing to do with this. And that didn't seem to make much difference."

Donald Rumsfeld had already, on September 11, ordered strike plans for Iraq. "Go massive," he said. "Sweep it all up. Things related and not."

Within a matter of days, Bush announced before a joint session of Congress that the United States was embarking on a global war: "From this day forward, any nation that continues to harbor or support terrorism will be regarded by the United States as a hostile regime."

At home, twelve hundred men were quickly arrested and detained, another eight thousand sought for interrogation, mostly Muslims. Bush rushed a 362-page U.S.A. Patriot Act through Congress. Senators had no time to read the bill, let alone debate it.

Only Senator Russ Feingold of Wisconsin voted against it, insisting: "Preserving our freedom is one of the main reasons that we are now engaged in this new war on terrorism. We will lose that war without firing a shot if we sacrifice the liberties of the American people."

Bush cloaked White House deliberations in an unprecedented veil of secrecy and, in 2002, empowered the National Security Agency to conduct warrantless wiretaps and monitor U.S. citizens' emails on a massive scale in violation of legal reviews required by legislation passed in 1978 in reaction to intelligence abuses of the previous decades.

The administration barraged the public with constant alerts, heightened security, and a five-tier system of color-coded warnings. The system was at times being politically manipulated by Rumsfeld and Attorney General John Ashcroft, and, in 2005, Tom Ridge, secretary of the new Department of Homeland Security, decided to resign rather than be party to such deception.

Potential terror targets jumped from 160 sites in 2003 to more than 300,000 in the next four years. Amazingly, Indiana led all states, with 8,600 potential targets by 2006. The national database included petting zoos, doughnut shops, popcorn stands, ice cream parlors, and the Mule Day Parade in Columbia, Tennessee. The unreality of the time continued to heighten. At the start of World War II, Franklin Roosevelt warned, "War costs money. . . . That means taxes and bonds and bonds and taxes. It means cutting luxuries and other nonessentials." Bush instead cut

As Ike looks on, Paul Wolfowitz speaks with Donald Rumsfeld, Colin Powell, and Scooter Libby during a Cabinet Room meeting on September 12, 2001.

taxes on the wealthy and told Americans, "Fly and enjoy America's great destination spots. Take your families and enjoy life."

Ironically, it was the arch Cold Warrior Zbigniew Brzezinski who in 2007 decried Bush's "five years of almost continuous national brainwashing on the subject of terror. . . . Where is the U.S. leader ready to say, 'Enough of this hysteria, stop this paranoia'? . . . Even in the face of future terrorist attacks, the likelihood of which cannot be denied, let us show some sense. Let us be true to our traditions."

Terrorism, he stressed repeatedly, was a tactic, not an ideology, and declaring war on a tactic made absolutely no sense.

But the real weight of Bush's global crusade would be felt abroad. Less than a month after the terrorist attacks, the U.S. invaded Afghanistan, ostensibly to destroy some of the same Islamic fanatics the U.S. had helped arm and train to defeat the Soviets two decades earlier.

Critics of the war would point out later that no Afghans were among the nineteen 9/11 hijackers, fifteen of whom were Saudi, and that U.S.

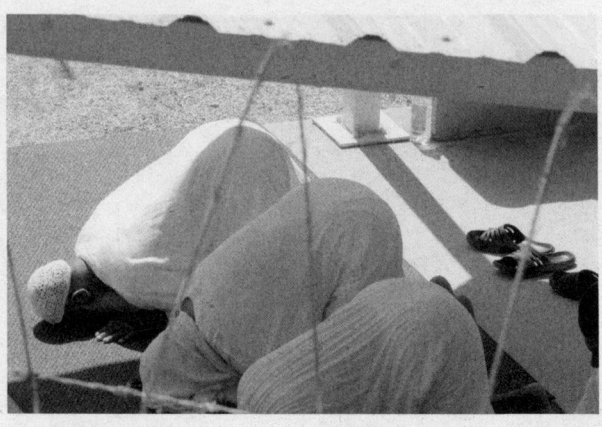

Detainees pray at the U.S. prison at Guantánamo Bay, Cuba. One FBI counterterrorism expert testified that of the nearly eight hundred detainees incarcerated at Guantánamo, fifty at most were worth holding.

bungling allowed Osama bin Laden and other Al-Qaeda leaders to escape into Pakistan in early December.

The CIA did round up thousands of suspects in Afghanistan and beyond. Although the U.S. had always considered its humane treatment of prisoners of war a sign of its moral superiority, the Bush administration branded detainees as "unlawful enemy combatants," waived the battlefield hearings required, and placed them outside the conventions of treatment mandated by the Geneva Convention of 1949. When foreign governments criticized his position, Bush backed down on the Taliban suspects but refused to change his policy for the Al-Qaeda fighters. Bush said: "I don't care what the international lawyers say, we are going to kick some ass."

The U.S. flew an unknown number of detainees to secret "black sites" around the world in such places as Thailand, Poland, Romania, and Morocco, where torture and other "harsh interrogation techniques" were implemented. Hundreds of others were imprisoned at the U.S. Naval Station at Guantánamo Bay, Cuba. At its peak in May 2003, the prison held roughly 680 men aged thirteen to ninety-eight. Five percent of these were captured by U.S. troops. More than 80 percent were turned over,

A protest poster compares waterboarding during the Spanish Inquisition to its modern-day practice by the United States at Guantánamo Bay, Cuba, under the Bush administration.

often for cash rewards, by a combination of Afghan warlord militias and both Afghan and Pakistani bounty hunters.

Government sources show that only 8 percent were Al-Qaeda fighters. Six hundred have been released, six convicted, and, according to the government, nine have died, most from suicide. As of 2012, 166 men from more than twenty countries remained in Guantánamo.

The Bush administration encouraged the CIA to employ ten enhanced interrogation methods that were the product of decades of research into torture, honed by allies in foreign countries. In February 2004, Major General Antonio Taguba reported that his investigation had turned up numerous instances of "sadistic, blatant, and wanton criminal abuses" at Abu Ghraib prison in Iraq. "There is no longer any doubt as to whether the current administration has committed war crimes. The only question that remains to be answered," Taguba explained, "is whether those who ordered the use of torture will be held to account." Arthur Schlesinger, Jr., a former Kennedy aide, said this torture policy was the "most dramatic, sustained, and radical challenge to the rule of law in American history. . . . No position taken has done more damage to the American reputation in the world—ever!"

Although the security situation in Afghanistan worsened over the next seven years, and the U.S. presence grew from twenty-five hundred to thirty thousand troops, Afghanistan was a distraction to Bush. His attention was focused on toppling his father's old adversary—Saddam Hussein.

Antiwar protesters gather at the Washington Monument. As the invasion of Iraq drew near, U.S. protesters were joined by millions around the world, including an estimated 3 million in Rome.

"Evidence from intelligence sources, secret communications, and statements by people now in custody reveal that Saddam Hussein aids and protects terrorists, including members of Al-Qaeda," Bush alleged.

As had Bill Casey in the 1980s and Lyndon Johnson in Vietnam, Bush used false intelligence to justify an invasion: "There is no question that the leader of Iraq is an evil man. After all, he gassed his own people—we know he's been developing weapons of mass destruction."

UN weapons inspectors searched high and low, visiting sites identified by the CIA. They found nothing, but Bush insisted the WMD were there: "The British government has learned that Saddam Hussein recently sought significant quantities of uranium from Africa."

Bush told Bob Woodward of the *Washington Post* around this time, "I do not need to explain why I say things. That's the interesting thing about being the president. Maybe somebody needs to explain to me why they say something, but I don't feel like I owe anybody an explanation."

These were extraordinary times. Words took on new meanings,

fulfilling George Orwell's prophecies of "double-speak" in his novel *1984*. First they steal the words, then they steal the meaning. Words like "axis of evil," "war against terror," "regime change," "simulated drowning," "enhanced interrogation," "preventive war." Civilians killed were now "collateral damage." CIA kidnappings were now "extraordinary renditions." And that most patriotic concept, "The Homeland," grew into a gargantuan new federal agency as labyrinthine as the Pentagon.

The French philosopher Voltaire in the eighteenth century observed, "Those who can make you believe absurdities can make you commit atrocities." The descent into unreality was dizzying. *Black Hawk Down*, a popular Oscar-nominated film, appeared in late 2001, glorifying American heroism and technology in 1990s Somalia.

Through technology, video games became more and more lifelike. And on television, increasingly bizarre and fanciful reality game shows soared in the ratings.

U.S. media beat the drums of war. MSNBC, which was owned by General Electric, canceled Phil Donahue's popular primetime show three weeks before the invasion. Network officials feared that the show would provide "a home for the liberal antiwar agenda at the same time our competitors are waving the flag at every opportunity."

And wave the flag they did. CNN, Fox, and NBC paraded more than seventy-five retired generals and other officers, almost all of whom were later revealed to be working directly for military contractors. Pentagon officials gave these "message force multipliers" talking points, portraying Iraq as an urgent threat.

Some later regretted having peddled lies to sell a war. Fox analyst Major Robert Bevelacqua, a retired Green Beret, complained, "It was them saying, 'We need to stick our hands up your back and move your mouth for you.'" NBC military analyst Colonel Kenneth Allard called the program "psyops on steroids." "I felt we'd been hosed," he admitted.

Major newspapers and magazines, including the *New York Times*, advanced the same message. One Bush insider told journalist Ron Suskind that Suskind represented "the reality-based community," but "that's not the way the world really works anymore. We're an empire now, and when we act, we create our own reality."

When France, Germany, and Russia, as well as most of the UN Security Council, refused to support the U.S. position, Bush was furious, and Rumsfeld sneered: "You're thinking of Europe as Germany and France. I don't. I think that's old Europe." French fries in the congressional cafeteria were renamed "Freedom Fries," just as sauerkraut became "liberty cabbage" during World War I.

Bush laid out his new strategy in a speech to the cadets at West Point in June 2002: "We must take the battle to the enemy, disrupt his plans, and confront the worst threats before they emerge," he declared.

The U.S. would act unilaterally and preemptively to overthrow any government deemed a threat to U.S. security. Cheney had laid bare the administration's dangerous reasoning: "If there's a one percent chance that Pakistani scientists are helping Al-Qaeda build or develop a nuclear weapon, we have to treat it as a certainty in terms of our response." "In the world we have entered, the only path to safety is the path of action, and this nation will act," Bush insisted.

Bush called for a moral crusade, saying that the United States must defend liberty and justice because these principles are right and true for all people everywhere. "Moral truth," he maintained, betraying a profound ignorance, "is the same in every culture, in every time, and in every place." Sixty countries made it onto Bush's potential hit list.

It was a bold statement of American exceptionalism. Bruce Bartlett, who served in both the Reagan and first Bush administrations, explained: "This is why George W. Bush is so clear-eyed about Al-Qaeda and the Islamic fundamentalist enemy. . . . He understands them, because he's just like them. . . . He truly believes he's on a mission from God. . . . The whole thing about faith is to believe things for which there is no empirical evidence."

Bush confided, "I have a sense of calm, knowing that the Bible's admonition, 'Thy Will Be Done,' is life's guide."

In early October 2002, Congress empowered Bush to go to war against Iraq on his own authority, whenever he deemed it appropriate, using whatever means, including nuclear weapons, he felt necessary.

The resolution drew a direct connection between Iraq and Al-Qaeda. Among those authorizing this were Senators John Kerry and Hillary

Clinton. This would cost both of them dearly in their runs for president. Not all were fooled. Congresswoman Barbara Lee was a voice of principle and reason: "Escalating this war and expanding this war does nothing in terms of our national security. It puts us more at risk. Iraq was not a haven for terrorists as it is now. Again, Iraq, Saddam Hussein and Al-Qaeda, there was no connection and we have to dispel that notion so the American people know the truth."

Millions of protesters hit the streets around the world. Three million in Rome, a million in London, hundreds of thousands in New York.

Time magazine surveyed several hundred thousand Europeans. Eighty-four percent thought the United States the greatest threat to peace; 8 percent thought Iraq was. Bush sent Secretary of State Colin Powell, the most respected member of his administration, before the United Nations to make a case for war. He told Powell: "Maybe they'll believe you."

Powell spoke for seventy-five minutes, telling the world, "My colleagues, every statement I make today is backed up by sources, solid sources. These are not assertions. What we're giving you are facts and conclusions based on solid intelligence. . . . We have firsthand descriptions of biological weapons factories on wheels and on rails. . . . We know that Iraq has at least seven of these mobile biological agent factories. The truck-mounted ones have at least two or three trucks each . . . the mobile production facilities . . . can produce anthrax and botulinum toxin. In fact, they can produce enough dry biological agent in a single month to kill thousands upon thousands of people. . . . Our conservative estimate is that Iraq today has a stockpile of between 100 and 500 tons of chemical-weapons agent. . . . [Saddam] remains determined to acquire nuclear weapons. . . . What I want to bring to your attention today is the potentially much more sinister nexus between Iraq and the Al-Qaeda terrorist network."

It was a thoroughly shameful performance, promoting false intelligence, that Powell later called a low point in his career. But the speech, although it fell flat overseas, had the desired impact on U.S. public opinion. Support for the war jumped from 50 percent to 63 percent.

The *Washington Post* pronounced the evidence on WMD "irrefutable." The U.S., without a Security Council resolution, was moving inexorably toward war. The truth was even darker. For Bush, Iraq was only the appetizer. After devouring Iraq, the neocons had their eyes set on the main course. Pentagon officials foresaw a five-year campaign with a total of seven targeted countries, beginning with Iraq, followed by Syria, Lebanon, Libya, Somalia, Sudan, and the biggest prize of all, Iran.

It would be a war to remake the world the neoconservative way.

Talk of empire abounded. The *New York Times* Sunday magazine cover for January 5, 2003, read: "American Empire: Get Used To It."

Bush clearly was a man with a boldness of vision. He'd always exhibited an outlaw side as a younger man. Now he would outdo his towering father by going beyond the laws of nations.

The eight-year Iraq War became the debacle critics predicted. Iraqi society was rent asunder. Like Vietnam, it warped America, polarizing it even further as costs and casualties mounted on all sides. Yet, remarkably, Bush won the 2004 election with a naked appeal to even more fervent patriotism.

By 2008, when Bush left office with the most dismal approval ratings since Harry Truman, he had not only thoroughly mismanaged two wars, as well as the federal relief efforts for New Orleans in the aftermath of Hurricane Katrina, but, most important, in the eyes of the public, he mismanaged the economy of the country, which nearly collapsed in 2008, ensuring the presidency to the Democrats.

His successor, Barack Hussein Obama, child of a black Kenyan father and white Kansas mother, who was raised in Indonesia and Hawaii, became, at forty-seven, president of the United States, evoking great hopes for change. His words and demeanor attested to the other side of America—constitutional, humanist, global, environmental.

Obama had spoken out strongly against the Iraq War and, financed by the Internet's multitude of small contributors, stunned the heavily favored and financed Democratic Party choice—Hillary Clinton—in the primaries. He now confronted an ex–military man, conservative John McCain, in the national election.

The wind was at Obama's back. Perhaps not since Roosevelt in the early 1930s had there been such populist anger at Wall Street and the unnecessary wars of empire.

But then an unexpected thing happened. Obama betrayed his earlier promise and became the first candidate to run in a general election to reject public financing in favor of private financing without limits. McCain, who took the public option, was badly outspent two to one.

In this period, Obama turned quietly to Wall Street funders with deep pockets like JP Morgan, Goldman Sachs, and Citigroup, as well as to General Electric and other defense contractors, computer giants, and the pharmaceuticals industry—Big Pharma—which, reversing years of supporting Republicans, gave Obama three times as much as McCain. Few of Obama's supporters complained at the time.

His victory in the national election was applauded across the world—a new America was here. Though conservatives would absurdly denounce Obama as a socialist, by far the biggest winner in the election turned out to be Wall Street. Obama brought back the same economic team— Timothy Geithner, Larry Summers, Peter Orszag, Rahm Emanuel—that, under Clinton, had done so much to deregulate the economy and set the stage for the current crisis. The *New York Times* referred to them as "a virtual Rubin constellation," acolytes of Robert Rubin, the most powerful Treasury secretary in decades.

After nearly wrecking the world economy with spectacular innovations in leveraging and speculation, several giant banks, insurance companies, and mortgage lenders, prophesying the collapse of the world's economy if they went under—they were, in other words, "too big to fail"—eagerly accepted a $700 billion bailout on remarkably easy terms. In addition, the Federal Reserve Board cut the interest rate for banks to zero percent. It became almost unpatriotic at the time to question the rightness of these financial rescues. But there were those who wondered—could not some of the sicker financial entities be let go and broken up? Could not these giants be confronted with the real market value of their toxic assets?

The public wanted revenge. It was a classic Depression backroom moment, as illustrated by Frank Capra in the powerful 1941 film *Meet John Doe*.

Former Federal Reserve chairman Paul Volcker urged Obama to act: "Right now, when you have your chance, and their breasts are bared, you need to put a spear through the heart of all these guys on Wall Street that for years have been mostly debt merchants."

But it didn't happen. The bailout was forced through a panicked Congress; the media applauded. The Treasury made no immediate demands that bankers make that money available in new loans to businesses or the public or, for that matter, cut their personal compensation. It made no demands that shareholders or bondholders absorb any losses. Taxpayers would fund the bailout alone.

The biggest losers over time would be workers, pensioners, older people with savings, homeowners, small businessmen, students with loans, and those, especially African Americans, who lost their jobs to a surging structural unemployment problem. Many simply lost their tenuous grip on the proverbial American dream of joining the "middle class." The myth of upward mobility was shattered. The bankers, or "banksters" as they were nicknamed during the Great Depression of the 1930s, had talked of voluntary restraint but received record compensation packages for the next two years.

Whereas CEOs in Britain or Canada earned 20 times as much as the average worker in 2010—and in Japan 11 times—in the U.S., CEOs made 343 times as much as the average worker.

The number of billionaires had jumped from 13 in 1985 to 450 in 2008. While the minimum wage stagnated at $5.15 an hour from 1997 to 2007, the poverty rate was higher than at any time since the 1960s. The net worth of the average American family actually dropped almost 40 percent, from $126,000 in 2007 to $77,000 in 2010. By 2011, the top one percent had more wealth than the bottom 90 percent.

Populist anger boiled over into the Occupy Wall Street movement, a kind of protest not seen since the 1930s. The gap between rich and poor had reached obscene proportions. And, some pointed out, these great "malefactors of wealth," as Teddy Roosevelt had called them, did not have to break the law in order to loot the economy. They, through their lawyers, lobbyists, and hand-picked legislators, had written the laws in the first place.

The right-wing Tea Party expressed a different kind of anger, fueled by advocacy groups like Americans for Prosperity, largely funded by the conservative, billionaire Koch brothers.

The confused American public, not knowing whom to blame for

persisting economic hardship, handed the Republicans a sweeping victory in 2010's midterm elections.

But only more gridlock and confusion pervaded Washington. Obama, who'd swept to office amid such euphoria, now walked a fine line, avoiding fatal mistakes but failing to deliver on hope or change. On his first day in office, the former constitutional law professor had promised "transparency and the rule of law will be the touchstones of this presidency."

Yet, in office, he refused to relinquish the expanded powers usurped by the Bush administration—as a passive population continued to consent to being stripped in front of airport screeners, permit eavesdropping on their communications, and pay for vast new security programs.

It did not make political sense for Obama to ease this heightened state of alert at the risk that a single terrorist incident would certainly result in renewed media hysteria and a Republican "I told you so" firestorm that could cost him his presidency. Reporter Diane Sawyer questioned Obama: "Ever in the middle of all this coming at you, you think maybe one term is enough?" Obama responded: "The one thing I'm clear about is that I'd rather be a really good one-term president than a mediocre two-term president."

Instead of fighting for transparency, however, Obama became a far more effective manager of the national security state. Like Bush, he repeatedly invoked the state secrets privilege in lawsuits involving torture, extraordinary rendition, and illegal NSA eavesdropping.

He blocked habeas corpus rights for enemy combatants, preserved military commissions, and authorized without due process the killing, in Yemen, of a U.S. citizen accused of having ties to Al-Qaeda.

Obama stunned civil libertarians when he took Bush-era investigations to the next level and began prosecuting government whistleblowers and reporters, using the World War I–era Espionage Act. Only three cases had been brought in ninety-two years. Obama initiated seven.

The cases were of dubious merit, most defendants claiming to have exposed unlawful activity in the government.

Most prominent were NSA analyst Edward Snowden and Chelsea Manning, an army intelligence analyst in Iraq who leaked more than

260,000 classified diplomatic cables and war reports, as well as videos, distributed by WikiLeaks, a nonprofit whistleblower media organization.

These revelations of U.S. war crimes in Iraq and Afghanistan and U.S. support for dictatorial regimes in the region proved to be a significant catalyst for the Arab Spring uprisings in Egypt, Tunisia, Yemen, Libya, and Bahrain.

Nonetheless, Obama's administration has severely impaired the operation of WikiLeaks and threatens to prosecute its cofounder.

These actions sent a clear message to all whistleblowers—commit war crimes like Bush and Cheney and you walk free. Expose them and you risk careers and huge fines, or, like Manning, you rot in jail.

One of the leading defenders of the new standards of conduct, Jack Goldsmith, former head of the Bush Office of Legal Counsel, reassured Cheney and other anxious neocons in an article saying that Obama was "like Nixon going to China . . . the changes he had made are destined to fortify the bulk of the Bush program for the long run."

This was a new shadow world. In 2010, the *Washington Post* called it an "alternative geography of the United States, a Top Secret America hidden from public view." Almost a million and a half people had top secret security clearances. More than three thousand government and private security corporations existed. One billion seven hundred thousand emails and communications were intercepted and stored every day by the National Security Agency.

Political commentator and constitutional lawyer Glenn Greenwald best described this assault on civil liberties when he wrote, "The core guarantee of western justice since the Magna Carta was codified in the U.S. by the fifth amendment to the constitution: No person shall . . . be deprived of life, liberty or property without due process of law."

He might well have added the Fourth Amendment to the Constitution, the right to privacy and protection against unreasonable search and seizure. Without due process and the right to privacy, each of us is essentially living at the mercy of the surveillance state. All this is being done in the name of stopping a terrorist threat blown wildly out of proportion.

Obama's foreign policy seemed more reasonable than Bush's, repudiating the unilateralism and preemption that had so outraged world opinion. But the goal—embracing U.S. global domination—differed little, and even the means were frustratingly similar. In 2011, Bush's former NSA and CIA director, General Michael Hayden, took comfort in the powerful continuity between two vastly different presidents, saying that "Americans have found a comfortable center line in what it is they . . . accept their government doing." He called it a "practical consensus."

His own experience in foreign affairs limited, Obama surrounded himself with hawkish advisors. Among them was a Bush holdover as secretary of defense, Robert Gates, a hardliner from the Bill Casey/CIA era of the 1980s. Hillary Clinton as secretary of state was equally hawkish. In an early speech, Clinton presented a version of American history steeped in unvarnished triumphalism and historical amnesia: "So let me say it clearly: The United States can, must, and will lead in this new century. . . . The third World War that so many feared never came. And many millions of people were lifted out of poverty and exercised their human rights for the first time. Those were the benefits of a global architecture forged over many years by American leaders from both political parties."

It would be difficult to find and ask the millions killed over many decades of American interference in their countries what they thought—the people of Hiroshima and Nagasaki, the Philippines, Central America, Greece, Iran, Brazil, Cuba, Congo, Indonesia, Vietnam, Cambodia, Laos, Chile, East Timor, Iraq, and Afghanistan, among others.

In Afghanistan, Obama, calling it a "war of necessity," doubled down on Bush. Pressured in late 2009 into sending more troops, he wavered. He was told by a military advisor, "I don't see how you can defy your military chain here," meaning that his high command might resign in protest. CIA director Leon Panetta told him, "No Democratic president can go against military advice, especially if he asked for it. So just do it. Do what they say."

When it came down to his decision, Obama did not show the courage of a John Kennedy. In December, he announced another thirty thousand troop increase to reach almost one hundred thousand, about the same number the Soviets had deployed in their disastrous invasion of Afghanistan.

He announced the troop increase at West Point, reminding the cadets that the U.S. invaded Afghanistan because it had provided sanctuary for

Al-Qaeda. But he neglected to mention that most of the preparations for September 11 took place not in Afghanistan but in apartments in Germany and Spain and flight schools in the U.S., or that only fifty to one hundred of Al-Qaeda's three hundred cadre were actually left in Afghanistan and that most were now in Pakistan—an ally.

That the president waging two wars would receive the Nobel Peace Prize that same month was surreal in the first place, but when the world heard Obama's defense of American unilateralism and preemption, the meaning of the prize was once more diminished, as it had been by Kissinger thirty-six years earlier. In his acceptance speech, he said, "I believe that the United States of America must remain a standard bearer in the conduct of war. That is what makes us different from those whom we fight."

Obama feared getting bogged down in Afghanistan, as Johnson had in Vietnam. What the backward, dirt poor, overwhelmingly illiterate Afghans needed was economic aid, education, and social reform—not more war. The U.S. spent $110 billion on military programs in Afghanistan in 2011 but only $2 billion for sustainable development. With big U.S. money floating around, as in Vietnam, corruption reached epic proportions. Mistrust between the supposed NATO and Afghan allies soared. The U.S.-backed Afghan president, Hamid Karzai, announced that he would support Pakistan if it should go to war with the U.S. By 2012, Afghan soldiers and police were killing U.S. troops with such regularity that the forces had to be increasingly separated.

Meanwhile, bedraggled, demoralized U.S. forces left Iraq in December 2011. Almost 4,500 U.S. troops would not come home and more than 32,000 were wounded, many of them severely. Iraqi death counts ranged from 150,000 to over a million. Two million Iraqis fled the country. The irony was exquisite. In deposing the Sunni Hussein, the United States had turned the new Shiite-dominated Iraq into a valuable ally of Iran, which ended up the war's biggest winner.

Bush officials had estimated the war to cost $50 to $60 billion. Rumsfeld had called anything above $100 billion "baloney." By 2008, when Bush left office, the U.S. had spent some $700 billion on the war, not including long-term care for veterans. Economists project total long-term costs as high as $4 trillion.

Secretary of State Hillary Clinton and Defense Secretary Robert Gates confer during a Cabinet Room meeting. A holdover from the Bush administration, Gates teamed with the hawkish Clinton to frustrate those who hoped for a reassessment of America's role in the world.

Obama welcomed the troops home at Fort Bragg, North Carolina, ensuring that the end of the war would be as dishonest as its beginning: "We're leaving behind a sovereign, stable, and self-reliant Iraq. . . . Unlike the old empires, we don't make these sacrifices for territory or for resources. We do it because it's right. . . . Never forget that you are part of an unbroken line of heroes spanning two centuries . . . to your grandparents and parents who faced down fascism and communism . . . and delivered justice to those who attacked us on 9/11." Thus, he sanctioned once again Bush's lie about the Iraqi connection to 9/11.

The words were barely out of his mouth before Iraq was racked with a new series of deadly suicide bombings. To this day, Iraq teeters on the edge of civil war and may recently have gone off the cliff.

Among the two wars' fiercest critics were the nation's mayors, who gathered in Baltimore in June 2011 and called for using $126 billion in savings resulting from ending these wars to rebuild the nation's cities. The mayor of Los Angeles observed regretfully, "That we would build

Obama and Afghan president Hamid Karzai converse during a March 2010 dinner at the Presidential Palace in Kabul. A shaky U.S. ally at best, Karzai has led a government that has proven both brutal and corrupt.

bridges in Baghdad and Kandahar and not Baltimore and Kansas City absolutely boggles the mind."

For the American people, deadened to these wars, a single bright spot in this foreign miasma came in May 2011. A bold cross-border raid at night by navy SEALs killed Osama bin Laden, who had been living comfortably in the shadow of Pakistan's premier military academy.

In the euphoria the raid created in the U.S., celebrating the skill and power of the SEALs who had executed bin Laden vigilante-style and dumped his body at sea, a new profile was created for Obama as, unlike Bush, an effective war president who would, by any means necessary, hunt down the enemy. In fact, really a wolf in sheep's clothing, the president calmly informed the American public, "After a firefight, they killed Osama bin Laden and took custody of his body."

A celebrated movie, *Zero Dark Thirty*, even implied torture was effective in finding bin Laden, though, in fact, it had been ordinary police and espionage work that located him after almost ten years. Nonetheless, America's capacity for self-love was again in full flower and there were no

*Obama and his national security team gather in the
White House Situation Room to receive updates on
the mission to assassinate Osama bin Laden.*

troubling discussions of bringing a wounded bin Laden back for imprisonment and trial, as the United States had done at Nuremberg, where
the Nazi defendants were unmasked and diminished.

But a trial was the last thing most Americans wanted. Those who accepted torture could tolerate vigilante justice.

But who was the real victor here? After trillions of dollars in projected
spending, two wars, hundreds of thousands of dead worldwide, an endless war on terror, the loss of civil liberties, one presidency failed and one
badly tarnished, and the near collapse of the empire's financial structure,
it can be said that the U.S. had won a Pyrrhic victory in which its losses
had made victory pointless.

Bin Laden, with his twisted vision of a new caliphate, was dead, but he
had achieved far more than he ever dreamed. He'd goaded the largest,
most powerful empire in history to reveal its worst nature—and, like the
Wizard of Oz, it didn't look so great and mighty.

Bin Laden's "martyrdom" in the eyes of his followers cemented his place
in history as a catalyst who weakened and perhaps helped destroy the old

world order. Some might liken him to a Hannibal or Attila to ancient Rome, a Robespierre to the old French Order, a Lenin to tsarist Russia, even a modern Hitler to the British Empire, which came to its end in his wake.

Bin Laden was gone. But what would the United States do now? Still tormented by its demons, it turned its gaze fully to China as a new threat and persisted in treating Russia as an old one, as well as vilifying Iran, North Korea, and Venezuela as regional threats.

Seeking to find a more efficient, leaner form of warfare, Obama in 2012 announced a 14 percent cut in future infantry strength, to be compensated for by an increased emphasis on outer space and cyberspace.

First used for surveillance in Vietnam, the drone, when equipped with missiles, was now becoming the modern face of warfare and Obama's weapon of choice. He personally began selecting those on the kill list. Before 9/11 the United States had opposed extrajudicial "targeted killing" by other nations, condemning Israel's targeting of Palestinians.

But by 2012, the air force and CIA were deploying a seven-thousand-drone armada, used mostly in Afghanistan, Iraq, and Pakistan. In 2009, Obama expanded its use to Yemen, where there were fewer than three hundred militants. By mid-2012, that number had increased to more than one thousand, as a steady barrage of U.S. drone attacks outraged Yemeni citizens. By 2012, Obama added Muammar Gaddafi's Libyan supporters and Islamic rebels in the Philippines and Somalia to the drone list. The repercussions of this style of warfare are yet to be experienced.

The number of civilian casualties of these attacks is fiercely contested by the U.S. government and several human rights organizations. When a judge asked the Pakistani-born U.S. citizen known as the "Time Square Bomber" how he could risk killing innocent woman and children, he replied that U.S. drones were regularly killing women and children in Afghanistan and Pakistan. To the Pakistanis, the victims were human beings. To the drone operators, they were "bug splats."

The cat was certainly out of the bag and, by 2012, more than fifty countries, some friendly and some hostile to the U.S., had purchased drones. Israel, Russia, India, and Iran claimed to have mastered manufacturing lethal ones, but the most dynamic program was China's. As with the nuclear bomb, a new arms race was on.

MQ-1 Predator (top) *and MQ-9 Reaper* (above) *drones fly combat missions above Afghanistan. U.S. officials touted these unmanned weapons as precise instruments for the targeted killing of enemy combatants, but their use led to numerous civilian deaths and helped usher in an era of drone proliferation across the globe.*

Bush had continued Clinton's expansion of NATO bases closer to Russia, breaking his father's promise to Gorbachev. Obama expanded NATO to Albania and Croatia. And despite abandoning 500 bases in Iraq, the Obama administration, in addition to an estimated 6,000 bases in the U.S., maintains close to 1,000 overseas bases that span the globe.

The U.S. had, by late 2007, gained a military presence, according to Stanford's Chalmers Johnson, in 151 of 192 UN member nations. In

2008, AFRICOM, based in Germany, was added as a sixth command responsible for a growing U.S. military presence in Africa.

SOUTHCOM, based in Miami, was reorganized in 2010 to increase U.S. military presence in Latin America with bases and surveillance systems and counterdrug and counterinsurgency programs targeting manifestations of "radical populism," as seen in Venezuela. The Fourth Fleet was reactivated in 2008 for the first time since World War II.

The navy now has ten carrier strike groups patrolling international waters. In 2011, the U.S. accounted for an astonishing 78 percent of the world's arms sales. In 2013, U.S. elite special operations forces were deployed to 134 countries.

During the Bush years, Pentagon spending more than doubled to $700 billion. Although the real Pentagon budget blurs into secret functions and different departments of government, by 2010, according to the National Priorities Project, the U.S. actually spent an estimated $1.2 trillion out of its $3 trillion annual budget on military, intelligence, and Homeland Security—a full-spectrum dominance of land, sea, air, space, and cyberspace. And while those expenditures have been cut in the aftermath of the Iraq War and as a result of Congressional budget battles, U.S. military spending still dwarfs that of its rivals.

In November 2011, Secretary of State Clinton threw down the gauntlet on China, writing, "As the war in Iraq winds down and America begins to withdraw its forces from Afghanistan, the United States stands at a pivot point." Calling this "America's Pacific Century," she proposed a substantially increased military involvement in the Asia/Pacific region to contain China.

Beginning with the Opium Wars in the nineteenth century, China has been humiliated time and again by stronger foes—including Britain, Japan, and Russia. It fought the U.S. to a standoff in Korea in the early 1950s. China is a proud nation—the world's second-largest economy. A hybrid—part state-owned, part capitalist—it has replaced the U.S. as Asia's main trading partner.

But in 1996, Chinese leaders were humiliated again by U.S. nuclear missile-rattling during another confrontation over Taiwan.

And with its economic interests and shipping lanes to protect, it set out to modernize its military. In 2012, the Pentagon estimated Chinese expenditures of $160 billion. But given the secrecy of the Chinese system, the real budget is unknowable at this time. Although it has only one foreign base, its hard line over disputed oil, gas, and mineral-rich islands and territories in the East and South China Seas has escalated tensions with its regional neighbors.

Internally, the government, communist in name only, remains politically backward—determined at any cost to modernize and brutally willing to stifle dissent where its one-party rule has been questioned. Western democracies, while doing business with China, have condemned these policies to little avail. But more ominously, China has again attracted the wrath of China-bashing American hardliners whose animosity dates back to the McCarthy era. A new faceoff is in the works.

The U.S. has returned to Asia, seeking to build new alliances, rebalance its fleet, and deploy its top stealth war planes to bases within striking distance of China by 2017. It has strengthened military alliances with China's neighbors, particularly Japan, South Korea, Taiwan, and the Philippines, sending twenty-five hundred marines to Australia—the first long-term troop increase in Asia since Vietnam.

The Chinese were deeply angry over the Obama administration's new arms sales of some $12 billion to Taiwan in 2010 and 2011. They have accused the U.S. of seeking to encircle them.

The fear of the U.S. by others cannot be underestimated. As the late conservative political scientist Samuel Huntington acknowledged in 1996, "The West won the world not by the superiority of its ideas or values or religion . . . but rather by its superiority in applying organized violence. Westerners often forget this fact; non-Westerners never do."

Progressive China experts fear the U.S. is once again employing Truman's 1946 playbook with the Soviet Union in an attempt to contain China. The same situation exists once again with Western revulsion for China's internal policies. But this time, holding $1 trillion in U.S. Treasury bonds, the Chinese could imperil the U.S. economy in ways the Soviets never could.

Historian Alfred McCoy delineated the real stakes when he wrote, "As early as 2020 the Pentagon hopes to patrol the entire globe ceaselessly, relentlessly via a triple canopy space shield reaching from stratosphere to exosphere, driven by drones armed with agile missiles. . . . The triple canopy should be able to . . . blind an entire army by knocking out ground communications, avionics, and naval navigation."

But, as McCoy cautions, the illusion of technological invincibility and information omniscience has failed arrogant nations in the past, as the fates of Germany in World War II and the U.S. in Vietnam attest.

With tragic irony McCoy reminds us that the U.S.'s "veto of global lethality" might be "an equalizer for any further loss of economic strength," and that the U.S.'s "fate might well be determined by which comes first in this century-long cycle: military debacle from the illusion of technological mastery, or a new technological regime powerful enough to perpetuate U.S. global dominion."

But, as a popular series of "Star Wars" movies shows, a nation dominating the world with its technology will soon become a tyranny that will be hated by those who are tyrannized.

China may become the first new empire to emerge in this nuclear-armed world. But an empire modeled on the U.S. or British versions would be a disaster. Great Han chauvinism would be no better than American exceptionalism. Former Defense official Joseph Nye observed that the dominant powers' failure to integrate the rising powers of Germany and Japan into the twentieth-century global system resulted in two catastrophic world wars. History must not be allowed to repeat itself.

The Chinese must shun the American example. And the U.S. must reverse course. Henry Wallace worried about how, if the U.S. treated the Soviets so badly when the U.S. was riding high economically and militarily, the Soviets would treat the U.S. when and if the situation was reversed. It never happened, but this race to the bottom, he understood, would have no winner.

As we close out this book, we must ask ourselves humbly, in looking back at the American Century, have we acted wisely and humanely in our relations to the rest of the world—a world in which, Oxfam reports, the richest 85 people have more wealth than the poorest 3.5 billion?

Have we been right to police the globe? Have we been a force for good, for understanding, for peace? We must look in the mirror. Have we perhaps in our self-love become the angels of our own despair? The claims of victory in World War II and justification for the atomic bomb dropped on Japan, though aimed at the Soviet Union, were the founding myths of our domination and national security state, and the nation's elites have benefited from that. The bomb has allowed us to win by any means necessary, which makes us, because we win, right. And because we are right, we are therefore good.

Under these conditions there is no morality but our own. As Secretary of State Madeleine Albright said, "If we have to use force, it is because we are America; we are the indispensable nation." Because we can threaten and have threatened humanity with the bomb, our mistakes are forgiven and our cruelties justified as benignly motivated aberrations.

But domination doesn't last. Five major empires have collapsed in the lifetime of a person born before World War II: Britain, France, Germany, Japan, and the Soviet Union. Three more empires collapsed earlier in the twentieth century: the Russian, Austro-Hungarian, and Ottoman. If history is a barometer, the United States domination will end as well.

We wisely resisted becoming a colonial empire, and most Americans would deny all imperial pretensions. Perhaps that is why we cling so doggedly to the myth of American exceptionalism—American uniqueness, benevolence, generosity. Maybe in that fanciful notion lie the seeds of American redemption—the hope that the United States will live up to that vision, which seemed within grasp in 1945 when Wallace almost became president, or in 1953 when Stalin died with a new U.S. president in office, or with JFK and Khrushchev in 1963, or Bush and Gorbachev in 1989, or Obama in 2008. History has shown us the curve of the ball could have broken differently. Those moments will come again in a different form—will we be ready?

Think back to Franklin Roosevelt, on the last day of his life, cabling Churchill: "I would minimize the general Soviet problem as much as possible because these problems, in one form or another, seem to arise every day and most of them straighten out."

Seeking calm in the situations that occur, letting things happen without overreacting, seeing the world through the eyes of our adversaries. This way lies in sharing in the needs of other countries—with true empathy and compassion—trusting a collective will of this planet to survive the coming period, ending the threats of nuclear annihilation and global warming.

Can we not surrender our notion of exceptionalism and our arrogance? Can we not cut out the talk of domination? Can we stop appealing to God to bless America over other nations? Hardliners and nationalists will object, but theirs has proven not to be the way. A young woman said to me in the 1970s, "We need to feminize this planet." I thought it strange then, but now I realize there's power in love—real power in real love.

Let us find a way back to respecting the law, not of the jungle, but of civilization, by which we first came together and put aside our differences to preserve the things that matter. Herodotus wrote in the fifth century before Christ that the first history was written "in the hope of preserving from decay the remembrance of what men have done."

And for that reason, the history of man is one not only of blood and death but also of honor, achievement, kindness, memory—and civilization.

There is a way forward by remembering the past, and then we can start, step by step, like a baby, reaching for the stars.

As President Kennedy eloquently reminded us more than a half century ago, "in the final analysis, our most basic common link is that we all inhabit this small planet. We all breathe the same air. We all cherish our children's futures. And we are all mortal."

PHOTO CREDITS

Benutzer: Fb78 via Wikimedia Commons: page 286

Corbis Images: pages 218, 219

Courtesy of Los Alamos National Laboratory: page 116

Courtesy of U.S. Department of Energy: page 105

Federal Bureau of Investigation: page 155

Franklin D. Roosevelt Presidential Library / National Archives: pages 37, 39, 47, 61, 63, 69, 98

George Bush Presidential Library and Museum/ National Archives: page 269

George W. Bush Presidential Library / National Archives: page 283

Gerald R. Ford Presidential Library: pages 227, 228, 229

German Federal Archive: pages 55, 70, 147

Harry S. Truman / National Archives: page 89

Harry S. Truman Presidential Library: pages 137, 142, 153

Harry S. Truman Presidential Library / National Archives: pages 87, 107, 127, 130

Information of New Orleans via Wikimedia Commons: page 266

Jim Kuhn via Wikimedia Commons: page 285

Jimmy Carter Library / National Archives: pages 232, 233

John F. Kennedy Presidential Library: pages 170, 179

John F. Kennedy Presidential Library / National Archives: pages 174, 181, 190

Library of Congress: pages 2, 7, 16, 17, 21, 24, 36, 42, 47, 67, 109, 172, 195, 199, 230

Library of Congress, University of Minnesota, National Archives: page 97

Library of Congress, Wikimedia Commons / Public Domain: pages 102, 103

Lyndon Baines Johnson Presidential Library: page 194

Lyndon Baines Johnson Presidential Library / National Archives: pages 201, 205, 207, 208

Nasser Sadeghi via Wikimedia Commons / Public Domain: page 157

PHOTO CREDITS

National Archives: pages 9, 22, 85, 99, 112, 113, 115, 135, 151, 161, 163, 175, 178, 196, 200, 204, 211, 231, 279

National Archives, Wikimedia Commons / Public Domain: page 115

National Museum of the U.S. Air Force: page 148

New Yorker Magazine: page 8

New York Times: page 77

Official White House Photograph: pages 297, 298, 299

Oliver Stone Personal Collection: page 203

Peter Kuznick Personal Collection: page 203

Photos of the Great War: World War I Image Archive: page 13

Public Domain: pages 19, 25, 26, 43, 241

Richard Nixon Presidential Library / National Archives: pages 210, 214

Ronald Reagan Presidential Library: pages 238, 239, 247, 248, 251

Ronald Reagan Presidential Library / National Archives: pages 247, 249, 257

Sue Ream via Wikimedia Commons: page 260

U.S. Air Force: page 301

U.S. Army: pages 191, 213

U.S. Department of Defense: pages 171, 235, 243, 261, 263, 266, 267

U.S. Information Agency: pages 67, 149

U.S. Marine Corps: pages 10, 116, 217, 243

U.S. Navy: page 284

Utilizator:Mihai.1954 via Wikimedia Commons: page 83

Wikimedia Commons / Public Domain: pages 111, 233

William J. Clinton Presidential Library / National Archives: page 271

INDEX

Page numbers in *italics* indicate photos and illustrations.

Mr. Smith Goes to Washington (film), 82, 121
mujahideen, 245, 251
Murray, Phil, 79, 81
Muslim community, 162, 234–235
Mussolini, Benito, 33, 52, 53, *55*, 106
Muste, A. J., 142
My Lai Massacre, 209–210, *213*

Nader, Ralph, 276
Nagasaki, bombing of, 112–114, *115*, *116*
Nasser, Gamal Abdel, 162
National Priorities Project, 302
National Recovery Administration (NRA), 37, 38
National Security Act, 134
National Security Agency (NSA), 293, 294
National Student Association, 202
Nehru, Jawaharlal, 156, 162
neoconservatives, 275, 276, 278, 290
Nevins, Allan, 95
New Deal, 35–36, 60, 226, 258
New York Journal, 4–5
New York Times, 44, 127, 131, 148, 154, 229, 234, 256, 262, 287, 290, 291
New York World, 4
news media, 252, 287
Newsweek, *97*, 263
Nicaragua
  contras, 240–241, *241*, 248–249, *251*, 253
  Sandinistas, 232, 253
Nicholas II, Tsar, 18, 20
Nimitz, Chester, 63, 109
9/11 attacks, 277–278, *279*, 281–282, 296

1984 (Orwell), 287
Nitze, Paul, 90, 150, 164–165, 181, 246
Nixon, Richard, 150, 165, 169, 192, *199*, 261
  and Chilean coup, 215
  domestic politics under, 225–226
  election of, 208, *210*
  Ford's pardon of, 215, 226
  and gold standard, 220, 226
  resignation of, 215
  and Vietnam War, 208–215, *214*
  and Watergate scandal, 214, 215, 226
Nkrumah, Kwame, 162
Nobel Peace Prize, 168, 202, 215, 296
Noriega, Manuel, 248, 260–261, *261*
Norman, Montagu, 33, 34
Normandy, Battle of, 76
Norris, George, 15
North Atlantic Treaty Organization (NATO), 138, 157, 162, 185, 259–260, 301
North Korea, 140, 276
North, Oliver, 240, 250, *251*
NSC-68 report (National Security Council), 150, 152
nuclear arms race, 104, 139, 155
nuclear fallout, 156
nuclear proliferation, 155
nuclear weapons
  Anti-Ballistic Missile Treaty, 276
  atomic attacks in North Korea, 149–150
  atomic bomb, 51–52, 64–65, 88, 94, 95, 103–104, 106–108, 110–120, 197
  "Atoms for Peace" program and, 155